FLORIDA HISTORY: A BIBLIOGRAPHY

compiled by

Michael H. Harris

The Scarecrow Press, Inc.
Metuchen, N. J.   1972

Library of Congress Cataloging in Publication Data

Harris, Michael H
  Florida history.

    1. Florida--Bibliography. I. Title.
Z1271.H35   016.9759   72-4222
ISBN 0-8108-0511-1

For all those who have written
or will write
about the history of Florida

PREFACE

Some years ago an acquaintance of mine lamented the fact that the student of Florida history was greatly handicapped by the lack of a comprehensive guide to the writings on that state's development. As a librarian with training and research interests in American history, I became intrigued with the idea of compiling such a guide. Little did I know of the task that awaited me. The project was begun in the fall of 1964, while I served on the reference staff of the Florida Atlantic University Library. Most of the work of compilation was done in 1964 and 1965. Then came a number of interruptions, including one of three years' duration occasioned by my doctoral studies in the Graduate Library School at Indiana University, all of which slowed progress on the bibliography considerably.

In 1970 and 1971 more time became available for work on the project, and in the fall of 1971, despite certain misgivings, this book was prepared for the press. My anxiety grew out of the awareness, developed after nearly a decade in pursuit of the voluminous and far-flung literature relating to Florida history, that this compilation was not complete. Up to the day that the final draft of the bibliography was typed more entries were being turned up. But then, the effort to prepare a perfect and definitive list might well have continued forever, and I decided that the time had come to make the bibliography available to all those interested in the history of Florida, in hopes that it might facilitate further investigation of the origins and development of one of the nation's most fascinating states. The compiler will welcome notes on errors of omission and commission from users of the bibliography.

Over the past seven years I have incurred many debts. The greatest of these is the one I owe to Dr. Samuel Proctor, editor of the Florida Historical Quarterly. Professor Proctor has been actively involved in this project since its inception in 1964, and despite a multitude of other responsibilities, his interest never flagged; his constant encouragement and incisive criticism have been invaluable to me.

Dozens of Florida historians and librarians helped me locate materials for inclusion in this list. Dr. Charlton Tebeau of the University of Miami took time out of his busy schedule to help me solidify my plans for the bibliography in June of 1965, and Dr. A. J. Hanna graciously hosted me in Winter Park while I examined the Union Catalog of Floridiana at Rollins College in April of 1966. Ruth Kent, Librarian of the St. Augustine Historical Society, contributed a number of entries for the bibliography and examined the typescript, pointing out a number of errors and omissions. Miss Kent had originally intended to share the task of compiling the bibliography, but other commitments and responsibilities made such demands upon her time that she was forced to withdraw from active involvement in the project.

It is also a pleasure to acknowledge financial support I received. In 1965, Edward Heiliger, then director of libraries of Florida Atlantic University, provided me with released time and some graduate assistant help in the early stages of the project. In 1966, the academic dean at Northern Illinois University, where I was serving as assistant reference librarian, awarded me a small grant which provided for a week's work in Winter Park and Gainesville. In 1970 the Kentucky Research Foundation of the University of Kentucky presented me with a grant which greatly facilitated work on the final stages of this project. The funds allowed me to spend two weeks working in the P. K. Yonge Library of Florida History at the University of Florida and helped underwrite the costs of preparing the manuscript.

I must also acknowledge the aid of two members of the University of Kentucky faculty. The first, Dr. Richard Lowitt, a professor of history who was formerly at Florida State University, has taken a personal interest in my work that is both flattering and encouraging. The second, Dr. Lawrence Allen, dean of the College of Library Science, has contributed more than he can know through his enlightened support of the research and investigation carried on by his faculty.

Finally, three persons have taken special pains in seeing the manuscript through the various stages of its development; they are Donita Gregory, Pamela Dawson Voris and Sally Allison Goodwin. Also, my wife Linda has helped in ways too numerous to recount.

All of these people and many more have contributed much to whatever merits this book may claim. Of course, any errors remaining are only my own.

Lexington, Kentucky   M. H. H.
December 1971

TABLE OF CONTENTS

PART TWO

INTRODUCTION

This bibliography is made up of citations to works on Florida history published through 1970. Three main classes of materials make up the bulk of the items listed: books and pamphlets, periodical articles, and theses and dissertations. Much of the best literature on Florida history has been published in periodicals, and particular pains were taken to locate as many of these articles as possible. As a result, the compiler is confident that this bibliography can act as an effective index to the papers on the history of Florida published in such periodicals as the Florida Historical Quarterly, Tequesta, Apalachee, and many others.

Several types of material posed real problems for the compiler, and they deserve some explanation here.

Travel and Description: In this category (section 16) the compiler attempted to include all items which could be located which dealt with Florida in any detail, and a representative selection of those which gave only slight attention to the state. A much fuller list of works which only touch on Florida can be constructed through the use of Thomas D. Clark's Travels in the South and Travels in the New South, and E. Merton Coulter's Travels in the Confederate States.

Manuscripts: Users of this bibliography will note that manuscript material is covered only as it is treated in published papers listed in section 1-B. Initially, the compiler had intended to include a lengthy chapter describing major manuscript collections within and outside of the state which related to Florida history. As a result a questionnaire was circulated to librarians and historians asking them to briefly describe the collections under their care. The results were both encouraging and frustrating. Encouraging because dozens of individuals carefully filled out the questionnaires and promptly returned them; frustrating because it became obvious that there were hundreds of important collections deserving attention, and that to give them even minimal coverage would require a book-length manuscript devoted to collections alone. In the light of this, the reluctant decision was made to omit any discussion of manuscript sources from this volume. What is really necessary is a book-length "Guide to Manuscript Material Relating to Florida History." The production of such a guide would require a large scale cooperative venture, and would be worthy of the attention of the Florida Historical Society and the Florida Library Association.

Government Documents: As a rule government documents were excluded from this bibliography. Their number and the fact that they are indexed elsewhere seemed to justify such a policy.

The arrangement of any bibliography is controlled by the philosophy of classification held by the compiler and the nature of the literature being organized. Both of these factors influenced my choice of a two-part arrangement for this list. Part One (sections 1-16) is chronologically arranged and contains those items which fall within the relatively neat chronological periods covered there. Part Two (sections 17-28) is arranged topically, and contains those items which deal with topics, such as "education," but which refuse to be neatly squeezed into the chronological sections.

The compiler was quite deliberate in citing each work only once in this bibliography. As a result it is imperative that the user turn to the subject index when searching for works on any aspect of Florida history. For instance, items dealing with St. Augustine are found under "The Spanish in Florida," "Education in Florida," "Local History," etc. However, all of these items can be conveniently located through the references found under "St. Augustine" in the subject index.

ABBREVIATIONS USED

Acad. Christ. Art J.	Academy of Christian Art Journal
Ag. Hist.	Agricultural History
ALA Bull.	American Library Association Bulletin
Ala. Hist. Q.	Alabama Historical Quarterly
Ala. Law	Alabama Lawyer
Ala. Rev.	Alabama Review
Am. Anthro.	American Anthropologist
Am. Antiquities	American Antiquities
Am. Coll. Dentists J.	American College Dentists Journal
Am. Eccles. Rev.	American Ecclesiastical Review
Am. Forests	American Forests
Am. Heritage	American Heritage
Am. Hist. Rev.	American Historical Review
Am. Irish Hist. Soc. J.	American Irish Historical Society Journal
Am. J. Econ. and Sociol.	American Journal of Economics and Sociology
Am. J. Med. Sci.	American Journal of Medical Sciences
Am. J. Pub. Health	American Journal of Public Health
Am. J. Sci. & Arts	American Journal of Science and Arts
Am. J. Surgery	American Journal of Surgery
Am. J. Trop. Med.	American Journal of Tropical Medicine
Am. Lit.	American Literature
Am. Mercury	American Mercury
Am. Neptune	American Neptune
Am. Philatelist	American Philatelist
Am. Printer	American Printer
Am. Speech	American Speech
An. Rep. Bur. Am. Ethnology	Annual Report of the Bureau of American Ethnology
Ann. Rep. Am. Hist. Assn.	Annual Report of the American Historical Association
Annals Med. Hist.	Annals of Medical History
Anthro. Q.	Anthropological Quarterly
Antioch R.	Antioch Revue
Atl. M.	Atlantic Monthly
Audubon Mag.	Audubon Magazine
Bibl. Nac. Rev.	Revista de la Biblioteca Nacional (Havana)
Bull. Am. Geo. Soc.	Bulletin of the American Geographical Society
Bull. Bureau Am. Ethnology	Bulletin of the Bureau of American Ethnology

Bull. Inst. Est. Asturianos	Instituto de Estudios Asturianos. Boletin
Can. Mining J.	Canadian Mining Journal
Cath. Hist. Rev.	Catholic Historical Review
Cath. World	Catholic World
Chron. Okla.	Chronicles of Oklahoma
Civil War Hist.	Civil War History
Coast Artillery J.	Coast Artillery Journal
D. A. R. Mag.	D. A. R. Magazine
Eccles. Rev.	Ecclesiastical Review
Eng. Hist. Rev.	English Historical Review
Engineers Mag.	Engineers Magazine
Eugenics Q.	Eugenics Quarterly
Everglades Nat. Hist.	Everglades Natural History
Everybody's Mag.	Everybody's Magazine
F. H. Q.	Florida Historical Quarterly
Filson Club Hist. Q.	Filson Club History Quarterly
Fla. Anthro.	Florida Anthropologists
Fla. Bar J.	Florida Bar Journal
Fla. Health Notes	Florida Health Notes
Fla. Highways	Florida Highways
Fla. Law J.	Florida Law Journal
Fla. Lib.	Florida Libraries
Fla. Lib. Bull.	Florida Library Bulletin
Fla. Mag.	Florida Magazine
Fla. Pub. Lib. Newsletter	Florida Public Library Newsletter
Fla. Pub. Works	Florida Public Works
Fla. State Univ. Studies	Florida State University Studies
Fla. Trend	Florida Trend
Ga. Hist. Q.	Georgia Historical Quarterly
Ga. Rev.	Georgia Review
Geog. Rev.	Geographical Review
Gulf State Hist. Mag.	Gulf State Historical Magazine
Gunton's Mag.	Gunton's Magazine
Harper's Mag.	Harper's Magazine
Harper's New Mo. Mag.	Harper's New Monthly Magazine
Hisp. Am. Hist. Rev.	Hispanic American Historical Review
Hist. Ed. Q.	History of Education Quarterly
Hist. Mag.	Historical Magazine
Hist. Mag. Prot. Episcopal Church	Historical Magazine of the Protestant Episcopal Church

Hist. Today	History Today
Hunt. Lib. Q.	Huntington Library Quarterly
Hunt's Merchants Mag.	Hunt's Merchants Magazine
Ind. Mag. Hist.	Indiana Magazine of History
Inter. J. Am. Linguistics	International Journal of American Linguistics
J. Am. Folklore Assn.	Journal of the American Folklore Association
J. Am. Hist.	Journal of American History
J. Fla. Med. Assn.	Journal of the Florida Medical Association
J. Geog.	Journal of Geography
J. Halifax Hist. Soc.	Journal of the Halifax Historical Society
J. Hist. Med.	Journal of the History of Medicine
J. Lib. Hist.	Journal of Library History
J. Neg. Ed.	Journal of Negro Education
J. Neg. Hist.	Journal of Negro History
J. N. Y. Botanical Garden	Journal of the New York Botanical Garden
J. Politics	Journal of Politics
J. S. Hist.	Journal of Southern History
Kan. Q.	Kansas Quarterly
L. J.	Library Journal
La. Hist.	Louisiana History
La. Hist. Q.	Louisiana Historical Quarterly
La. Studies	Louisiana Studies
Labor Hist.	Labor History
Lib. Q.	Library Quarterly
Lit. Fla.	Literary Florida
Mag. Am. Hist.	Magazine of American History
Mass. Audubon Soc. Bul.	Massachusetts Audubon Society Bulletin
Miami Law Q.	Miami Law Quarterly
Mil. Engineer	Military Engineer
Miss. Hist. Soc. Pub.	Mississippi Historical Society Publications
Miss. Q.	Mississippi Quarterly
Miss. Val. Hist. Assoc. Proc.	Mississippi Valley Historical Association Proceedings
Miss. Val. Hist. Rev.	Mississippi Valley Historical Review
Monthly Labor Rev.	Monthly Labor Review
N. Am. Rev.	North American Review

Nat. Hist.	Natural History
Nat. Geo. Mag.	National Geographic Magazine
Nat. Parks Mag.	National Parks Magazine
Nat. Rep.	National Republic
Nature Mag.	Nature Magazine
N. C. Hist. Rev.	North Carolina Historical Review
Neg. Hist. Bull.	Negro History Bulletin
Notes in Anthro.	Notes in Anthropology
N. Y. Hist. Soc. Q. Bull.	New York Historical Society Quarterly Bulletin

Proc. Am. Ant. Soc.	Proceedings, American Antiquarian Society
Proc. Fla. Med. Assn.	Proceedings of the Florida Medical Association
Proc. S. Hist. Assn.	Proceedings of the Southern History Association
Proc. U. S. Naval Institute	Proceedings of the U. S. Naval Institute
Pub. Am. Jewish Hist. Soc.	Publications of the American Jewish Historical Society
Pub. Health Nursing	Public Health Nursing
Pub. Health Report	Public Health Report
Pub. La. Hist. Soc.	Publications of the Louisiana Historical Society
Pub. Miss. Hist. Soc.	Publications of the Mississippi Historical Society

Q. J. Fla. Am. & M. Col.	Quarterly Journal of Florida A & M College

Railway and Locomotive Hist. Soc. Bull.	Railway and Locomotive Historical Society Bulletin
Rel. in the Making	Religion in the Making
Rev. Meritime	Revue Meritime
Rollins Coll. Bull.	Rollins College Bulletin
Rutgers U. Lib. J.	Rutgers University Library Journal

S. Atl. Q.	South Atlantic Quarterly
Sat. Even. Post	Saturday Evening Post
S. C. Hist. Geneal. Mag.	South Carolina History and Genealogical Magazine
S. C. Hist. Mag.	South Carolina Historical Magazine
Scientific Am. Supp.	Scientific American Supplement
Scientific Mo.	Scientific Monthly
Scribner's Mag.	Scribner's Magazine
S. E. Geog.	Southeastern Geographer
S. E. Lib.	Southeastern Librarian
S. Folklore Q.	Southern Folklore Quarterly
S. Indian Stud.	Southern Indian Studies
S. Lumberman	Southern Lumberman
S. Observer	Southern Observer

Smithsonian J. Hist.	Smithsonian Journal of History
Speech Mono.	Speech Monographs
Susquehanna U. Studies	Susquehanna University Studies
Tenn. Hist. Q.	Tennessee Historical Quarterly
Trans. Am. Philos. Soc.	Transactions of the American Philosophical Society
U. Colo. Studies	University of Colorado Studies
U. Fla. Law R.	University of Florida Law Review
U. S. N. Inst. Proc.	United States Naval Institute Proceedings
Va. Cavalcade	Virginia Cavalcade
Wilson Lib. Bull.	Wilson Library Bulletin
Wm. Mary Q.	William and Mary Quarterly

Florida History: A Bibliography

PART ONE

I. GUIDES TO SOURCES

 A. Bibliographies

1. Bergquist, Constance C. "A Bibliography of Florida Library History," J. Lib. Hist. 5(1970):48-65.

2. Brunner, Kenneth August. Guide to Florida State and Local Government, With Special Reference to Pinellas County and the City of St. Petersburg. St. Petersburg: Cypress Press, 1957.

3. Calvert, J. M. "Annotated Bibliography of Florida Periodicals." Master's thesis, University of Mississippi, 1968.

4. Cole, Theodore Lee. "Bibliography of the Statute Law of the Southern States; Part 3: Florida," Proc. S. Hist. Assn. 1 (1935):211-25.

5. "A Digest of Florida Material in Niles' Register (1811-1849)," F. H. Q. 18(1940):227-28.

6. Florida. Agricultural Experiment Station. Catalog of the Official Publications of the Florida Agricultural Experiment Station and Florida Agricultural Extension Service, 1888-1937. Gainesville: University of Florida, 1938.

7. Florida. State Dept. of Education. A Suggested Library Book List for Florida Schools; a Handbook on Book Selection for All Grade Levels... Tallahassee, Fla.: State Dept. of Education, 1939. (Its Florida program for improvement of schools. Bulletin no. 8, December, 1939)

8. Florida. State Library. Florida Material in the Volumes of Niles' Register, National Intelligencer, and De Bow's Review in Florida State Library. Tallahassee: State Library, 1932.

9. Florida. University, Gainesville. Bibliography on Seminole Indians. Gainesville: University of Florida, N. Y. A. Project, 1940.

10. Florida Historical Society. Catalogue of Books, Manuscripts, Relics, and Photographs. Jacksonville: Florida Historical Society, 1916. (List for November 1916. pp. 1-15)

11. Florida Library Association. "Preliminary Checklist of Flo-
     ridiana, 1500-1865, in the Libraries of Florida," Fla. Lib.
Bull. 2(1930):1-16.

12. "Florida Newspaper Files in the Library of Congress," Gulf
     States Hist. Mag. 1(1903):277-80.

13. Floridiana, a Bibliography on Florida for Use by Public School
     Teachers and Others. Compiled by Carita Doggett Crose, A.
R. Mead, J. M. Leps, and others. Gainesville: 1945.

14. George Peabody College for Teachers. "A Bibliography and
     Checklist of Fiction on Florida, 1831-1940." Nashville:
George Peabody College for Teachers. Contribution to Education
no. 410: 1949.

15. Gipson, Laurence H. A Bibliographical Guide to the History
     of the British Empire 1748-1776: The British Empire Before
the American Revolution. New York: Alfred A. Knopf, 1969.

16. Goggin, J. M. "Source Materials for the Study of the Florida
     Seminole Indians." University of Florida, Anthropology
Laboratory, Laboratory Notes 3(1959):1-19.

17. Griffen, William B. "The Stetson Collection," Fla. Anthro.
     13(1960):33-36.

18. Hanna, Alfred Jackson. Recommended Readings for the
     Florida Centennial. Union Catalog of Floridiana. Winter
Park: Rollins College, 1945.

19. _____ . "The Union Catalog of Floridiana." Reprint from
     Proceedings of the Second Convention of the Inter-American
Bibliographical and Library Association. New York: 1939.

20. Hasbrouck, Alfred. "A Union Catalog of Floridiana," F. H. Q.
     16(1937):119-26.

21. Hendry, B. L. "Bibliography of Published Materials Concern-
     ing or Relating to the Geology of Florida From Earliest Times
to 1954." Master's thesis, Florida State University, 1958.

22. Historical Records Survey. Florida. Catalogue of the F. W.
     Hoskins Library, Panama City, Florida; Material Relating to
Florida. With Supp... Jacksonville: Historical Records Survey,
1937.

23. Historical Records Survey. Florida. Catalogue of the T. T.
     Wentworth, Jr. Collection of Floridiana. Pensacola: His-
torical Records Survey, 1936.

24. Historical Records Survey. Florida. "A Preliminary Short-
     title Check List of Books, Pamphlets, and Broadsides Printed

in Florida, 1784-1860." Compiled by Douglas C. McMurtrie.
American Imprints Inventory. Imprints Memoranda, no. 1. Jacksonville: 1937.

25. Julien C. Yonge Library. Catalogue of Julien C. Yonge Collection, Pensacola, Florida. Assembled by Historical Records Survey, 1936-37. Miami: 1938.

26. Key West Administration. Key West Bibliography; Preliminary Survey of Literature Pertaining to Key West, in Key West. Vol. 1, no. 1. Key West: Key West Historical Society, 1934.

27. Kuehl, Warren F. A Bibliography of the Writings of Hamilton Holt. Winter Park: Rollins College, 1959.

28. Larsen, William Frederick. Bibliography of Florida Government. Gainesville: Dept. of Reference and Bibliography, University of Florida Libraries, 1955.

29. Lloyd, Dorothy G. "Official Publications of Florida, 1821-1941." Master's thesis, University of Illinois, 1943.

30. Mason, Walter Scott. The People of Florida as Portrayed in American Fiction. Nashville: Bureau of Publications, 1949.

31. McGuire, Vincent. Florida in Literature. Gainesville: 1956.

32. McMurtrie, Douglas C. "The Beginnings of Printing in Florida," F. H. Q. 23(1944):63-93.

33. _____. The First Printing in Florida. Atlanta: Privately Printed, 1931.

34. McRory, Mary O. Florida in Fiction, a Bibliography. Tallahassee: Florida State Library, 1958.

35. N. Y. A. Project. Bibliography on Seminole Indians. Gainesville: 1940.

36. O'Connor, Martine J. Florida Imprints, 1782-1876. Photoreproductions of typescript. A. T. Union Catalog Division, Library of Congress.

37. Sapp, C. A. Toward a Bibliography of Florida Promotional Materials as Found in Books, Pamphlets and Reports 1865-1900. Tallahassee: State University, 1949.

38. Saunders, Harold Rinalden. "English Books Written by Floridians, Residents and Visitors." Master's thesis, University of Florida, 1929.

39. Sellards, E. H. "Bibliography of Florida Geology." In Florida

Geological Survey. Annual Report, I, 1907-08. Tallahassee:
1908.

40. Servies, James A., comp. Pensacola and West Florida: A
     Chronological Checklist of Printed Works, 1542-1969. Pen-
sacola: John C. Pace Library, University of West Florida, 1970.

41. Shea, John Gilmary. Ancient Florida. Edited by Justin Win-
     sor. Boston and New York: Houghton Mifflin, 1884-89.

42. Taylor, G. Elizabeth Woodal and A. Elizabeth Alexander. A
     Bibliography and Subject Index of Publications; Issued by Offi-
cial Florida Agencies 1942-51. Gainesville: Department of Reference and Bibliography, University of Florida Libraries, 1953.

43. Temple, Doris L. and Louis Richardson. Keeping Up With
     Florida: A Selected Reading List. Tallahassee: State Uni-
versity Library, 1953.

44. Thompson, Lawrence S. "Foreign Travellers in Florida,
     1900-1950," F. H. Q. 31(1952):92-108.

45. U. S. Library of Congress, Division of Bibliography. "List
     of Books Relating to Florida." Washington: 1921.

46. "Union Catalog of Floridiana," F. H. Q. 21(1943):362-64.

47. Willey, Gordon Randolph. Archeology of the Florida Gulf
     Coast. Washington: Smithsonian Institution, 1949.

48. Winters, C. Z. Florida History. A Course of Study Espe-
     cially Designed for Florida Club Women. Gainesville: Uni-
versity of Florida. n. d.

     B.   Guides to Manuscripts

49. Archivo Nacional de Cuba. Catalogo de los Fondos de las
     Floridas. Havana, 1944.

50. Arnade, Charles W. "Florida History in Spanish Archives;
     Reproductions at the University of Florida," F. H. Q. 34(1955):
36-50.

51. _____. "A Guide to Spanish Florida Source Material,"
     F. H. Q. 35(1956):320-25.

52. Beer, William. "List of Original Authorities on the History
     of the British Province of West Florida, in the Record Office,
London," Pub. La. Hist. Soc. 1(1896):34.

53. Bell, Herbert C., David W. Parker, and others. Guide to
     British West Indian Archive Materials, in London and in the

Islands, for the History of the United States.   Papers of the Department of Historical Research, 1926.

54.   Coker, William S., and Jack D. L. Holmes. "Sources for the History of the Spanish Borderlands," F.H.Q. 49(1971): 380-93.

55.   "Colonial Land Claims in East and West Florida," F.H.Q. 17(1939):243-44.

56.   Drewry, Elizabeth B. "Material in the National Archives Relating to Florida, 1789-1870," F.H.Q. 23(1944):97-115.

57.   Emig, Elmer J. "A Check-list of Extant Florida Newspapers, 1845-1876," F.H.Q. 9(1932):77-87.

58.   "Florida Material in the W. L. Clements Library," F.H.Q. 22(1943):103-04.

59.   Florida State Library. Florida Material in U.S. Congressional Documents in Florida State Library. Tallahassee: State Library, 1932.

60.   Gannon, Michael V. "Mission of Nombre de Dios Library," Cath. Hist. Rev. 51(1965):373-78.

61.   Griffin, Charles and Roscoe R. Hill. Descriptive Catalogue of the Documents Relating to the History of the United States in the Archivo Histórico Nacional. n. d.

62.   Hanna, Alfred Jackson. "Diplomatic Missions of the United States to Cuba to Secure the Spanish Archives of Florida." In Hispanic American Essays, a Memorial to James Alexander Robertson, edited by A. Curtis Wilgus. Chapel Hill: University of North Carolina Press, 1942.

63.   Historical Records Survey. Florida. Check List: Records Required by Law in Florida Counties. Jacksonville: Historical Records Survey, 1939.

64.   _____. Guide to Depositories of Manuscript Collections in the United States. Jacksonville: Florida Historical Records Survey, 1940.

65.   _____. Guide to Public Vital Statistics Records in Florida. Jacksonville: Historical Records Survey, 1941.

66.   _____. Inventory of the Church Archives of Florida: Baptist Bodies. Jacksonville: Historical Records Survey, 1939-41.

67.   _____. Inventory of the County Archives of Florida. Jacksonville: Historical Records Survey, 1938-42.

68. "The Historical Records Survey and State Archives Survey of
     Florida, " F. H. Q. 17(1938):59-63.

69. Holmes, Jack D. L. A Guide to Spanish Louisiana, 1762-
     1806. Louisiana Collection Series of Books and Documents
on Colonial Louisiana. Vol. 2. New Orleans: 1970.

70. _____. "Resources Outside the United States and Research
     Opportunities for Spanish Florida, 1781-1821, " In In Search of
Gulf Coast Colonial History. Ed. by Ernest W. Dibble and Earle
W. Newton (DeLand, Fla., 1970), 1-22.

71. Jacksonville, Florida. Public Library. Genealogical Material,
     Local and State History in the Jacksonville Public Library.
Compiled by Pattie Porter Frost. Jacksonville: Arnold Ptg. Company, 1929.

72. Kruse, R. C. "Library Resources for the Florida History of
     Elementary Schools. " Master's thesis, Kent State, 1958.

73. McAvoy, Thomas T. and Laurence J. Bradley, comps. Guide
     to the Microfilm Edition of the Records of the Diocese of
Louisiana and the Floridas, 1576-1803. Notre Dame: University
of Notre Dame Archives, 1967.

74. Major, H. A. "With the Spanish Records of West Florida, "
     Proceedings of the Historical Society of East and West Baton
Rouge 2(1918):60-64.

75. Manning, Mable M. "The East Florida Papers in the Library
     of Congress, " Hisp. Am. Hist. Rev. 10(1930):392-97.

76. Manucy, Albert C. "Florida History (1650-1750) in the Span-
     ish Records of North Carolina State Department of Archives
and History, " F. H. Q. 25(1947):319-32; 26(1947):77-91.

77. _____. "Notes on the Catalogo de Los Fondos de Las
     Floridas: and the Distribution of Other Florida Archival Ma-
terial for the Second Spanish Period, " F. H. Q. 25(1946):44-63.

78. "Manuscripts of Florida Interest at the University of North
     Carolina, " F. H. Q. 20(1941):210-11.

79. Mowat, Charles L. "Material Relating to British East Florida
     in the Gage Papers and Other Manuscript Collections in the
William L. Clements Library, " F. H. Q. 18(1939):46-60.

80. Neill, Wilfred T. "Surveyors' Field Notes as a Source of
     Historical Information, " F. H. Q. 34(1956):329-33.

81. Peña Y Cámara, Jose María de la. Archivo General de Indias
     de Sevilla, Guía del Visitante. Madrid: Dirrecion General de
Archivos y Bibliotecas, 1958.

82. Register Henry Shelton Sanford Papers, General Sanford Mem-
     orial Library, Sanford, Florida. Nashville: Tennessee State
Library and Archives, 1966.

83. Renz, James H. "Floridiana Collection, " L. J. 83(1958):
     2368-69.

84. "Resources for the History of the British Floridas, " F. H. Q.
     24(1946):218-38.

85. Robertson, James A. "Archival Distribution of Florida Man-
     uscripts, " F. H. Q. 10(1931):35-50.

86. _____. "The Spanish Manuscripts of the Florida State His-
     torical Society, " Proc. Am. Ant. Soc. 39(1929):16-37.

87. Shaw, B. "University of Florida's Chinsequt Hill Library, "
     L. J. 81(1956):118-20.

88. Sociedad Colombista Panamericana. Documents Pertaining to
     the Floridas Which Are Kept in Different Archives of Cuba.
Havana: 1945.

89. Survey of Federal Archives. Florida. Inventory of Federal
     Archives in the States. Jacksonville: Survey of Federal Ar-
chives, 1940-41.

90. Tanner, Helen H. "List of Documents Pertaining to the His-
     tory of East Florida in the Gage Papers [American Series]. "
In the William L. Clements Library, Ann Arbor, Mich. Typescript,
1952.

91. _____. "List of Documents Pertaining to the History of
     Florida in the Amherst Papers. " At the Clements Library,
Ann Arbor, Mich. Typescript, 1951.

92. _____. "List of Documents Pertaining to the History of
     Florida in the Gage Papers [English Series]. " At the William
L. Clements Library, Ann Arbor, Mich. Typescript, 1950.

93. Thomas, David Y. "Report Upon the Historic Buildings, Mon-
     uments, and Local Archives of St. Augustine, Florida, " Ann.
Rep. Am. Hist. Assn. 1(1905):339-52.

94. _____. "Report on the Public Archives of Florida, " Ann.
     Rep. Am. Hist. Assn. 2(1906):149-58.

95. "Typescripts of Manuscripts Made by Florida Historical Re-
     cords Survey, " F. H. Q. 18(1940):216-24.

96. U. S. Library of Congress. Florida's Centennial... With a
     Catalog of the Exhibition. Washington: Government Printing
Office, 1946.

97.   Wright, Irene A. "The Odyssey of the Spanish Archives of
      Florida." In Hispanic American Essays, a Memorial to
James Alexander Robertson, edited by A. Curtis Wilgus. Chapel
Hill: University of North Carolina Press, 1942. pp. 169-207.

98.   Wroth, Lawrence C. "Source Materials of Florida History
      in the John Carter Brown Library of Brown University," F.
H. Q. 20(1941):3-46.

      C. Historiography

99.   Akerman, Hugh, Jr. "The Novel's Place in History: A
      Study of Florida Fiction." Master's thesis, University of
Florida, 1955.

100. Arana, Luis Rafael. "The Exploration of Florida and Sources
      on the Founding of St. Augustine," F. H. Q. 44(1965):1-16.

101. Arnade, Charles W. "Cycles of Conquest in Florida," Te-
      questa 23(1963):23-31.

102. _____. "Recent Problems of Florida History," F. H. Q.
      42(1963):1-15.

103. Buckman, H. H. "The Geological Background of Florida
      History," Jacksonville Historical Society Annual (1933-34):1-8.

104. Campbell, A. C. "Study of the Aspects of Good Citizenship
      Found in a Selected Number of Titles About Florida." Mas-
ter's thesis, Atlanta, 1961.

105. Corse, Carita Doggett. "Florida History--a Field of Color-
      ful Original Sources," F. H. Q. 6(1927):33-39.

106. Davis, T. Frederick. "Florida's Great Seas; Its Historical
      Inaccuracies," F. H. Q. 3(1924):16-19.

107. Doherty, Herbert J., Jr. "Florida Bibliography and Histori-
      ography; Writings in Florida History on the Period 1821-
1860," F. H. Q. 37(1958):160-74.

108. _____. "Florida Books From University Presses," F. H.
      Q. 42(1963):170-73.

109. Eddy, Henrie M. "The Guide to Historical Literature."
      Master's thesis, Columbia University, 1933.

110. _____. "A Study of Bibliographic Guides Available for the
      Formation of a Collection of Florida History and Literature
With Special Study of the Guide to Historical Literature as a Means
of Selecting Regional Material." Master's thesis, Columbia University, 1933.

111. Fletcher, Duncan U. "Address Before the Florida Historical
      Society, " F. H. Q. 4(1925):22-30.

112. Florida State Historical Society. Charter and By-laws of the
      Florida State Historical Society. Deland: Florida State His-
torical Society, 1922.

113. _____ . Historical Society of Florida. Organized in St.
      Augustine, 1856. New York: J. A. Gray, 1856.

114. Gadsden, James. "Florida, " N. Am. Rev. 26(1828):478-97.

115. Griffin, William B. "Suggestions for Research in the Cul-
      ture and Society of Spanish Florida, " F. H. Q. 38(1960):
226-38.

116. Hale, Nathan. "Florida, " N. Am. Rev. 13(1821):62-100.

117. Hanke, Lewis. Bartolomé de las Casas, Historian; an Es-
      say in Spanish Historiography. Gainesville: University of
Florida Press, 1952.

118. Held, Ray E. "Spanish Florida in American Historiography,
      1821-1921. " Ph. D. dissertation, University of Florida,
1955.

119. Jacksonville Community Service. Florida Historical Pa-
      geant, Official Program, Presented at Jacksonville, Florida,
April 20, 21, 22, 1922. Jacksonville: Tutewiler Press, 1922.

120. Johnson, James G. "Myths, Legends, Miracles, Related
      by the First Historians of Florida, " Ga. Hist. Q. 8(1924):
292-303.

121. Jones, E. V. W. "The Use of Florida Historical Material
      by a Journalist, " F. H. Q. 18(1939):127-31.

122. Kimber, Sidney A. "The Relation of a Late Expedition to
      St. Augustine. " Papers of the Bibliographic Society of
America 28(1934):81-96.

123. Lamson, Herbert. "History of the Jacksonville Historical
      Society, " Papers of the Jacksonville Historical Society
1(1947):113-21.

124. _____ . "History of the Jacksonville Historical Society, "
      Papers of the Jacksonville Historical Society 2(1949):90-92.

125. _____ . "History of the Jacksonville Historical Society,
      1949-1954, " Papers of the Jacksonville Historical Society
3(1954):178-180.

126. Lazear, E. A. "Extent and Availability of Locally Prepared
      Indexes to Florida Materials With Emphasis on Periodicals."
Master's thesis, Florida State, 1961.

127. Manucy, Albert C. "Barcia's History of Florida," F. H. Q.
      31(1953):290-301.

128. Marchman, Watt. "The Florida Historical Society, 1856-
      1861, 1879, 1902-1940," F. H. Q. 19(1940):3-65.

129. _____. "Research Projects on Florida Subjects," F. H. Q.
      20(1942):362-79.

130. McDuffee, Lillie B. "Writing Local History," F. H. Q.
      24(1946):210-15.

131. Patrick, Rembert W. "The Collection of Historical Material
      in Florida," Papers of the Jacksonville Historical Society
      1(1947):1-15.

132. Robertson, James Alexander. "The Preservation of Florida
      History," N. C. Hist. Rev. 4(1927):351-65.

133. _____. "The Significance of Florida's History," F. H. Q.
      6(1927):25-32.

134. Smith, Hale G. "Florida Bibliography and Historiography;
      the Development of Knowledge Regarding the Florida Indians,"
      F. H. Q. 37(1958):156-60.

135. Stetson, J. B., Jr. "Florida as a Field for Historical Re-
      search," Report of the American Historical Association for
      1922. Vol. 1, pp. 191-98.

136. Tebeau, C. W. "Florida Bibliography and Historiography;
      Historical Writing on Twentieth Century Florida," F. H. Q.
      37(1958):174-77.

137. Vinten, C. R. "The Conservation of Historic Sites in Flori-
      da," F. H. Q. 23(1944):122-26.

138. Warren, Harris G. "Textbook Writers and the Florida Pur-
      chase Myth," F. H. Q. 41(1963):325-31.

139. Wilgus, A. Curtis. "James Alexander Robertson," F. H. Q.
      18(1939):3-10.

140. Wysor, Fred J. Sources for Facts About Florida. Tampa:
      F. J. Wysor, n. d.

II. MAPS

141. Arana, Luis Rafael. "The Alonso Solana Map of Florida, 1683, " F. H. Q. 42(1964):258-66.

142. Arnade, Charles W. "Three Early Spanish Tampa Bay Maps [18th Cent.], " Tequesta 25(1965):83-96.

143. Barlow, R. H. "A Hitherto Unknown Map of the Pensacola Coastal Region, 1762, " F. H. Q. 22(1943):41.

144. Baxter, John Matthews. "An Annotated Checklist of Florida Maps, " Tequesta 1(1941):107-15.

145. Beazley, Jon S. "Florida State Road Department Re-mapping Program [1936-48], " Surveying and Mapping 9(1949):28-38.

146. Boyd, Mark F. , ed. "A Map of the Road From Pensacola to St. Augustine, 1778, " F. H. Q. 17(1938):15-24.

147. Bushong, Allen D. "Research on the Southeast by Geographers, 1946-1967, " S. E. Geog. 9(1969):48-84.

148. Carr, Kenneth L. Map of Lost, Buried, Sunken Treasures of the Florida Keys. Produced by Caribbean Instrument Co. and Algomah Instrument Co. West Palm Beach: F. L. Coffman, 1952.

149. Chambers, Henry Edward. West Florida and Its Relation to the Historical Cartography of the United States. Baltimore: The Johns Hopkins press, 1898.

150. Coffman, Ferris La Verne. Treasure Map of Florida. Produced by Caribbean Instrument Company, West Palm Beach, Fla. , and Algomah Instrument Company, Mackinaw City, Mich. West Palm Beach: F. L. Coffman, 1952.

151. Craig, Alan K. , and Christopher S. Peebles. "Captain Young's Sketch Map, 1818, " F. H. Q. 48(1969):176-79.

152. Cumming, William P. "Mapping of the Southeast: The First Two Centuries, " S. E. Geog. 6(1966):3-19.

153. _____ . The Southeast in Early Maps. Princeton, N. J.: Princeton University Press, 1958. Revised and Supplemented edition, Chapel Hill, N. C.: University of North Carolina Press, 1962.

154. Harley, A. F. "Bernard Romans' Map of Florida Engraved by Paul Revere, and Other Early Maps in the Library of the Florida Historical Society, " F. H. Q. 9(1930):47-57.

155. Hurst, Robert R., Jr. "Mapping Old St. Joseph, Its Rail-
      roads, and Environs," F. H. Q. 39(1961):354-65.

156. Karpinski, Louis C. "Manuscript Maps Relating to American
      History in French, Spanish, and Portuguese Archives," Am.
Hist. Rev. 33(1928):328-30.

157. _____. "Mapping Florida," Print Connoisseur 9(1929):
      291-310.

158. Lanzas, Pedro Torres. Relacion Descriptiva de Los Mapas,
      Planos, &c. de Mexico Y Floridas, Existentes en el Archivo
General de Indias. Sevilla: El Mercantil San Eloy, 1900.

159. McMullen, Edwin Wallace. English Topographic Terms in
      Florida, 1563-1874. Ann Arbor: University Microfilms,
1950.

160. Raisz, Erwin and John R. Dunkle, eds. Atlas of Florida.
      Gainesville: University of Florida Press, 1964.

161. Roehrig, J. P. "Toward a Carto Bibliography of Florida
      Maps Before 1784 With References to Their Locations in
Florida Libraries and Major Libraries in the United States." Master's thesis, Florida State, 1955.

162. Seckinger, Ron L. "Observations on the Origin and Date of
      a Seventeenth-Century Florida Map," F. H. Q. 43(1965):385-87.

163. True, David O. "The Freducci Map of 1514-1515: What it
      Discloses of Early Florida History," Tequesta 1(1944):50-55.

164. _____. "Some Early Maps Relating to Florida," Imago
      Mundi (Leiden) 11(1954):73-84.

165. Wilson, Emily F. "The Plantation Area--Maps," J. of the
      Halifax Hist. Soc. 2(1957):15-23.

III. GENERAL WORKS

166. Bauskett, J. S. Story of Florida. Dansville, N. Y.: F. A.
      Owen Publishing Company, 1913.

167. Beater, Jack. Islands of the Florida Coast; Stories of Ad-
      venture. Fort Myers: Jack Beater, 1956.

168. _____. True Tales of the Florida West Coast. Fort
      Myers, Florida: Wordshop House, 1959.

169. Bolton, Herbert Eugene. The Spanish Borderlands; A Chron-
      icle of Old Florida and the Southwest. New Haven: Yale
University Press, 1921.

170. Bowe, Richard J. Pictorial History of Florida. Tallahassee:
      Historical Publications, 1965.

171. Brevard, Caroline Mays. A History of Florida. New York:
      American Book Company, 1904.

172. _____. A History of Florida From the Treaty of 1763 to
      Our Own Times. 2 vols. Edited by James Alexander
Robertson. Deland: The Florida State Historical Society, 1924-25.

173. Brinton, Daniel Garrison. Notes on the Floridian Peninsula,
      Its Literary History, Indian Tribes, and Antiquities. Phila-
delphia: J. Sabin, 1859.

174. Brooks, Thomas Joseph. Brief History and Civics of the
      State of Florida; also, the State Capitol, State Flag and Seal,
State Flower and Bird, State Song and State Government. Tallahassee: N. Mayo, Commissioner of Agriculture, 1953.

175. Campbell, Richard L. Historical Sketches of Colonial Flori-
      da. Cleveland, Ohio: The Williams Publishing Company,
1892.

176. Carson, Ruby Leach, and Charlton W. Tebeau. Florida:
      From Indian Trail to Space Age. 3 vols. Delray Beach:
Southern Publishing Company, 1966.

177. Cash, William Thomas. The Story of Florida. 4 vols.
      New York: The American Historical Society, Inc., 1938.

178. Chapin, George M. Florida, 1513-1913, Past, Present and
      Future; Four Hundred Years of Wars and Peace and Indus-
trial Development. 2 vols. Chicago: S. J. Clarke Publishing
Company, 1914.

179. Copeland, Leeila S., and Dovell, J. E. La Florida: Its
      Land and People. Austin, Texas: Steck Company, 1957.

180. Covington, James Warren. The Story of Southwestern Flori-
      da. 2 vols. New York: Lewis Historical Publishing Com-
pany, 1957.

181. Cutler, Harry Gardner. History of Florida, Past and Pre-
      sent, Historical and Biographical... 3 vols. Chicago: The
Lewis Publishing Company, 1923.

182. Dau, Frederick W. Florida Old and New. New York: Put-
      nam, 1934.

183. Dibble, Ernest F. and Earle W. Newton, eds. In Search of
     Gulf Coast Colonial History: Proceedings of the First Gulf
Coast History and Humanities Conference. Pensacola: Historic
Pensacola Preservation Board, 1970.

184. Dodd, Dorothy. "The Flags of the State of Florida," F. H. Q.
     23(1945):160-69.

185. Douglas, Marjory Stoneman. Florida: The Long Frontier.
     New York: Harper and Row, 1967.

186. Dovell, Junius Elmore. Florida: Historic, Dramatic, Con-
     temporary. 4 vols. New York: Lewis Historical Publish-
ing Company, [1952].

187. Dunn, Hampton. Re-discover Florida. [Miami]: Hurricane
     House, 1969.

188. Fairbanks, George Rainsford. The Early History of Florida.
     St. Augustine: Florida Historical Society, 1857.

189. _____. Florida, Its History and Its Romance. Jackson-
     ville: H. & W. B. Drew Company, 1898.

190. _____. History of Florida From Its Discovery by Ponce
     de Leon, in 1512, to the Close of the Florida War, in 1842.
Philadelphia: J. B. Lippincott & Company; Jacksonville: C. Drew,
1871.

191. Fairlie, Margaret Carrick. History of Florida. [Kingsport,
     Tenn.] Priv. print.: [Kingsport Press], [1935].

192. Farney, Charles M. Florida Handbook of Facts. [St. Paul:
     Webb Publishing Company], [1931].

193. Florida. Department of Agriculture. Florida, the Land of
     Romance [since 1493]. Tallahassee: Peninsular Publishing
Company, 1956.

194. Flynn, Stephen J. Florida, Land of Fortune. Washington,
     D. C.: Luce, 1962.

195. Fritz, Florence Irene. Unknown Florida. Coral Gables:
     University of Miami Press, 1963.

196. Goggin, John M. Indian and Spanish Selected Writings.
     Coral Gables: University of Miami Press, 1964.

197. Greenhow, Robert. The History of Florida, Louisiana, Texas,
     and California... From the Discovery to Their Incorporation
With the United States of America. New York: n. p., 1856.

198. Hanna, Alfred Jackson, and Kathryn Trimmer (Abbey) Hanna.
     Florida's Golden Sands. Indianapolis: Bobbs-Merrill, [1950].

199. Hanna, Kathryn Trimmer. Florida: Land of Change [1513-
     1947]. 2nd rev. ed. Chapel Hill: University of North Car-
     olina Press, [1948].

200. Harrison, Benjamin. "Old Pictures of the New Florida;
     Ponce de Leon and His Land, " F.H.Q. 3(1924):29-36.

201. Jenkinson, Richard C. Florida. [Woodstock, Vermont:
     Elm Tree Press, 1928].

202. Jernigan, Ernest Harris. Florida: Past, Present, Future.
     Ocala: Florida Research Press, 1964.

203. La Gorce, J. O. "Florida: The Fountain of Youth, " Nat.
     Geo. Mag. 57(1930):1-93.

204. Leake, James Miller. A Short History of Florida. Boston:
     Heath, [1924].

205. Long, Ellen C. Florida Breezes: or, Florida New and Old.
     Jacksonville: Ashmead Brothers, 1882.

206. McKay, D. B., ed. Pioneer Florida. 3 vols. Tampa:
     Southern Publishing Company, 1959.

207. McNeer, May Yonge. The Story of Florida. New York:
     Harper, 1947.

208. Nance, Ellwood Cecil, et. al. The East Coast of Florida,
     a History, 1500-1961. 3 vols. Delray Beach: Southern
     Publishing Company, 1962.

209. Nightingale, Lloyd Turner. Florida: The Strange and the
     Curious. New York: Vantage Press, 1969.

210. Patrick, Rembert Wallace. Florida Under Five Flags. 4th
     ed. Gainesville: University of Florida Press, 1967.

211. _____, Eleanor B. Patrick, and Hester G. Fisackerly.
     The Story of Florida. Austin, Texas: Steck Company, 1957.

212. Ranson, Robert. Chronology of the Most Important Events
     Connected With Florida History During Four Hundred and
     Seventeen Years, 1513 to 1930. 2nd ed. St. Augustine: R. Ranson,
     1930.

213. Reese, Montana Lisle. Bean Soup; or, Florida With a Span-
     ish Accent. Jacksonville: Crawford, 1964.

214. Rerick, Rowland H. Memoirs of Florida; Embracing a General History of the Province, Territory and State. 2 vols. Edited by Francis P. Fleming. Atlanta, Georgia: The Southern Historical Association, 1902.

215. Simpson, J. Clarence. "Middle Florida Place Names," Apalachee 2(1946):68-77.

216. Smith, Mary Ellen. South Florida Frontiers. Miami: Florida Power and Light, 1957.

217. Snodgrass, Dena. "Collected Papers," Papers of the Jacksonville Historical Society 5(1969):entire issue.

218. Tebault, Alfred George. Chronicles of Florida. Norfolk, Virginia: J. W. Bancroft, 1886.

219. Tebeau, Charlton W., et. al. Florida From Indian Trail to Space Age; A History... Delray Beach: The Southern Publishing Company, 1965.

220. Tebeau, Charlton W. A History of Florida. Miami: University of Miami Press, 1971.

221. Vignoles, Charles Blacker. The History of the Floridas, From the Discovery by Cabot, in 1497, to the Cession of the Same to the United States, in 1821. Brooklyn, N.Y.: G. L. Birch, 1824.

222. _____. Observations Upon the Floridas. New York: E. Bliss & E. White, 1823.

223. Wentworth, Theodore T. Historical Reproductions From The Collection of T. T. Wentworth, Jr., Pensacola. Florida. Pensacola: n.p., 1937.

IV.   DISCOVERY AND EXPLORATION TO 1565

A.   General Studies

224. Arana, Luis Rafael. "The Exploration of Florida and Sources on the Founding of St. Augustine," F. H. Q. 44(1965):1-16.

225. Arnade, Charles W. "Tristan de Luna and Ochuse (Pensacola Bay) 1559," F. H. Q. 37(1959):201-222.

226. Bennett, Charles E. Settlement of Florida. Gainesville: University of Florida Press, 1968.

227. Bolton, Herbert Eugene. Coronado; Knight of Pueblos and Plains. Albuquerque: University of New Mexico, 1949.

228. Brebner, John Bartlet. The Explorers of North America, 1492-1806. London: A. & C. Black Ltd., 1933.

229. Buhler, Curt Ferdinand. Novello Cattanio: Un Viaggio Fatto Alli Paesi del Continente Nuovo. Essays Honoring Lawrence C. Wroth. Portland, Maine: Anthoensen Press, 1951.

230. Buker, George Edward. "The Seven Cities; the Role of a Myth on the Discovery and Exploration of America." Master's thesis, University of Florida, 1965.

231. Cabeza de Vaca, Alvar Nunez. The Journey of Alvar Nunez Cabeza de Vaca and his Companions From Florida to the Pacific, 1528-1536. New York: A. S. Barnes, 1905.

232. _____. Naufragios y Relacion de la Journada gue Hizo a la Florida Con el Adelantado Ponfilo Norvaez. Madrid: Blass, 1928.

233. _____. The Power Within Us. Cabez de Vaca's Relation of His Journey From Florida to the Pacific 1528-1536. New York: Sloan and Pearce, 1944.

234. Connolly, Mathew J. "Four Contemporary Narratives of the Founding of St. Augustine," Cath. Hist. Rev. 51(1965):305-34.

235. Drake, Samuel Gardner. "Narrative of the Captivity of John Ortiz, a Spaniard, Who Was Eleven Years a Prisoner Among the Indians of Florida." In Tragedies of the Wilderness..., by S. G. Drake, pp. 9-20. Boston: Antiquarian Bookstore and Institute, 1844.

236. Escalente Fontaneda, Hernando d'. Memoirs of D° d'Escalente Fontaneda Respecting Florida. Translated by Buckingham Smith. Edited by David O. True. Miami: University of Miami and the Historical Association of Southern Florida, Miscellaneous Publications, No. I, 1944.

237. "Explorations and Settlements in the Spanish Borderlands: Their Religious Motivations." Papers Read at the Historical Symposium Sponsored by the Mission Nombre de Dios Under the Auspices of the St. Augustine Foundation, October 26, 1966. St. Augustine: St. Augustine Mission Nombre de Dios, 1967.

238. French, Benjamin Franklin, ed. Historical Collections of Louisiana and Florida, Including Translations of Original Manuscripts Relating to Their Discovery and Settlement, With Numerous Historical and Biographical Notes. 2d ser. Historical Memoirs and Narratives, 1527-1702. New York: A. Mason, 1875.

239. Fuller, A. W. F. "An Original Sixteenth Century Painting
      of Natives of Florida by LeMoyne With Historical Notes and
Observations Relating To It." In International Congress of Ameri-
canists. 20th Rio de Janeiro, 1922. Vol. 2. Annaes...Rio de
Janeiro, 1928.

240. Garcia, Genaro, ed. Dos Antiquas Relaciones de la Florida;
      Publicadas Por Primera Vez Genar o Garcia. Mexico: Tip.
y lit. de J. Aguilar Vera y Comp., 1902.

241. Hanna, A. J. "Beginnings of Florida," Am. Heritage
      4(1952):62-64.

242. Headley, J. T. "The First Colonists of Florida," Harpers
      Mag. 20(1860):503-13.

243. Kohl, J. G. "A History of the Discovery of the East Coast
      of North America,..." In Collections of the Maine Historical
Society. 2d ser. Portland: Bailey and Noyes, 1869.

244. Lawson, Edward W. The Discovery of Florida and Its Dis-
      coverer Juan Ponce de Leon. St. Augustine: E. W. Law-
son, 1946.

245. Long, Daniel. Interlinear to Cabeza de Vaca: His Relation
      of the Journey From Florida to the Pacific, 1528-1536.
Santa Fe: Writers' Editions, 1936.

246. Lowery, Woodbury. The Spanish Settlements Within the Pre-
      sent Limits of the United States, 1513-1561. Vol. I. 1562-
1574. Vol. II. New York: G. P. Putnam's Sons, 1901.

247. Muniz, Jose Rivero. "Primeros Viajes de los Espanoles a
      la Florida [1512-68] Cuba," Bibl. Nac. Rev. 6(1955):133-59.

248. Priestley, Herbert Ingram, ed. The Luna Papers: Docu-
      ments Relating to the Expedition of Don Tristan de Luna Y
Arellano for the Conquest of La Florida in 1559-1561. 2 vols.
Translated by H. I. Priestley. De Land: The Florida Historical
Society, Publications of the Florida State Historical Society, No. 8,
1928.

249. _____. Tristan de Luna, Conquistador of the Old South;
      a Study of Spanish Imperial Policy. Glendale, California:
Arthur H. Clark Company, 1936.

250. Roberts, William. An Account of the First Discovery, and
      Natural History of Florida...Collected From the Best Author-
ities... London: T. Jeffreys, 1763.

251. Slaughter, Frank G. "Who Discovered Florida?" Papers of
      the Tallahassee Historical Society 4(1960):1-19.

252. Trumball, Henry. History of the Discovery of America:
      ... To Which is Annexed the Particulars of Almost Every
Important Engagement With the Savages in the United States and
Territories... Boston: George Clark, 1840.

          B. Pedro Menendez de Aviles

253. Barrientos, Bartolome. Pedro Menendez de Aviles, Founder
      of Florida. Translated by Anthony Kerrigan. Gainesville:
University of Florida Press, 1965.

254. Bellamy, Ruthjeanne. "The Personality of Pedro Menendez,"
      F. H. Q. 5(1927):202-07.

255. Camin, Alfonso. El Adelantado de la Florida, Pedro Menen-
      dez de Aviles. Mexico: Revista Norte, 1944.

256. Connor, Jeannette Thurber (trans.). Pedro Menendez de Aviles.
      Adelantado, Governor, and Captain General of Florida. Mem-
orial of Gonzalo Solis de Meras. Translated by Jeannette Thurber
Connor. DeLand: Florida State Historical Society, No. 3, 1923.

257. Covinton, James W. "A Floride: 1565," F. H. Q. 41(1963):
      274-81.

258. Hoffman, Paul Everett. "The Background and Development
      of Pedro Menendez's Contribution to the Defense of the Span-
ish Indies." Master's thesis, University of Florida, 1965.

259. _____. "The Narrow Waters Strategies of Pedro Menen-
      dez," F. H. Q. 45(1966):12-17.

260. Lowe, E. R. "Association of the Caloosa Indians With the
      Spanish Explorer Pedro Menendez," Martello no. 1(1964):
      15-16.

261. Manucy, Albert C. Florida's Menendez, Captain General of
      the Ocean Sea. St. Augustine: St. Augustine Historical So-
ciety, 1965.

262. _____. "The Man Who Was Pedro Menendez," F. H. Q.
      44(1965):67-80.

263. Mendoza Grajales, Francisco Lopez de. ... The Founding of
      St. Augustine. Memoir of the Happy Result and Prosperous
Voyage of the Fleet Commanded by the Illustrious Captain-General
Pedro Menendez de Aviles, Which Sailed From Cadiz on the Morn-
ing of Thursday, June 28th, for the Coast of Florida, and Arrived
There on the 28th of August, 1565. Boston: Directors of the Old
South Work, 1897.

264. Menendez De Aviles, Pedro. "Translations of the Letters of
      Menendez to Phillip II in 1565," Proc. Mass. Hist. Soc. 2d
ser. 8(1894):417-68.

265. Reding, Katherine, ed. "Letter of Gonzalo Menendez de
      Canzo, Governor of Florida, to Phillip II of Spain of June
28, 1600," Ga. Hist. Q. 8(1924):215-28.

266. Ruidiaz y Caravia, Eugenio. ...La Florida; su Conquista y
      Colonizacion por Pedro Menendez de Aviles; Obra Premiada
por la Real Academia de la Historia... 2 vols. Madrid: Imp.
de los hijos de J. A. Garcia, 1893.

267. Reese, Nancy Bryan. "Menendez, the man," Jacksonville
      Historical Society Annual (1933-34):29-43.

268. Vigil, Ciriaco Miguel. Noticias Biographico--Genealogicas
      de Pedro Menendez de Aviles, Primer Adelantado y Conquis-
tador de la Florida. Aviles: La Union, 1892.

269. Vigneras, L. A. "A Spanish Discovery of North Carolina
      in 1566," N. C. Hist. Rev. 46(1969):398-407.

      C.   Ponce de Leon

270. Arnade, Charles W. "Who Was Juan Ponce de Leon?" Te-
      questa 27(1967):29-58.

271. Ballesteros Gaibrois, Manuel. La Idea Colonial de Ponce
      de Leon: Un Ensayo de Interpretacion. San Juan, Puerto
Rico: Instituto de Cultura Puertorriquena, 1960.

272. Davis, T. Frederick. "History of Juan Ponce de Leon's
      Voyages to Florida," F. H. Q. 14(1935):1-70.

273. _____. "Ponce de Leon's Discovery of Florida (map),"
      F. H. Q. 11(1933):opposite p. 172.

274. _____. "The Record of Ponce de Leon's Discovery of
      Florida, 1513," F. H. Q. 11(1932):5-15.

275. Irving, Washington. Voyages and Discoveries of the Com-
      panions of Columbus. New York: Ungar, 1956.

276. Jerome, Father. Juan Ponce de Leon. St. Leo, Florida:
      Abbey Press, 1962.

277. King, Ethel. The Fountain of Youth and Juan Ponce de Leon.
      Brooklyn: Theodore Gaus & Sons, Inc., 1963.

278. Lamson, Herbert. "Juan Ponce de Leon," Jacksonville His-
      torical Society Annual (1933-34):9-13.

279. Lawson, Edward W. Determination of the First Landing
     Place of Juan Ponce de Leon on the North American Conti-
nent in the Year 1513. [St. Augustine?]: 1954.

280. _____. The Discovery of Florida and its Discoverer Juan
     Ponce de Leon. St. Augustine: Edward W. Lawson, 1946.

281. Mann, Florian A. The Story of Ponce de Leon, Soldier,
     Knight, Gentleman, Whose Quest for the Fountain of Youth
in the Land of Bimini Led to the Discovery of Florida. De Land:
E. O. Painter & Co., 1903.

282. Murga Sanz, Mincente. Juan Ponce de Leon. San Juan:
     Universidad de Puerto Rico Press, 1959.

283. Olschki, Leonardo. "Ponce de Leon's Fountain of Youth:
     History of a Geographic Myth, " Hisp. Am. Hist. Rev.
21(1941):361-85.

284. Over, Frederick A. Juan Ponce de Leon. Heroes of Amer-
     ican History Series. New York: Harper & Brothers, 1908.

285. Scisco, Louis Dow. "Ponce de Leon's Patents for Coloniza-
     tion, " Records of the American Catholic Historical Society
of Philadelphia 23(1912):201-11.

286. _____. "The Track of Ponce de Leon in 1513, " Bull.
     Am. Geo. Soc. 45(1913):721-35.

287. Zabriskie, George Albert. "Landing of Ponce de Leon in
     Florida, " N. Y. Hist. Soc. Q. Bull. 29(1945):197-201.

     D. Hernando DeSoto

288. Abbott, John S. C. Ferdinand de Soto... New York: Dodd,
     Mead and Company, 1903.

289. Andrews, Daniel Marshall. Desoto's Route From Cofitache-
     qui, in Georgia, to Cosa, in Alabama. Lancaster, Pennsyl-
vania: New Era Printing Company, 1917.

290. Baber, Adin. "Food Plants of the Desoto Expedition, 1539-
     1543, " Tequesta 1(1942):34-40.

291. Boyd, Mark F. "The Arrival of De Soto's Expedition in
     Florida, " F. H. Q. 16(1938):188-220.

292. Bullen, Ripley P. "De Soto's Ucita and the Terra Ceia site
     [1539], " F. H. Q. 30(1952):317-23.

293. Choate, Charles A. "De Soto in Florida, " Gulf States Hist.
     Mag. 1(1903):342-44.

294. "Concession Made by the King of Spain to Hernando De Soto
      of the Government of Cuba and Conquest of Florida, With
the Title of Adelantado, " F. H. Q. 16(1938):179-87.

295. Daly, Dominick, tr. Adventures of Roger L'Estrange:
      Sometime Captain in the Florida Army of His Excellency the
Marquis Hernando de Soto...An Autobiography. London: Swan
Sonnenschein & Company, Limited, 1896.

296. De Soto, Hernando. "Letter Written to the Secular Cabildo
      of Santiago de Cuba by Hernando De Soto (July 9, 1539), "
F. H. Q. 16(1938):174-78.

297. Gibson, John L. "The DeSoto Expedition in the Mississippi
      Valley, I: Evaluation of the Geographical Potential of the
Lower Ouachita River Valley With Regard to the DeSoto-Moscoso
Expedition, " La. Studies (1968):203-12.

298. Goggin, John Mann. "Are there De Soto Relics in Florida?"
      F. H. Q. 32(1954):151-62.

299. Hernandez Diaz, Jose. ...Expedicion del Adelantado Her-
      nando DeSoto a la Florida; Notas y Documentos Relativos a
su Organizacion.... Sevilla: Impr. de la Garidia, 1938.

300. Irving, Theodore. The Conquest of Florida Under Hernando
      de Soto. London: Edward Churton, 1835.

301. King, Grace. DeSoto and His Men in the Land of Florida.
      New York: Macmillan Company, 1898.

302. "Letter to the King of Spain From Officers at Havana in the
      Army of De Soto, " F. H. Q. 16(1938):221-23.

303. Lewis, Theodore Hayes. "The Chronicle of DeSoto's Expe-
      dition, " Publications of the Mississippi Historical Society
7(1903):379-97.

304. McWilliams, Tennant S. "The DeSoto Expedition in the Mis-
      sissippi Valley, II [Spanish] Armada on the Mississippi, " La.
Studies (1968):213-27.

305. Phinney, A. H. "Narvaez and DeSoto; Their Landing Places
      and the Town of Espirito Santo, " F. H. Q. 3(1925):15-21.

306. Robertson, James Alexander. True Relation of the Hardships
      Suffered by Governor Hernando de Soto and Certain Portu-
guese Gentlemen During the Discovery of the Province of Florida.
Translated and Edited by a gentleman of Elvas. 2 vols. DeLand:
The Florida State Historical Society, 1933.

307. Schell, Rolfe. DeSoto Didn't Land at Tampa. Fort Myers
      Beach, Florida: Island Press, 1966.

308. Serrano y Sanz, Manuel. Expedicion de Hernando de Soto a
      la Florida (fragmentos del discurso preparado por el senor
Serrano para su ingreso en la Academia de la historia) Precedidos
de una Noticia Biobibliografica del Autor, por Vicente Castaneda.
Madrid: Tip. de Archivos, 1933.

309. Shipp, Barnard. The History of Hernando de Soto and Flor-
      ida; or, Record of the Events of Fifty-six Years, From 1512
to 1568. Philadelphia: Collins, 1881.

310. Steck, Francis Borgia. "Neglected Aspects of the DeSoto
      Expedition, " Mid-America 15(1932):3-26.

311. Swanton, John Reed. "De Soto and Terra Ceia, " F. H. Q.
      31(1953):196-207.

312. _____. "De Soto's First Headquarters in Florida, " F. H.
      Q. 30(1952):311-16.

313. _____. "Ethnological Value of the DeSoto Narratives, "
      Am. Anthro. 34(1932):570-90.

314. _____. "The Landing Place of DeSoto, " F. H. Q. 16(1938):
      149-73.

315. Vasques, Alonzo. "Memorial of Alonzo Vazquez to the King
      of Spain, Asking for Certain Priviledges, and Permission to
Reside in Florida; With the Testimony of Persons as to His Services in the Army of Hernando DeSoto, During the Invasion at the
Province. " Translated by Buckingham Smith. Hist. Mag. 4(1860):
257-61.

316. Wilkinson, Warren Hager. Opening the Case Against the U.
      S. De Soto Commission's Report, Being a "Thorough-going
Examination" of the Part in Re present Florida of the Final Report
of the U. S. De Soto Expedition Commission. Vicariously Sponsored
by the 75th Congress, 1st session (House document no. 71) U. S. G.
P. O. , 1939. Jacksonville Beach: Alliance for the Preservation of
Florida Antiquities, 1960.

V. THE FRENCH IN FLORIDA, 1562-1568

317. Barnwell, Joseph W. "European Settlements in the East
      Coast of North America, " S. C. Hist. Geneal. Mag. 25(1924):
88-93.

318. Bennett, Charles E. "A Footnote on Rene Laudonniere, " F.
      H. Q. 45(1967):289-91.

319.   . Laudonniere and Fort Caroline: History and
Documents. Gainesville: University of Florida Press, 1964.

320.   . Settlement of Florida. Gainesville: University
of Florida Press, 1968.

321.   , tr. "A 16th Century French Manuscript Bearing
the Only Known Signature of Rene Laudonniere, " F. H. Q.
39(1961):256-59.

322.   , tr. "A 16th Century French 'Mug Book' Brings
to Light Interesting Comments on Florida History--Saturiba
Being Featured, " F. H. Q. 39(1961):260-65.

323. Bertolette, Daniel Floyd K. "The French Huguenots in Early
Florida. " In his Motives in Education and Other Essays.
Boston: The Gorham Press, 1916.

324. Besson, P. "Massacre de la Florida, 1565, " Societe de
l'histoire du Protestantisme Francais Bulletin 61(1912):364-
73.

325. Biggar, H. P. "Jean Ribaut's Discovery of Terra Florida, "
Eng. Hist. Rev. 32(1917):253-70.

326. Bourne, Edward Gaylord. "French and Spaniard in Florida
(1558-1568). " In Spain in America. New York: Harper and
Brothers, 1904.

327. Charlevoix, Pierre Francois Xavier de. History and General
Description of New France. Translated by John Gilmary
Shea, New York: J. G. Shea, 1866-72.

328. Colee, Harold. "The Huguenots in Florida, " Jacksonville
Historical Society Annual (1933-34):14-20.

329. Davis, T. Frederick. "The First Protestant Service in
North America, " F. H. Q. 18(1940):192-97.

330. Delpeuch, Maurice. "Un Glorieux Episode Maritime et Colonial des Guerres de Religion; le Capitaine de la marine Royale
Dominique de Gourgue et le Massacre de la Colonie Protestante de
la Floride (1565-8), " Rev. Maritime (Paris) 155(1902):2150-91.

331. Folmer, Henry. Franco-Spanish Rivalry in North America,
1564-1763. Glendale, California: Arthur H. Clark Company,
1953.

332. Gorman, M. Adele Francis. "Jean Ribaut's Colonies in Florida, " F. H. Q. 44(1965):51-66.

333. Green, Evelyn E. Dominiques Vengence, a Story of France
and Florida. London: T. Nelson and Sons, 1897.

334. Guenin, Eugene. Premiers Essais de Colonisation; les
      Francais en Bresil et en Floride (1530-1568). Paris: E.
Bigot, 1910.

335. Hammond, A. E., ed. and tr. "A French Document Relat-
      ing to the Destruction of the French Colony in Florida at the
Hands of the Spanish, 1565, " F. H. Q. 39(1960):55-61.

336. Hawkins, John M. "The Voyage Made by John M. Hawkins
      Esquire. " In Early English and French Voyages Chiefly
From Hakluyt. Edited by Henry S. Burrage. New York: Barnes
and Noble, 1934.

337. Higginson, Thomas W. "The French Voyageurs, " Harper's
      Mag. 66(1883):505-19.

338. Kleber, Louis C. "Spain and France in Florida, " History
      Today 18(1968):487-94.

339. La Ronciere, Charles de. ...La Floride Francaise, Scene
      de la vie Indienne, Pientes en 1564. Paris: Les Editions
Nationalies, 1928.

340. Laudonniere, Rene. A Notable History Containing Four Voy-
      ages Made by Certain French Captains Into Florida. Edited
by Martin Basanier. Translated by Richard Hakluyt. Franham,
Surrey, England: Henry Stevens, Son & Stiles, 1964.

341. Le Challeux, Nicolas. A True and Perfect Description of
      the last Voyage or Navigation, Attempted by Capitaine John
Rybaut, Deputie and Generall For the French Men, into Terra
Florida, This Year Past, 1565 (1563?). Truely Set Forth by Those
That Returned From Thence, Wherein are Contayned Things as
Lamentable to Heare as They Haue Bene Cruelly Executed. Lon-
don: Printed by Henry Denham for Thomas Hacket, [1566].

342. Lorant, Stefan, ed. The New World: Notes on the French
      Settlements in Florida, 1562-1565. New York: Duell, Sloan,
1946.

343. Lowery, W. "Jean Ribaut and Queen Elizabeth, " Am. Hist.
      Rev. 9(1909):456-59.

344. Otis, R. R. French Intrusion Into Spain's La Florida. At-
      lanta: Privately Printed, 1949.

345. Parkman, Francis. "The Fleur-de-Lis at Port Royal, " Atl.
      M. 12(1863):30-35.

346. _____. "The Fleur-de-Lis in Florida, " Atl. M. 12(1863):
      225-40.

347. _____ . Pioneers of France in the New World. Boston:
Little, Brown & Company, 1898.

348. _____ . "The Spaniard and the Heretic, " Atl. M. 12(1863):
537-55.

349. _____ . The Struggle for a Continent. Edited by Pelham
Edgar. Boston: Little, Brown & Company, 1907.

350. _____ . "The Vengeance of Dominic de Gourgues, " Atl.
M. 14(1964):530-37.

351. Porter, Emma Rochelle and Garrett Porter. The Huguenot
Colonization at Fort Caroline Near the Mouth of the St. Johns
River, Florida, 1562-65. Jacksonville: The Drew Press, 1923.

352. Simms, William Gilmore. The Lily and the Totem, or, The
Huguenots in Florida. New York: Baker and Scribner, 1850.

353. Sparks, Jared. Life of John Ribault. Library of American
Biography, 2d series. Boston: Charles C. Little and James
Brown, 1845.

354. Spratt, J. W. "The French Occupation of Florida, " Jacksonville Historical Society Annals (1933-34):21-28.

355. Wenhold, Lucy L., tr. "Manrique De Rojas' Report on
French Settlement in Florida, 1564, " F. H. Q. 38(1959):45-62.

VI.   THE SPANISH IN FLORIDA, 1565-1763

      A.   General Studies

356. Arnade, Charles W. "Celi's Expedition to Tampa Bay: A
Historical Analysis, " F. H. Q. 47(1968):1-7.

357. _____ . "The Failure of Spanish Florida, " Americas
16(1960):271-81.

358. _____ . Florida on Trial, 1593-1602. Coral Gables: University of Miami Press, 1959.

359. _____ . "The Juan Baptista Franco Document of Tampa
Bay, 1756, " Tequesta 28(1968):99-101.

360. Arrendondo, Antonio de. Arrendondo's Historical Proof of
Spain's Title to Georgia. A Contribution to the History of
One of the Spanish Borderlands. Edited by Herbert E. Bolton.
Berkeley: University of California, 1925.

361.   Barcia, Don Andreas Gonzales. Ensayo Cronologico Para
        la Historia General de la Florida, por Gabriel de Cardenas
z Cano. Madrid, 1723.

362.   Boyd, Mark F., ed. "Diego Pena's Expedition to Apalachee
        and Apalachicola in 1716; A Journal Translated and with an
introduction by Mark F. Boyd," F. H. Q. 28(1949):1-27.

363.   _____. "Documents Describing the Second and Third Ex-
        peditions of Lieutenant Diego Pena to Apalachee and Apalachi-
cola in 1717 and 1718," F. H. Q. 31(1952):109-39.

364.   _____. "The Expedition of Marcos Delgado From Apalache
        to the Upper Creek Country in 1686; Based on Original Doc-
uments...," F. H. Q. 16(1937):3-32.

365.   Bushnell, Clyde G. "La Influencia de los Españoles en la
        Florida [1492-1819]." Master's thesis, Universidad Nacional
de Mexico, 1948.

366.   Capron, Louis. "The Spanish Dance," F. H. Q. 38(1959):91-
        95.

367.   Clausen, Carl J. A 1715 Spanish Treasure Ship. Contribu-
        tions of the Florida State Museum, Social Sciences No. 12.
Gainesville: University of Florida Press, 1965.

368.   Connor, Jeannette Thurber, ed. and trans. Colonial Records
        of Spanish Florida, Letters and Reports of Governors and
Secular Persons. 2 vols. DeLand: The Florida State Historical
Society, 1925-30.

369.   Covington, James W., ed. Pirates, Indians, and Spaniards:
        Father Escobedo's "La Florida". St. Petersburg: Great
Outdoors Publishing Company, 1963.

370.   Cox, Isaac Joslin. "Florida, Frontier Outpost of New Spain."
        In A. Curtis Wilgus (ed.) Hispanic American Essays, a Mem-
orial to James Alexander Robertson. Chapel Hill: University of
North Carolina Press, 1942. pp. 151-65.

371.   Davis, T. Frederick. "Pioneer Florida: An Interpretation
        of Spanish Laws and Land Titles," F. H. Q. 24(1945):113-20.

372.   DeCoste, Fredrik. First Child [Martin de Arquelles] at
        Spanish Florida; the Strange Case of an Officer who Made
History. Jacksonville: Convention Press, 1965.

373.   Dupre Brown, Grace. "La es Pada y la Cruz en las Flori-
        das Españolas." Master's thesis, Universidad Nacional Auto-
naoma, 1941.

374.   Fairbanks, George Rainsford. The Spaniards in Florida,
        Comprising the Notable Settlement of the Huguenots in 1564,
and the History and Antiquities of St. Augustine, founded A. D.
1565. By George R. Fairbanks... Jacksonville, Florida: C.
Drew, 1868.

375.   Fernandez-Florez, Dario. Drama y Adventura de los Es-
        pañoles en Florida. Madrid: Ediciones Cultura Hispanica,
1963.

376.   _____. The Spanish Heritage in the United States. Ma-
        drid: Publicaciones Españoles, 1968.

377.   Gillaspie, William R. "Juan de Ayala y Escobar, Procura-
        dor and Entrepreneur: A Case Study of the Provisioning of
Florida, 1683-1716." Ph. D. dissertation, University of Florida,
1961.

378.   _____. "Sergeant Major Ayala y Escobar and the Threat-
        ened St. Augustine Mutiny," F. H. Q. 47(1968):151-64.

379.   Griffen, William B. "Spanish Pensacola, 1700-1763," F. H.
        Q. 37(1959):242-62.

380.   Harman, Joyce E. Trade and Privateering in Spanish Flori-
        da, 1732-1763. St. Augustine: St. Augustine Historical So-
ciety, 1969.

381.   Helps, Sir Arthur. The Spanish Conquest of America and Its
        Relation to the History of Slavery and to the Government of
the Colonies... Vol. 4. London and New York: John Lane, 1900-
1904.

382.   Higgs, Charles D. "Spanish Contacts With the AIS (Indian
        River) Country," F. H. Q. 21(1942):25-39.

383.   Historical Records Survey. Florida. Spanish Land Grants
        in Florida; Brief Translations From the Archives of the
Boards of Commissioners for Ascertaining Claims and Titles to
Land in the Territory of Florida... 2 Vols. Prepared by the
Historical Records Survey, Division of Professional and Service
Projects, Work Projects Administration. Tallahassee: State Li-
brary Board, 1940.

384.   Hoffman, Paul E. and Eugene Lyon. "Accounts of the Real
        Hacienda, Florida, 1565 to 1602," F. H. Q. 48(1969):57-69.

385.   Holmes, Jack D. L. "Dauphin Island's Critical Years: 1701-
        1722," Ala. Hist. Q. 29(1967):39-63.

386.   _____. "Indigo in Colonial Louisiana and the Floridas,"
        La. Hist. 8(1967):329-49.

387. _____, and John D. Ware. "Juan Baptisa Franco and Tampa Bay, 1756," Tequesta 28(1968):91-97.

388. Jackson, William Richard. Early Florida Through Spanish Eyes. Coral Gables: University of Miami Press, 1954.

389. _____. "Florida in Early Spanish Colonial Literature [16th and 17th centuries]." Master's thesis, University of Illinois, 1952.

390. Jerome, Father. Wytfliet's Florida, 1597. St. Leo.: Abbey Press, 1965.

391. Johnson, James G. "The Colonial Southeast, 1732-1763: An International Contest for Territorial and Economic Control," U. Colo. Studies 19(1932).

392. Lawson, Katherine Swan. Martin de Arguelles, the First Spaniard Born in St. Augustine and the First European Child Born on the Atlantic Coast of the United States in a Permanent European Settlement. St. Augustine: St. Augustine Historical Society and Institute of Science, 1941.

393. Leon, Alonso, and Fray Damian Massanet. "Letter of Fray Damian Massanet to Don Carlos de Siguenza, 1690; Itinerary of the de Leon Expedition of 1689; Itinerary of the de Leon Expedition of 1690." In Spanish Exploration in the Southwest, 1542-1706, edited by Herbert Eugene Bolton. New York: Charles Scribner's Sons, 1916.

394. Leonard, Irving A. Spanish Approach to Pensacola, 1689-1693. Quivira Society Publications, vol. 9. Albuquerque: The Quivira Society, 1939.

395. _____. "The Spanish Re-exploration of the Gulf Coast in 1686," Miss. Val. Hist. Rev. 22(1936):547-57.

396. Link, Marion Clayton. "The Spanish Camp Site and the 1715 Plate Fleet Wreck," Tequesta 26(1966):21-30.

397. Lowery, Woodbury. The Spanish Settlements Within the Present Limits of the United States. 2 vols. Florida 1513-1561 Vol. 1. Florida 1562-1574. Vol. 2. New York: G. P. Putnam's Sons, 1905.

398. Marks, Henry S. "The Earliest Land Grants in the Miami Area," Tequesta 18(1958):15-21.

399. _____. "A Forgotten Spanish Land Grant in South Florida," Tequesta (1960):51-55.

400. Mendelis, Louis J. "Colonial Florida," F.H.Q. 3(1924):4-15.

401.   Merriman, Roger Bigelow.   "Florida."   In his Rise of the
       Spanish Empire in the Old World and in the New.   Vol. 4.
New York: Macmillan Company, 1934.

402.   Okenfuss, Max J.   "First Impressions: The Earliest Des-
       cription of Florida to Circulate in Russia (1710)," Tequesta
30(1970):69-71.

403.   "Publicity in 1669; Excerpts From a London Advertisement
       Found in an Annapolis, Maryland Library," Hobbies 46(1941):
116-17.

404.   Sauer, Carl Ortwin.   The Early Spanish Main.   Berkeley:
       University of California Press, 1966.

405.   Serrano y Sanz, Manuel, ed.   ...Documentos Historicos de
       la Florida y la Luisiana, Siglos XVI al XVIII.   Madrid: V.
Suarez, 1912.

406.   Smith, Hale G.   "Two Historical Archaeological Periods in
       Florida," Am. Antiquities 13(1948):313-19.

407.   TePaske, John J.   "Funerals and Fiestas in Early Eighteenth-
       Century St. Augustine," F.H.Q.   44(1965):97-104.

408.   Ugarte, Ruben Vargas.   ...Los Martires de la Florida, 1566-
       1572.   Lima: Talleres Graficos de la Editorial "Lumen,"
1940.

409.   Ware, John D.   "A View of Celi's Journal of Surveys and
       Chart of 1757," F.H.Q.   47(1968):8-24.

       B.   Governors

410.   Arana, Luis Rafael.   "The Day Governor Cabrera Left Flori-
       da [1667]," F.H.Q.   40(1961):154-63.

411.   Arnade, Charles W., trans.   "Florida in 1643 as Seen by Its
       Governor," F.H.Q.   34(1955):172-76.

412.   Bouza Brey, Fermin.   "El Almirante Don Gonzalo Mendez de
       Cancio, Gobernador y Capitain General de la Florida (1544?-
1622)," Bull. Inst. Est. Asturianos 6(1952):305-31.

413.   Held, Ray E.   "Hernando de Miranda, Governor of Florida,
       1575-1577," F.H.Q.   28(1949):111-30.

414.   Hinkley, Nancy E.   "The Administration of Don Pablo de
       Hita Salazar, Governor of Spanish Florida, 1675-1680." Mas-
ter's thesis, University of Florida, 1956.

415.   Lanning, John Tate. "The Legend That Governor Moral
       Sanchez was Hanged, " Ga. Hist. Q. 38(1954):349-55.

416.   Lawson, Katherine S. "Governor Salazar's Wheat Farm
       Project, 1645-1657, " F. H. Q. 24(1946):196-200.

417.   Seckinger, Ron Leroy. "Spanish Conquest and Control on
       the Florida Frontier: The Endeavors of Governor Pedro De
Ibarra, 1603-1609. " Master's thesis, University of Florida, 1964.

418.   Tepaske, John J. "Economic Problems of Florida Governors,
       1700-1763, " F. H. Q. 37(1958):42-52.

419.   _____. "The Governorship of Spanish Florida, 1700-1763."
       Ph. D. dissertation, Duke University, 1959.

420.   _____. The Governorship of Spanish Florida, 1700-1763.
       Durham, N. C.: Duke University Press, 1964.

       C.   The Defenses

421.   Arana, Luis R. "The Spanish Infantry: The Queen of
       Battles in Florida, 1671-1702. " Master's thesis, University
of Florida, 1960.

422.   Arnade, Charles W. "Piribiriba on the Salamototo; Spanish
       Fort on the St. Johns River, " Papers of the Tallahassee
Historical Society 4 (1960):65-84.

423.   Boyd, Mark F. "The Fortifications at San Marcos de Apa-
       lache (St. Marks, Wakulla Co., Florida), " F. H. Q. 15(1936):
3-34.

424.   Chatelain, Verne E. "The Defenses of Spanish Florida,
       1565-1763. " Ph. D. dissertation, University of Minnesota,
1943.

425.   _____. The Defenses of Spanish Florida 1565-1763.
       Washington: Carnegie Institute of Washington, Pub. #511,
1941.

426.   Connor, Jeannette Thurber. "The Nine Old Wooden Forts
       of St. Augustine, " F. H. Q. 4(1926):103-11;171-80.

427.   Faye, Stanley. "Spanish Fortifications of Pensacola, 1698-
       1765, " F. H. Q. 20(1941):151-68.

428.   Goggin, John Mann. "Fort Pupo: A Spanish Frontier Out-
       post [St. Johns River, Fla., 1716?-1740], " F. H. Q. 30(1951):
139-92.

429.   Graff, Mary B.   "Fort Picolata," Papers of the Jacksonville
       Historical Society 1(1947):50-66.

430.   Ivers, Larry E.   "The Battle of Fort Mosa," Ga. Hist. Q.
       51(1967):135-53.

431.   Reding, Katherine, ed.   "... Plans for the Colonization and
       Defense of Apalache, 1675," Ga. Hist. Q. 9(1925):169-76.

432.   Vigneras, L. A.   "Fortifications de la Florida," Anuario
       de Estudios Americanos (Seville) 16(1959):533-52.

       D.   English, Spanish, and French Rivalry

433.   Abbey, Kathryn T.   "Efforts of Spain to Maintain Sources of
       Information in the British Colonies Before 1779," Miss. Val.
Hist. Rev. 15(1928):56-68.

434.   Arnade, Charles W.   "The English Invasion of Spanish Flori-
       da, 1700-1706," F. H. Q. 61(1962):29-37.

435.   _____ .   The Seige of St. Augustine in 1702.   Gainesville:
       University of Florida Press in cooperation with the St. Aug-
ustine Historical Society, 1959.

436.   Covington, James W.   "Drake Destroys St. Augustine; 1585,"
       F. H. Q. 44(1965):81-93.

437.   De Bethancourt, Antonio.   "Felipe V y la Florida [1697-
       1742]," Anuario de Estudios Americanos 7(1950):95-123.

438.   Dunn, William Edward.   "The Occupation of Pensacola Bay,
       1689-1700," F. H. Q. 4(1926):140-54.

439.   _____ .   Spanish and French Rivalry in the Gulf Region
       of the United States, 1678-1702; The Beginnings of Texas
and Pensacola.   Austin: University of Texas, 1917.   (Also a
Ph. D. dissertation at Columbia University.)

440.   Faye, Stanley.   "The Contest for Pensacola Bay and Other
       Gulf Ports 1698-1722," F. H. Q. 24(1946):167-95;302-28.

441.   Ford, Lawrence Carrol.   The Triangular Struggle for Span-
       ish Pensacola 1689-1739.   Washington: Catholic University
of America Press, 1939.   (Catholic University Studies in Hispanic
American History II), (Also a Ph. D. dissertation at Catholic University).

442.   Gold, Robert L.   "The Settlement of the East Florida Span-
       iards in Cuba, 1763-1766," F. H. Q. 42(1964):216-31.

443. _____ . "The Settlement of the Pensacola Indians in New Spain, 1763-1770," Hisp. Am. Hist. Rev. 45(1965):657-76.

444. Johnson, J. G. "The International Contest for the Colonial Southeast, 1566-1763." Ph. D. dissertation, University of California, 1924.

445. Kimber, Edward. A Relation, or Journal of a Late Expedition to the Gates of St. Augustine, in Florida; Conducted by the Hon. General James Oglethorpe, With a Detachment of His Regiment, etc. from Georgia. In a Letter to the Reverend Mr. Isaac K---r in London. By a gentleman, volunteer in the said expedition. London: T. Astley, 1744.

446. Kleber, Louis C. "Spain and England in Florida, [1565-1818]," Hist. Today (1969):46-52.

447. Luther, Edith Allin. "Sir Francis Drake's Raid on St. Augustine, 1586: Transcription, Modernization, and Translation of Certain Documents of the Stetson Collection." Master's thesis, University of Florida, 1957.

448. "A Ranger's Report of Travels with General Ogelthorpe in Georgia and Florida, 1739-1742." In Travels in the American Colonies, edited by Newton D. Mereness, pp. 218-36. New York: Macmillan, 1916.

449. Russell, Charles C. "General James Edward Oglethorpe," Papers of the Jacksonville Historical Society 1(1947):28-49.

450. Siebert, Wilbur H. "The Departure of the Spaniards from East Florida, 1763-64," F. H. Q. 19(1940):145-54.

451. _____ . "How the Spaniards Evacuated Pensacola in 1763," F. H. Q. 11(1932):48-57.

452. Wenhold, Lucy L., ed. and trans. "The Trials of Captain Don Isidoro de Leon, with an Introduction and Additional Notes by Albert C. Manucy," F. H. Q. 35(1957):246-65.

453. Wright, Irene A., ed. and trans. Further English Voyages to Spanish America, 1583-1594: Documents From the Archives of the Indies at Sevilla, Illustrating English Voyages to the Caribbean, the Spanish Main, Florida, and Virginia. London: Hakluyt Society, 1951.

454. Wright, J. Leitch, Jr. "Sixteenth Century English-Spanish Rivalry in la Florida," F. H. Q. 38(1960):265-79.

455. Zuniga y Zerda, Joseph de. "The Siege of Saint Augustine by Governor Moore of South Carolina in 1702 as reported to the King of Spain by Don Joseph de Zuniga y Zerda, Governor of

Florida." Translated by Mark F. Boyd. F. H. Q. 26(1948):345-54.

VII. AN ENGLISH COLONY, 1763-1784

A. General Studies

456. Arnade, Charles W. "Florida Keys: English or Spanish in 1763?" Tequesta 15(1955):41-53.

457. Bohnenberger, Carl. "The Settlement of Charlotia (Rolles Town), 1765," F. H. Q. 4(1925):43-49.

458. Boyd, Mark F., ed. "From a Remote Frontier. Letters and Reports Passing Between the Commanders at Apalache (St. Marks), Governor Grant at St. Augustine, General Haldimand at Pensacola, and General Gage, Commander-in-Chief at New York, 1766-1767," F. H. Q. 19(1941):179-245, 402-12; 20(1942):382-97; 21(1943):44-52, 135-46.

459. Brown, Vera Lee. "Anglo-American Relations in America in the Closing Years of the Colonial Era [1763-1779]," Hisp. Am. Hist. Rev. 5(1922):325-483.

460. Carter, Clarence E. "British Policy Towards the American Indians in the South, 1763-8," Eng. Hist. Rev. 33(1918):37-56.

461. Caughey, John Walton. Bernardo de Galvez in Louisiana, 1776-1783. Berkeley: University of California Press, 1934.

462. Chester, Peter. "The Correspondence of Peter Chester." Edited by Mrs. Dunbar Rowland. Miss. Hist. Soc. Pub., Centenary Series 5(1925):1-184.

463. Covington, James. "English Gifts to the Indians, 1765-1766," Fla. Anthro. 13(1960):71-75.

464. DeVorsey, Louis, Jr. The Indian Boundary in the Southern Colonies, 1763-1775. Chapel Hill: University of North Carolina Press, 1966.

465. Drude, Kenneth. "Fort Baton Rouge [est. 1779 by British]," La. Studies 7(1968):258-69.

466. Fuller, B. D. "How England Gained and Lost One Loyal Colony," J. Am. Hist. 25(1931):141-49.

467. Gipson, Lawrence Henry. "The Florida Frontier." In his The British Empire Before the American Revolution. Vol.

4. New York: Alfred A. Knopf, 1939.

468. Goggin, John M. "A Florida Indian Trading Post, circa
      1763-1784, " S. Indian Stud. 1(1949):35-38.

469. Gold, Robert L. Borderland Empires in Transition: The
      Triple-Nation Transfer of Florida. Carbondale: Southern
Illinois University Press, 1969.

470. _____ . "Politics and Property During the Transfer of
      Florida From Spanish to English Rule, 1763-1764, " F. H. Q.
      42(1963):16-34.

471. _____ . "The Transfer of Florida From Spanish to
      British Control, 1763-1765. " Ph. D. dissertation, University
of Iowa, 1964.

472. Hanna, Alfred Jackson. "Florida, an English Colony. "
      Bachelor's thesis, Rollins College, 1917.

473. Kennett, Lee, ed. & trans. "A French Report on St. Aug-
      ustine in the 1770's, " F. H. Q. 44(1965):133-35.

474. Kerr, Wilfred B. "The Stamp Act in the Floridas 1765-
      1766, " Miss. Val. Hist. Rev. 21(1935):463-70.

475. Lawson, Katherine S. "Luciano DeHerrera, Spanish Spy in
      British St. Augustine, " F. H. Q. 23(1945):170-76.

476. Lockey, Joseph B. "The Florida Banditti, 1783, " F. H. Q.
      24(1945):87-107.

477. May, Philip S. "Zephaniah Kingsley, Nonconformist (1765-
      1843), " F. H. Q. 23(1945):145-59.

478. Mahon, John K. "British Strategy and Southern Indians:
      War of 1812, " F. H. Q. 44(1966):285-302.

479. Mowat, Charles. "The First Campaign of Publicity for
      Florida, " Miss. Val. Hist. Rev. 30(1943):359-76.

480. _____ . "The Southern Brigade: A Sidelight on the
      British Military Establishment in America, 1763-1775, " J.
S. Hist. 10(1944):59-77.

481. Panagopoulos, Epaminondas Peter. "The Background of the
      Greek Settlers in the New Smyrna Colony [Florida, 1766-
68], " F. H. Q. 35(1956):95-115.

482. "Proclamation of George the III (Upon the Acquisition of
      East and West Florida), " F. H. Q. 3(1925):36-42.

483. Sioussat, St. George L. "The Breakdown of the Royal Man-
      agement of Lands in the Southern Provinces, 1773-1775, "
Ag. Hist. 3(1929):67-98.

484. Tingley, Helen Eloise Boor. "Florida Under the English
      Flag, 1763-83, " J. Am. Hist. 11(1917):66-102.

      B. East Florida

485. "Address of the 'Principal Inhabitants of East Florida' to
      Governor Tonyn, June 6, 1783, " F. H. Q. 8(1930):169-73.

486. Beeson, Kenneth H., Jr. "Janas in British East Florida, "
      F. H. Q. 44(1965):121-32.

487. Carter, Clarence E., ed. "Observations of Superintendent
      John Stuart and Governor James Grant of East Florida on
the Proposed Plan of 1764 for the Future Management of Indian Affairs, " Am. Hist. Rev. 20(1915):815-31.

488. Caughey, John Walton. "The Panis Mission to Pensacola,
      1778, " Hisp. Am. Rev. 10(1930):480-89.

489. Corbitt, Duvon C. "Spanish Relief Policy and the East Flor-
      ida Refugees of 1763, " F. H. Q. 27(1948):67-82.

490. Corse, Carita Doggett. "DeBrahm's Report on East Florida,
      1773, " F. H. Q. 17(1939):219-26.

491. Covington, James W., ed. The British Meet the Seminoles;
      Negotiations Between British Authorities in East Florida and
the Indians: 1763-68. Contributions of the Florida State Museum,
Social Sciences, no. 7. Gainesville: University of Florida, 1961.

492. Gipson, Lawrence Henry. "East Florida as a British Pro-
      vince, 1763-65. " In his The British Empire Before the
American Revolution. Vol. 9. New York: Alfred A. Knopf,
1956.

493. Gold, Robert L. "The East Florida Indians Under Spanish
      and English Control: 1763-1765, " F. H. Q. 44(1965):105-20.

494. Harlan, Rogers C. "A Military History of East Florida
      During the Governorship of Enrique White: 1796-1811. "
Master's thesis, Florida State University, 1971.

495. Kennett, Lee, ed. and trans. "A French Report on St.
      Augustine in the 1770's, " F. H. Q. 44(1965):133-35.

496. "[Land Grants in British East Florida], " F. H. Q. 6(1927):
      120-30.

497. Lawson, Edward W. "What Became of the Man Who Cut Off Jenkin's Ear," F. H. Q. 37(1958):33-41.

498. Lockey, Joseph Byrne, comp. East Florida, 1783-1785: A File of Documents Assembled and Many of Them Translated by Josephy Byrne Lockey. Edited by John Walton Caughey. Berkeley: University of California Press, 1949.

499. Mowat, Charles Loch. East Florida as a British Province, 1763-1784. Berkeley and Los Angeles: University of California Press, 1943.

500. _____. "The Enigma of William Drayton," F. H. Q. 22(1943):3-33.

501. _____. "The Land Policy in British East Florida," Ag. Hist. 14(1940):75-77.

502. _____. "Material Relating to British East Florida in the Gage Papers and Other Manuscript Collections in the William L. Clements Library," F. H. Q. 18(1939):46-60.

503. _____. "St. Augustine Under the British Flag, 1763-1775," F. H. Q. 20(1941):131-50.

504. _____. "St. Francis Barracks, St. Augustine; a Link With the British Regime," F. H. Q. 23(1943):266-80.

505. _____. "That 'Odd Being,' De Brahm," F. H. Q. 20(1943): 323-45.

506. _____. "The Tribulations of Denys Rolle," F. H. Q. 23(1944):1-14.

507. Siebert, Wilbur H. "The Port of St. Augustine During the British Regime, Part I," F. H. Q. 24(1946):247-65; Part II F. H. Q. 25(1946):76-93.

508. Stout, Joseph and Mary. "The Case of Some Inhabitants of East Florida, 1767-1785." Edited by Barbara Gorely Teller. F. H. Q. 33(1954):97-110.

509. Tanner, Helen Hornbeck. "Vicente Manuel de Zéspedes and the Restoration of Spanish Rule in East Florida, 1784-1790." Ph. D. dissertation, University of Michigan, 1961.

510. _____. Zéspedes in East Florida, 1784-1790. Coral Gables: University of Miami Press, 1963.

511. Tucker, Philip C. "Notes on the Life of James Grant Prior and Subsequent to His Governorship at East Florida," F. H. Q. 8(1929):112-19.

C. West Florida

512. Abbey, Kathryn T. "Peter Chester's Defense of the Missis-
      sippi After the Willing Raid, " Miss. Val. Hist. Rev. 22(1935):
      17-32.

513. Born, John Dewey. "British Trade in West Florida, 1763-
      1783. " Ph. D. dissertation, University of New Mexico, 1963.

514. Brewster, Lawrence F. "The Later History of British West
      Florida, 1770-1781. Governor Peter Chester and the Hey-
      dey of the Province.... " Master's thesis, Columbia University,
      1932.

515. "British Proclamation of Oct. 7, 1763, Creating the Govern-
      ment of West Florida, " La. Hist. Q. 13(1930):610-16.

516. Carter, Clarence E. "The Beginnings of British West Flori-
      da, " Miss. Val. Hist. Rev. 4(1917):314-41.

517. _____ . "Some Aspects of British Administration in West
      Florida, " Miss. Val. Hist. Rev. 1(1914):364-75.

518. Dart, Henry P., ed. "British Proclamation of October 7,
      1763, Creating the Government of West Florida, " La. Hist.
      Q. 13(1930):199-201.

519. Farmar, Robert. "The Siege of Pensacola in 1781: Robert
      Farmar's Journal of One Siege at Pensacola, " Hist. Mag.
      4(1860):166-72.

520. Galvez, Bernardo de. "Diary on the Operations Against
      Pensacola, 1781, " La. Hist. Q. 1(1917):44-84.

521. Gauld, Charles A. "A Scottish View of West Florida in
      1769, " Tequesta 29(1969):61-66.

522. Gipson, Lawrence Henry. "West Florida as a British Pro-
      vince. " In his The British Empire Before the American
      Revolution. Vol. 9. New York: Alfred A. Knopf, 1956.

523. Haarmann, Albert W. "The Spanish Conquest of British
      West Florida, 1779-1781, " F. H. Q. 39(1960):107-34.

524. Hamilton, Peter J. "Acts of the Assembly at British West
      Florida; 1766-1778, " Gulf States Hist. Mag. 2(1904):273-79.

525. _____ . "British West Florida, " Pub. Miss. Hist. Soc.
      7(1903):399-426.

526. Howard, Clinton N. "Alleged Spanish Grants in British West
      Florida, " F. H. Q. 22(1943):74-85.

527. _____ . The British Development of West Florida, 1763-1769. University of California Publications in History, vol. 34. Berkeley and Los Angeles: University of California Press, 1947.

528. _____ . "Colonial Pensacola: The British Period, Part I, " F. H. Q. 19(1940):109-27.

529. _____ . "Colonial Pensacola: The British Period, Part II, " F. H. Q. 19(1941):246-69.

530. _____ . "Colonial Pensacola: The British Period, Part III, The Administration of Governor Chester, 1770-1781, " F. H. Q. 19(1941):368-402.

531. _____ . "The Distribution of Land in British West Florida, " La. Hist. Q. 16(1933):539-53.

532. _____ . "Early Settlers in British West Florida, " F. H. Q. 24(1945):45-55.

533. _____ . "Expansion in West Florida, 1770-1779, " Miss. Val. Hist. Rev. 20(1934):481-96.

534. _____ . "Governor Johnstone in West Florida, " F. H. Q. 27(1939):281-303.

535. _____ . "The Interval of Military Government in West Florida, " La. Hist. Q. 22(1938):18-30.

536. _____ . "The Military Occupation of British West Florida, 1763, " F. H. Q. 17(1939):181-99.

537. _____ . "Some Economic Aspects of British West Florida, 1763-1768, " J. S. Hist. 6(1940):20-21.

538. Howard, Milo B. and Robert R. Rea, eds. and trans. The Memoire Justificatif of the Chevalier Montauit de Monberaut: Indian Diplomacy in British West Florida, 1763-1765. University, Alabama: University of Alabama Press, 1965.

539. Ingram, Earl Glynn. "A Critical Study of the British West Florida Legislative Assembly. " Master's thesis, Auburn University, 1969.

540. Johnson, Cecil S. "British West Florida, 1763-1783. " Ph. D. dissertation, Yale University, 1932.

541. _____ . British West Florida, 1763-1783. New Haven: Yale University Press, 1943.

542. _____ . "The Distribution of Land in British West Florida," La. Hist. Q. 16(1933):539-53.

543.   . "Expansion in West Florida, 1770-1779," Miss.
Val. Hist. Rev. 20(1934):481-96.

544.   . "A Note on Absenteeism and Pluralism in British
West Florida," La. Hist. Q. 19(1936):196-98.

545.   . "Pensacola in the British Period: Summary and
Significance," F. H. Q. 37(1959):263-80.

546.   . "West Florida Revisited," J. Miss. Hist.
28(1966):121-32.

547.   Long, Jeannette M. "Immigration to British West Florida,
1763-1781." Master's thesis, University of Kansas, 1969.

548.   McMurtrie, Douglas C., ed. "A Newly-discovered Broadside, Printed at New Orleans in 1768 by Denis Brand, Of-
fering Amnesty to Deserters From the British Forces Who Should
Return to Service at Pensacola...With an Explanatory Note...."
Chicago: R. H. Johnson, 1941.

549.   Murdoch, Richard K. "A British Report on West Florida
and Louisiana, November, 1812," F. H. Q. 43(1964):36-51.

550.   Murphy, W. S. "The Irish Brigade of Spain at the Capture
of Pensacola, 1781," F. H. Q. 38(1960):216-25.

551.   Ogden, Jonathan. "Pensacola in 1770." Edited by Charles
C. Cumberland. Rutgers U. Lib. J. 13(1949):7-13.

552.   Osborn, George C. "Major-General John Campbell in West
Florida," F. H. Q. 27(1949):311-39.

553.   . "Relations With the Indians of West Florida During the Administration of Governor Peter Chester, 1770-
1781," F. H. Q. 31(1953):239-72.

554.   Padgett, J. A., ed. "Commission, Orders and Instructions
Issued to George Johnstone, British Governor at West Florida, 1763-1767," La. Hist. Q. 21(1938):1021-68.

555.   . "Governor Peter Chester's Observations on the
Boundaries of British West Florida, About 1775," La. Hist.
Q. 26(1943):5-11.

556.   . "Minutes of the West Florida Assembly, 1766-
1769," La. Hist. Q. 22(1939):311-84.

557.   Pittman, Lieutenant. "Apalachee During the British Occupation; a Description Contained in a Series of Four Reports by
Lieut. Pittman, R. E.," F. H. Q. 12(1934):114-22.

558. Rea, Robert R., and Holmes, Jack D. L. "Dr. John Lori-
      mer and the Natural Sciences in British West Florida," S.
      Hum. Rev. (1970):363-72.

559. Rea, Robert R. "Graveyard for Britons ; West Florida,
      1763-1781," F. H. Q. 47(1969):345-64.

560. _____. "Henry Hamilton and West Florida [1779]," Ind.
      Mag. Hist. 54(1958):49-56.

561. _____. "The King's Agent for British West Florida,"
      Ala. Rev. 16(1963):141-53.

562. _____. "Military Deserters From British West Florida,"
      La. Hist. 9(1968):123-37.

563. _____. "A Naval Visitor [John Blankett] in British West
      Florida [1764-65]," F. H. Q. 40(1961):142-53.

564. Worcester, Donald E., tr. "Miranda's Diary of the Siege
      of Pensacola, 1781," F. H. Q. 29(1951):163-96.

VIII. FLORIDA AND THE AMERICAN REVOLUTION

565. Abbey, Kathryn T. "Florida as an Issue During the Ameri-
      can Revolution." Ph. D. dissertation, Northwestern University,
      1926.

566. _____. "Spanish Projects for the Reoccupation of the
      Floridas during the American Revolution," Hisp. Am. Hist.
      R. 9(1929):265-85.

567. Barrs, Burton. East Florida in the American Revolution.
      Jacksonville: Guild Press, 1932.

568. Boyd, Mark F. and Jose Navarro Latorre. "Spanish Interest
      in British Florida, and in the Progress of the American Rev-
      olution," F. H. Q. 32(1953):92-130.

569. Bullen, Ripley P. "Fort Tonyn and the Campaign of 1778,"
      F. H. Q. 29(1951):253-60.

570. Callahan, North. Flight From the Republic: The Tories of
      the American Revolution. Indianapolis: Bobbs-Merrill Co.,
      1967.

571. Cross, John H. "A Matron of the Revolution," F. H. Q.
      2(1909):39-41.

572.   Fritot, Jessie Robinson, comp.   Pension Records of Soldiers
        of the Revolution Who Removed to Florida.   Jacksonville:
Published by the Jacksonville Chapter of the National Society of
Daughters of the American Revolution, 1946.

573.   Manucy, Albert and Alberta Johnson.   "Castle St. Mark and
        the Patriots of the Revolution," F. H. Q.   21(1942):3-24.

574.   Miranda, Francisco de.   "Miranda's Diary of the Siege of
        Pensacola, 1781."   Translated by Donald E. Worcester.
F. H. Q.   29(1951):163-96.

575.   Olson, Gary D.   "Loyalists and the American Revolution:
        Thomas Brown [later of St. Augustine] and the South Caro-
lina Backcountry, 1775-76," S. C. Hist. Mag.   69(1968):44-56.

576.   Pennington, Edgar Legare.   "East Florida in the American
        Revolution, 1775-1778," F. H. Q.   9(1930):24-46.

577.   Peters, Thelma.   "The American Loyalists and the Planta-
        tion Period in the Bahama Islands."   Ph. D. dissertation,
University of Florida, 1960.

578.   _____.   "The American Loyalists in the Bahama Islands:
        Who They Were," F. H. Q.   40(1962):226-40.

579.   _____.   "The Loyalist Migration From East Florida to
        the Bahama Islands [during the Revolution]," F. H. Q.   40(1961):
123-41.

580.   Roberts, William.   "The Losses of a Loyalist Merchant in
        Georgia During the Revolution," Ga. Hist. Q.   52(1968):270-76.

581.   Rush, N. Orwin.   The Battle of Pensacola, March 9 to May
        8, 1781; Spain's Final Triumph Over Great Britain in the
Gulf of Mexico.   Tallahassee: Florida State University, 1966.

582.   Siebert, Wilbur H.   East Florida as a Refuge of Southern
        Loyalists, 1774-1785.   Worcester, Mass.:   The Antiquarian
Society, 1928.

583.   _____.   Loyalists in East Florida, 1774-1785; the Most
        Important Documents Pertaining Thereto...With an Accompany-
ing Narrative.   2 vol.   De Land: The Florida State Historical Society, 1929.

584.   _____.   "The Loyalists in West Florida and the Natchez
        District," Miss. Val. Hist. Rev.   2(1916):465-83.

585.   _____.   "The Port of St. Augustine During the British
        Regime: Part II: The Port During the Revolution," F. H. Q.
25(1946):76-93.

586. _____. "Privateering in Florida Waters and Northwards in the Revolution," F. H. Q. 22(1943):62-73.

587. Smith, Paul H. "The American Loyalists: Notes on Their Organization and Numerical Strength," Wm. Mary Q. 25(1968): 259-77.

588. _____. Loyalists and Redcoats: A Study in British Revolutionary Policy. Chapel Hill: University of North Carolina Press for the Institute of Early American History and Culture, 1964.

589. Sosin, Jack M. The Revolutionary Frontier, 1763-1783. New York: Holt, Rinehart, and Winston, 1967.

590. Taylor, Garland. "Colonial Settlement and Early Revolutionary Activity in West Florida Up to 1779," Miss. Val. Hist. Rev. 22(1935):351-60.

IX. SPAIN IN FLORIDA, 1784-1821

A. General Studies

591. Arnade, Charles W. "The Failure of Spanish Florida," The Americas 16(1960):271-81.

592. Corbitt, D. C. "The Administrative System in the Floridas, 1783-1821," Tequesta 1(1942):41-62;2(1943):57-67.

593. _____. "The Contention Over the Superintendencia of the Floridas," F. H. Q. 15(1936):113-17.

594. _____, ed. and tr. "Papers Relating to the Georgia-Florida Frontier, 1784-1800," Ga. Hist. Q. 21(1937):73-83, 185-88, 274-93, 372-81; 22(1938):72-76, 184-91, 286-91, 391-94; 23(1939):77-79, 189-202, 300-03, 381-87; 24(1940):77-83, 150-57, 257-71, 374-81.

595. _____. "The Return of Spanish Rule to the St. Marys and the St. Johns, 1813-1821," F. H. Q. 20(1941):47-68.

596. Covington, James W. "Stuart's Town, the Yamasee Indians, and Spanish Florida," Fla. Anthro. 21(1968):8-13.

597. Davis, T. Frederick. "The Alagon, Punon Rostro, and Vargas Land Grants," F. H. Q. 25(1946):175-90.

598. Ellicott, Andrew. The Journal of Andrew Ellicott, Late Commissioner on Behalf of the United States During the Year

1796, the Years 1797, 1798, 1799, and Part of...1800: For De-
termining the Boundary Between the United States and [Spanish]
Containing Occasional Remarks on...the Whole of West Florida,
and Part of East Florida....   Philadelphia: Budd & Bartrom for
Thomas Dobson, 1803.

599.   Galvez, Bernardo de.   Diario de las Operaciones de la Ex-
          pedicion Contra la Plaza de Panzacola Concluida por las
Armas de S. M. Catolica, Baxo las Ordenes del Mariscal de
Campo D. Bernardo de Galvez.   Edited by N. Orwin Rush.   Facsimile reprint published by Friends of Florida State University Library, 1967.

600.   Glunt, J. D.   "Plantation and Frontier Records of East and
          Middle Florida, 1789-1868." Ph. D. dissertation, University
of Michigan, 1931.

601.   Halbert, H. S. and T. H. Ball.   The Creek War of 1813 and
          1814.   University: University of Alabama Press, 1969.

602.   Holmes, Jack D. L.   Gayoso: The Life of a Spanish Gover-
          nor in the Mississippi Valley, 1789-1799.   Baton Rouge:
Louisiana State University Press, 1965.

603.   _____.   "Two Spanish Expeditions to Southwest Florida,
          1783-1793," Tequesta 25(1965):97-107.

604.   Hull, Ambrose and Stella.   "Settlers From Connecticut in
          Spanish Florida...." Edited by Robert E. Rutherford. F. H. Q.
30(1952): 324-40;31(1952): 33-48.

605.   Kinnaird, Lawrence, ed.   Spain in the Mississippi Valley,
          1765-1794: [translations of materials from the Spanish ar-
chives in the Bancroft Library].   3 vol.   Washington, D. C.:
American Historical Association, 1946-49.

606.   Leary, Lewis.   "James Holme's Florida Plantation, 1804,"
          F. H. Q. 20(1941):69-71.

607.   Lockey, Joseph B.   "The Florida Intrigues of José Alvarez
          de Toledo," F. H. Q. 12(1934):145-178.

608.   _____, ed.   "The St. Augustine Census of 1786," F. H. Q.
          18(1939):11-31.

609.   Murdoch, Richard K.   "Documents Concerning a Voyage to
          the Miami Region in 1793," F. H. Q. 31(1952):16-32.

610.   _____.   "Documents Pertaining to the Georgia-Florida
          Frontier, 1791-1793," F. H. Q. 38(1960):319-338.

611.   _____.   "France to the Rescue: an Episode of the Flori-
          da Border, 1797," F. H. Q. 30(1951):203-24.

612. _____. The Georgia-Florida Frontier, 1793-1796. Spanish Reaction to French Intrigue and American Designs. Berkeley: University of California Press, 1951.

613. Patrick, Rembert W. Florida Fiasco; Rampant Rebels on the Georgia-Florida Border, 1810-1815. Athens: University of Georgia Press, 1954.

614. Río Cossa, José del. "Descripción de la Florida Oriental Hecha en 1787. Por el Teniente de Navio, D. José del Río Cossa," Soc. Geog. Nac. Bol. 75(1935):420-32, 456-60.

615. Rutherford, Robert Erwin. "Spain's Immigration Policy for the Floridas, 1780-1806." Master's thesis, University of Florida, 1952.

616. Shambaugh, Marion Francis. "The Development of Agriculture in Florida During the Second Spanish Period." Master's thesis, University of Florida, 1953.

617. Tanner, Helen Hornbeck. "The Delaney Murder Case," F. H. Q. 44(1965):136-49.

618. _____. General Greene's Visit to St. Augustine in 1785. Ann Arbor, Mich.: William L. Clements Library, 1964.

619. _____. "The 1789 Saint Augustine Celebration," F. H. Q. 38(1960):280-93.

620. _____. "Zespedes and the Southern Conspiracies," F. H. Q. 38(1959):15-28.

621. Upchurch, John C. "Aspects of the Development and Exploration of the Forbes Purchase," F. H. Q. 48(1969):117-39.

622. Ware, John D. "St. Augustine, 1784: Decadence and Repairs," F. H. Q. 48(1969):180-87.

623. Whitaker, Arthur Preston. "Commerce of Louisiana and the Floridas at the End of the Eighteenth Century," Hisp. Am. Hist. R. 8(1928):190-203.

624. _____, ed. and tr. Documents Relating to the Commercial Policy of Spain in the Floridas, with Incidental Reference to Louisiana. De Land: The Florida State Historical Society, 1931.

625. Wright, J. Leitch, Jr. "British Designs on the Old Southwest: Foreign Intrigue on the Florida Frontier, 1783-1803," F. H. Q. 44(1966):265-84.

66   Florida History

B.   East Florida

626.   The Case of the Inhabitants of East-Florida With an Appendix, containing Papers, by Which All the Facts Stated in the Case, are Supported. St. Augustine: Printed by John Wells, 1784.

627.   Davis, T. Frederick. "Elotchaway, East Florida, 1814," F. H. Q. 8(1930):143-55.

628.   _____. "Florida Historical Material in Niles' Register," F. H. Q. 9(1940):155-62.

629.   _____, ed. MacGregor's Invasion of Florida, 1817; Together With an Account of his Successors, Irwin, Hubbard and Aury on Amelia Island, East Florida. Jacksonville: The Florida Historical Society, 1928.

630.   "Governors of Spanish East Florida, 1784-1821," F. H. Q. 6(1927):117.

631.   Lockey, Joseph. East Florida, 1783-1785. Berkeley: University of California Press, 1949.

632.   McQueen, Juan. Letters...to His Family Written From Spanish East Florida, 1791-1807. Columbia, S. C.: Bostwick and Thomlen, 1943.

633.   Murdoch, Richard K. "Elijah Clarke and Anglo-American Designs on East Florida, 1797-1798," Ga. Hist. Q. 35(1951): 173-90.

634.   _____. "Governor Zéspedes and the Religious Problem in East Florida, 1786-1787," F. H. Q. 26(1948):325-44.

635.   _____. "Indian Presents: To Give or Not to Give. Governor White's Quandary," F. H. Q. 35(1957):326-46.

636.   _____, ed. "Report of the Forest Resources of Spanish East Florida in 1792," Ag. Hist. 27(1953):147-51.

637.   Skinner, John. "Letters Relating to Macgregor's Attempted Conquest of East Florida, 1817," F. H. Q. 5(1926):54-57.

638.   Tanner, Helen Hornbeck. "The Transition From British to Spanish Rule in East Florida, 1783-1785." Master's thesis, University of Florida, 1949.

639.   _____. "Vicente Manuel de Zespedes and the Restoration of Spanish Rule in East Florida, 1784-1790." Ph. D. dissertation, University of Michigan, 1961.

640.   _____. Zespedes in East Florida, 1784-1790. University of Miami Hispanic American Studies, no. 19. Coral Gables:

University of Miami Press, 1963.

C. West Florida

641. Arthur, Stanley Clisby. The Story of the West Florida Re-
        bellion. St. Francisville, La.: The St. Francisville Demo-
crat, 1935.

642. Brown, Gilburt S. The Amphibious Campaign for West Flor-
        ida and Louisiana, 1814-1815: A Critical Review of Strategy
and Tactics at New Orleans. University, Alabama: University of
Alabama Press, 1968.

643. Burns, F. P. "West Florida and the Louisiana Purchase,"
        La. Hist. Q. 15(1932):391-416.

644. Corbitt, D. C. "The Last Spanish Census of Pensacola,
        1820," F. H. Q. 24(1945):30-38.

645. Cox, Isaac Joslin. "The American Intervention in West
        Florida," Am. Hist. Rev. 17(1912):290-311.

646. _____. "The Border Missions of General George
        Mathews," Miss. Val. Hist. Rev. 12(1925):309-33.

647. _____. "General Wilkinson and his Later Intrigues With
        the Spaniards," Am. Hist. Rev. 19(1914):794-812.

648. _____. The West Florida Controversy, 1798-1813; a
        Study in American Diplomacy. Baltimore: Johns Hopkins
Press, 1918.

649. "Documents Relating to Colonel Edward Nicholls and Captain
        George Woodbine in Pensacola, 1814," F. H. Q. 10(1931):51-54.

650. Egan, Clifford L. "The United States, France, and West
        Florida, 1803-1807," F. H. Q. 47(1969):227-52.

651. Favrot, H. L. "Some of the Causes and Conditions That
        Brought About the West Florida Revolution in 1810," Pub.
La. Hist. Soc. 1 Pt. 2 (1895):37-46.

652. _____. "The West Florida Revolution and Incidents Grow-
        ing Out of It," Pub. La. Hist. Soc. 1 Pt. 3 (1896):17-30.

653. Faye, Stanley. "British and Spanish Fortifications of Pensa-
        cola, 1781-1821," F. H. Q. 20(1942):277-92.

654. "Governors of Spanish West Florida, 1781-1821," F. H. Q.
        6(1927):118-19.

655.   Harrison, Frances Kathryn. "The Indians as a Means of
       Spanish Defense of West Florida, 1783-1795." Master's
thesis, Alabama, 1950.

656.   Holmes, Jack D. L. and J. Leitch Wright, Jr., trs. and
       eds. "Luis Bertucat and William Augustus Bowles: West
Florida Adversaries in 1791," F. H. Q. 49(1970):49-62.

657.   _____. "Two Spanish Expeditions to Southwest Florida,
       1783-1793," Tequesta 25(1965):97-107.

658.   _____. "Spanish Treaties With West Florida Indians,
       1784-1802," F. H. Q. 48(1969):140-54.

659.   Kendall, J. S., ed. "Documents Concerning the West Flori-
       da Revolution, 1819," La. Hist. Q. 17(1934):80-95.

660.   Latour, Arsène Lacarrière. Historical Memoir of the War
       in West Florida and Louisiana in 1814-15. n. p.: John Con-
rad and Co., 1816.

661.   McAlister, L. N. "Pensacola During the Second Spanish
       Period," F. H. Q. 37(1959):281-327.

662.   Morales, Don Juan Ventura. Louisiana (Province) Intendant.
       Regulations Governing Grants of Land in the Provinces of
Louisiana and West Florida, Promulgated on July 17, 1779. Evans-
ton, Ill.: Private Printing, 1942.

663.   Ogg, F. A. and Dunbar Rowland. "The American Interven-
       tion in West Florida," Miss. Val. Hist. Assoc. Proc.
4(1912):47-58.

664.   Padgett, James A., ed. "Official Records of the West Flor-
       ida Revolution and Republic," La. Hist. Q. 21(1938):685-805.

665.   Plaisance, Aloysius, ed. "Pensacola in 1810," F. H. Q.
       32(1953):44-48.

666.   Price, Grady Daniel. "The United States and West Florida,
       1803-1812." Master's thesis, University of Texas, 1939.

667.   Prichard, W., ed. "An Original Letter on the West Florida
       Revolution of 1810," La. Hist. Q. 18(1935):354-62.

668.   Renaut, F. P. "La Politique des Etats-Unis dans l'Amerique
       du Nord Espagnole Sous de Joseph Bonaparate, 1808-1814,"
Rev. Sci. Pol. 39(1918):76-93.

669.   Sterkx, Henry Eugene and Brooks Thompson. "Philemon
       Thomas and the West Florida Revolution," F. H. Q. 39(1961):
378-86.

670. Szaszdi, Adam. "Governor Folch and the Burr Conspiracy," F. H. Q. 38(1960):239-51.

671. "West Florida and Its Attempt on Mobile, 1810-1811," Am. Hist. Rev. 2(1907):699-705.

D. Panton, Leslie, Bowles and Innerarity

672. Boyd, Mark F. "Events at Prospect Bluff on the Apalachicola River: An Introduction to Some Letters of Edmund Doyle, Trader," Tallahassee Historical Society Annual 3 (1937):82-102.

673. _____. "Events at Prospect Bluff on the Apalachicola River, 1808-1818; an Introduction to Twelve Letters of Edmund Doyle, trader," F. H. Q. 16(1937):55-96.

674. Brown, J. A. "Panton, Leslie and Company, Indian Traders of Pensacola and St. Augustine," F. H. Q. 37(1959):328-36.

675. Corbitt, D. C. and John Tate Lanning, eds. "A Letter of Marque issued by William Augustus Bowles as Director of the State of Muskogee," J. S. Hist. 11(1945):246-61.

676. Corse, Carita Doggett. "Denys Rolle and Rollestown, a Pioneer for Utopia," F. H. Q. 7(1928):115-34.

677. Cotterill, Robert S. "A Chapter of Panton, Leslie and Company," J. S. Hist. 10(1944):275-92.

678. Douglass, Elisha P. "The Adventurer Bowles," Wm. Mar. Q. 6(1949):3-23.

679. Forbes, John. "A Journal of John Forbes, May, 1803; the Seizure of William Augustus Bowles," F. H. Q. 9(1931):279-89.

680. Greenslade, Marie Taylor. "John Innerarity, 1783-1854," F. H. Q. 9(1930):90-95.

681. _____. "William Panton," F. H. Q. 14(1935):107-29.

682. Innerarity, James. "The Forbes Purchase; a Letter From James Innerarity to William Simpson, Partners of John Forbes and Company 24 Sept., 1804," F. H. Q. 10(1931):102-08.

683. _____. "A Letter of James Innerarity on William Panton's Estate," F. H. Q. 10(1932):185-94.

684. _____. "Letters of James Innerarity; the War of 1812," F. H. Q. 10(1932):134-38.

685.   Innerarity, John.   "The Creek Nation, Debtor to John Forbes
       and Co., Successors to Panton, Leslie and Co.; a Journal
of John Innerarity, 1812," F. H. Q. 9(1930):67-89.

686.   _____.   "Letters of John Innerarity...," F. H. Q. 11(1933):
       140-41; 12(1933):37-41, 84-88.

687.   "John Forbes and Co., Successors to Panton, Leslie and Co.,
       vs. the Chickasaw Nation; a Journal of an Indian Talk, July,
1805," F. H. Q. 8(1930):131-42.

688.   Key, Margaret.   "William Augustus Bowles in the Tallahas-
       see Area," Apalachee 4(1950-56):44-65.

689.   Kinnaird, Lawrence.   "The Significance of William Augustus
       Bowles' Seizure of Panton's Apalachee Store in 1792," F. H.
Q. 9(1931):156-92.

690.   McAlister, Lyle N., ed.   "The Marine Forces of William
       Augustus Bowles and His 'State of Muskogee'; Illustrative
Documents," F. H. Q. 32(1953):3-27.

691.   McAlister, Lyle N.   "William Augustus Bowles and the State
       of Muskogee," F. H. Q. 40(1962):317-328.

692.   "The Panton, Leslie Papers," F. H. Q. 11(1932):33-39, 88-90,
       190-92; 12(1933):123-34, 198-99; 13(1934):51-53, 105-10, 165-66,
236-40; 14(1935):130-32, 217-20, 275-80; 15(1936):65-67, 125-34, 173-74,
249-51; 16(1937):44, 130, 251-64; 17(1938):54-58, 237-42, 312-18;
18(1939):61-63, 135-40.

693.   Sherlock, John V.   "Panton, Leslie and Company."   Master's
       thesis, Florida State University, 1948.

694.   Upchurch, John C.   "Aspects of the Development and Ex-
       ploration of the Forbes Purchase," F. H. Q. 48(1969):117-39.

695.   West, Elizabeth Howard, ed.   "A Prelude to the Creek War
       of 1813-1814; in a Letter of John Innerarity to James Innera-
rity," F. H. Q. 18(1940):247-66.

696.   Wright, J. Leitch, Jr.   William Augustus Bowles: Director
       General of the Creek Nation.   Athens: University of Georgia
Press, 1967.

E.   Genet's Projected Attack

697.   Crandall, Regina K.   "Genet's Projected Attack on Louisiana
       and the Floridas, 1793-94."   Ph. D. dissertation, University
of Chicago, 1902.

698. Murdoch, Richard K. "Citizen Manqourit and the Projected Attack on East Florida in 1794," J. S. Hist. 14(1948):522-40.

699. _____. "French Intrigue Along the Georgia-Florida Frontier, 1793-1796." Ph.D. dissertation, University of California at Los Angeles, 1947.

700. Turner, Frederick Jackson, ed. "Correspondence of the French Ministers to the United States, 1791-1797." In Annual Report of the American Historical Association for the Year 1903. Washington: Government Printing Office, 1904.

701. _____. "The Manqourit Correspondence in Respect to Genet's Projected Attack Upon the Floridas, 1793-1794." In American Historical Association Annual Report for 1897. Washington: Government Printing Office, 1898.

702. _____. "The Origin of Genet's Projected Attack on Louisiana and the Floridas," Am. Hist. Rev. 3(1898):650-71.

F. War of 1812

703. Clarke, George I. F. "The Surrender of Amelia," F.H.Q. 4(1925):90-95.

704. Cooper, James. Secret Acts, Resolutions, and Instructions Under Which East Florida Was Invaded by the United States Troops, Naval Forces, and Volunteers; in 1812 and 1813; Together With the Official Correspondence of the Agents and Officers of the Government.... Washington: G. S. Gideon Printer, 1860.

705. Davis, T. Frederick. "United States Troops in Spanish East Florida, 1812-13," F.H.Q. 9(1930):3-23; Part II 9(1930):96-116; Part III 9(1931):135-55; Part IV 9(1931):259-78; Part V 10(1931):24-34.

706. _____. "U.S.S. Peacock in the War of 1812; a Fight off the Florida East Coast," F.H.Q. 16(1938):231-41.

707. Haarmann, Albert W. "The Siege of Pensacola: An Order of Battle," F.H.Q. 44(1966):193-99.

708. Hasbrouck, Alfred. "Our Undeclared War With Spain," Journal of American Military History 11(1938):115-25.

709. Kruse, Paul. "A Secret Agent in East Florida: General George Mathews and the Patriot War [1811-12]," J. S. Hist. 18(1952):193-217.

710. Mahon, John K. "British Strategy and Southern Indians: War of 1812," F.H.Q. 44(1966):285-302.

71

James. "James Monroe, Secretary of State, to Matthews," F.H.Q. 6(1928):235-37.

, Richard K. "A British Report on West Florida siana, November 1812," F.H.Q. 43(1964):36-51.

713. Owsley, Frank L., Jr. "British and Indian Activities in Spanish West Florida During the War of 1812," F.H.Q. 46(1967):111-23.

714. Patrick, Rembert W., ed. "Letters of the Invaders of East Florida, 1812," F.H.Q. 28(1949):53-65.

715. Phinney, A. H. "First Spanish-American War," F.H.Q. 4(1926):114-29.

716. Wyllys, R. K. "The East Florida Revolution of 1812-1814," Hisp. Am. Hist. Rev. 9(1929):415-45.

G. Indian Removal and Seminole War, 1817-1818

717. Copp, Belton A. "The Patriot War, a Contemporaneous Letter," F.H.Q. 5(1927):162-67.

718. "Debate, in the House of Representatives of the United States, on the Seminole War, in January and February, 1819." Washington: Printed at the Office of the National Intelligencer, 1819.

719. Giddings, Joshua Reed. The Exiles of Florida; or, The Crimes Committed by Our Government Against the Maroons, Who Fled From South Carolina, and Other Slave States, Seeking Protection Under Spanish Laws. Columbus, Ohio: Follett, Foster and Co., 1858.

720. Mahon, John K. "The Treaty of Moultrie Creek 1823," F.H.Q. 40(1962):350-73.

721. Paine, Charles Raymond. "The Seminole War of 1817-1818." Master's thesis, Oklahoma, 1938.

722. Tebbel, John and Keith Jennison. "The First Seminole War." In their The American Indian Wars. New York: Harper and Bros., 1960.

723. U. S. Congress. House Committee on Military Affairs. Views of the Minority of the Committee on Military Affairs, on the Subject of the Seminole War, and the Trial and Execution of Arbuthnot and Armbrister. Washington, 1819.

724. Wright, J. Leitch, Jr. "A Note on the First Seminole War As Seen by the Indians, Negroes, and Their British Ad-

visers," J. S. Hist. 34(1968):565-75.

H. Jackson in Florida, 1814-1821

725. Bassett, John Spencer. "Jackson in Florida." In his Life of Andrew Jackson. New York: Macmillan, 1931.

726. Bruce, H. A. "Andrew Jackson and the Acquisition of Florida," Outlook 88(1908):730-42.

727. Clark, Anna. "Jackson's Administration of Florida," F. H. Q. 5(1926):44-49.

728. Cresson, W. P. "The Seminole War and the Florida Treaty." In his James Monroe. Chapel Hill: University of North Carolina Press, 1946.

729. Davis, T. Frederick. "Pioneer Florida: Jackson's Premature Proclamation, 1821," F. H. Q. 24(1945):39-44.

730. Doherty, Herbert J., Jr. "Andrew Jackson vs. the Spanish Governor," F. H. Q. 34(1955):142-58.

731. _____. "The Governorship of Andrew Jackson," F. H. Q. 33(1954):3-31.

732. Dovell, Junius Elmore. "The Influence of Andrew Jackson on the History of Florida." Master's thesis, Stetson University (De Land, Florida), 1934.

733. Eaton, John Henry. Life of Major General Andrew Jackson, Containing a Brief History of the Seminole War, and Cession and Government of Florida. Philadelphia: M'Carty and Davis, 1828.

734. An Examination of the Civil Administration of Governor Jackson in Florida... The Acts of General Andrew Jackson as a Legislator. Washington, 1828. 9 articles signed "Henry" reprinted from the National Intelligencer. June 21-Sept. 23, 1828.

735. Fisher, Ruth Anna. "The Surrender of Pensacola as Told by the British," Am. Hist. Rev. 54(1949):326-29.

736. Florida (Ter.) Laws, statutes, etc. Ordinances, by Major-General Andrew Jackson, Governor of the Provinces of the Floridas, Exercising the Powers of the Captain-general, and of the Intendant of the Island of Cuba, Over the Said Provinces, and of the Governors of Said Provinces Respectively. St. Augustine: Printed by R. W. Edes, 1821.

737. Florida (Ter.) Laws, statutes, etc. Ordinances of the Provinces of the Floridas, but Relating Specifically to West

Florida, as Proclaimed by Major General Andrew Jackson and Printed in Broadside Form at Pensacola in 1821, reproduced in facsimile from the only known copies, preserved in the National Archives, Washington, D. C.   Edited with an introduction by Douglas C. McMurtrie.   Chicago: John Calhoun Club, 1941.

738.   Gadsden, Captain James.   "The Defenses of the Floridas; a Report of Captain James Gadsden, Aide-de-Camp to General Andrew Jackson, August 1, 1818, " F. H. Q. 15(1937):242-48.

739.   Griffin, John W.   "An Archeologist at Fort Gadsden, "   F. H. Q. 28(1950):254-61.

740.   Holland, James W.   "Andrew Jackson and the Creek War: Victory at the Horseshoe [Bend, 1814], " Ala. Rev. (1968): 143-75.

741.   Innerarity, John.   "Letters of John Innerarity; the Seizure of Pensacola by Andrew Jackson, November 7, 1814, " F. H. Q. 9(1931):127-34.

742.   Jackson, Andrew.   "Two Uncollected Letters of Andrew Jackson, " F. H. Q. 15(1937):169-72.

743.   James, Marquis.   "The Florida Adventure. "   In his Andrew Jackson; the Border Captain.   Indianapolis: Bobbs-Merril Co. , 1933.

744.   Lowe, Richard G.   "American Seizure of Amelia Island [1817], " F. H. Q. 45(1966):18-30.

745.   Mays, Elizabeth.   "The March of Andrew Jackson in the First Seminole War."   Master's thesis, Emory, 1923.

746.   McQueen, Ray A.   "The Role of Andrew Jackson in the Acquisition of the Floridas. "   Ph. D. dissertation, University of Pittsburgh, 1942.

747.   Milgram, James Willard.   "A Florida Cover Under American Occupation of Spanish Territory, " F. H. Q. 40(1961):93-98.

748.   Parton, James.   [Jackson and Florida.]   In his Life of Andrew Jackson.   Boston: Houghton Mifflin, 1888.

749.   Perkins, Samuel.   General Jackson's Conduct in the Seminole War, Delineated in a History of that Period, Affording Conclusive Reasons Why He Should Not be the Next President.   Brooklyn, Conn.:   Advertiser Press, 1828.

750.   Phinney, A. H.   "The Second Spanish-American War, " F. H. Q. 5(1926):103-11.

751. Schouler, James. "The Jackson and Van Buren Papers," Atl. M. 95(1905):217-25.

752. _____. [Jackson in Florida.] In his History of the United States of America Under the Constitution. 3d ed. New York: Dodd, Mead, 1894.

753. _____. "Monroe and the Rhea Letter," Mag. Am. Hist. 12(1884):308-22.

754. Souter, Shelton. "Jackson in Florida." Master's thesis, Emory, 1924.

755. Stenberg, Richard R. "Jackson's Rhea Letter Hoax," J. S. Hist. 2(1936):480-90.

756. Sumner, William Graham. [Jackson in Florida.] In his Andrew Jackson. Boston: Houghton, Mifflin, 1899.

757. Van Ness, William Peter. A Concise Narrative of General Jackson's First Invasion of Florida, and of His Immortal Defence of New-Orleans. 2d ed. New York: Printed by E. M. Murden & A. Ming, Jr., 1827.

758. A Vindication of the Measures of the President and His Commanding Generals, in the Commencement and Termination of the Seminole War. By a citizen of the state of Tennessee. Washington: Printed by Gales & Seaton, 1819.

759. Wyllys, R. K. "The Filibusters of Amelia Island," Ga. Hist. Q. 12(1928):297-325.

760. Young, Captain Hugh. "A Topographical Memoir on East and West Florida With Itineraries of General Jackson's Army, 1818," F. H. Q. 13(1934):16-50, 82-104, 129-64.

I. Formal Acquisition by the U. S. A.

761. Bailey, Hugh C. "Alabama and West Florida Annexation," F. H. Q. 35(1957):219-32.

762. _____. "Alabama's Political Leaders and the Acquisition of Florida," F. H. Q. 35(1956):17-29.

763. Bécker, Jerónimo. "La Cesión de las Floridas." España Moderna, 240(1908):41-70.

764. Bemis, Samuel Flagg. [The Florida Question]. In his John Quincy Adams and the Foundations of American Foreign Policy. New York: Alfred A. Knopf, 1949.

765. Bisceglia, Louis R.   "The Florida Treaty and the Gallatin-
      Vives Misunderstanding," F. H. Q. 48(1970):247-63.

766. Brooks, Philip C.   "The Adam's-Onis Treaty of 1819 as a
      Territorial Agreement."   Ph. D. dissertation, University of
California, 1933.

767. _____.   Diplomacy and the Borderlands, the Adams-Onis
      Treaty of 1819.   Berkeley, Calif.: University of California
Press, 1939.

768. Catterall, R. C. H.   "A French Diplomat and the Treaty
      With Spain, 1819," Am. Hist. Rev. 11(1906):495-96.

769. Cubberly, Frederick.   "John Quincy Adams and Florida,"
      F. H. Q. 5(1926):88-93.

770. Curry, J. L. M.   "The Acquisition of Florida," Mag. Am.
      Hist. 19(1888):286-301.

771. Dewhurst, W. W.   Disputes Between the United States and
      Spain Over Florida Settled by the Treaty of 1819.   Proceed-
of the fifteenth annual session of the Florida State Bar Association,
Orlando, Florida, June 14-16, 1922.

772. Fuller, Hubert Bruce.   The Purchase of Florida; its History
      and Diplomacy.   Cleveland: The Burrows Brothers Co.,
1906.

773. Griffin, Charles Carrol.   The United States and the Disrup-
      tion of the Spanish Empire, 1810-1822.   New York: Colum-
bia University Press, 1937.

774. Harris, Lester.   "The Cession of Florida and John Quincy
      Adams, Secretary of State, U. S. A." F. H. Q. 36(1958):223-38.

775. Jameson, J. Franklin, ed.   "Calhoun's Correspondence,"
      American Historical Association Annual Report 2(1899):93-
1212.

776. Leary, Lewis.   "Philip Freneau on the Cession of Florida,"
      (a poem) F. H. Q. 21(1942):40-43.

777. "Letter of William Wirt, 1819," Am. Hist. Rev. 25(1920):
      692-95.

778. Lowe, Richard G.   "American Seizure of Amelia Island,"
      F. H. Q. 45(1966):18-30.

779. Memorias de la Vida del Exmo. Senor D. José Garcia de
      Leon Y Pizarro Escritas por el Mismo. 3 vol. Madrid:
1894-97.

780. Monroe, James. ...Monroe's Messages on Florida. Boston: Directors of the Old South Work, 1902.

781. Onis, Luis de. Memoir Upon the Negotiations Between Spain and the United States of America, Which Led to the Treaty of 1819. Translated by Tobias Watkins. Baltimore: F. Lucas, Jr., 1821.

782. _____. Memoria Sobre las Negociaciones Entre España y los Estados Unidos de America. Madrid: Ediciones Jose Porrua Turanzas, 1969.

783. Patrick, Rembert W. "A New Letter of James Monroe on the Cession of Florida," F. H. Q. 23(1945):195-201.

784. Pazos Kanki, Vincente. The Exposition, Remonstrance and Protest of Don Vincente Pazos, Commissioner on Behalf of the Republican Agents Established at Amelia Island, in Florida, Under the Authority and in Behalf of the Independent States of South America; With an Appendix. Presented to the executive of the United States, on the ninth day of February, 1818. Translated from the Spanish. Philadelphia: 1818.

785. Rattenberry, J. F. "Remarks on the Cession of the Floridas to the United States of America, and on the Necessity of Acquiring the Island of Cuba by Great Britain," Pamphleteer (London) 15(1819):261-80.

786. Spain. Legacion. U. S. Official Correspondence Between Don Luis de Onis...and John Quincy Adams...in Relation to the Floridas and the Boundaries of Louisiana.... London: E. Wilson, 1818.

787. Webster, Daniel. "Acquisition of the Floridas," Proc. Mass. Hist. Soc. 11(1871):329-30.

788. Young, Rogers W. "The Transfer of Fort San Marcos and East Florida to the United States," F. H. Q. 14(1936):231-43.

X.   A UNITED STATES TERRITORY, 1821-1845

A.   General Studies

789. Abbey, Kathryn T., ed. "Documents Relating to El Destino and Chemonie Plantations, Middle Florida, 1828-1868," F. H. Q. 7(1929):179-213, 291-329; 8(1929):3-46; 9(1929):79-111.

790. Alverez, Eugene. "James Buckland: The Mystery of an Early Florida Visitor," F. H. Q. 43(1965):266-69.

791. Appleyard, Lula Dee Keith. "Plantation Life in Middle
      Florida, 1821-1845." Master's thesis, Florida State Univer-
sity, 1940.

792. Barfield, William D. "The First Civil Governor and the
      Capital of Florida, " Papers of the Jacksonville Historical
Society 2(1949):75-89.

793. Bellamy, Jeanne, ed. "The Perrines at Indian Key, Florida,
      1838-1840, " Tequesta 7(1947):69-78.

794. Bevis, W. P. "Legislative Information and Important Events
      Concerning Territorial Florida From 1822 Until 1845, " Tal-
lahassee Historical Society Annual 1(1934):17-24.

795. Bittle, George C. "Richard Keith Call's 1836 Campaign, "
      Tequesta 29(1969):67-72.

796. Campbell, James T. "The Charles Hutchinson Letters From
      Territorial Tallahassee, 1839-1843, " Apalachee 4(1950-56):
13-28.

797. "Capital Removal, " F. H. Q. 4(1925):3-10.

798. Carter, Clarence Edwin, ed. The Territory of Florida,
      1821-1824. The Territorial Papers of the United States.
Vol. 22. Washington: United States Government Printing Office,
1956.

799. _____ . The Territory of Florida, 1824-1828. The Ter-
      ritorial Papers of the United States. Vol. 23. Washington:
The National Archives, 1958.

800. _____ . The Territory of Florida, 1828-1834. The Ter-
      ritorial Papers of the United States. Vol. 24. Washington:
The National Archives, 1959.

801. _____ . The Territory of Florida, 1834-1839. The Ter-
      ritorial Papers of the United States. Vol. 25. Washington:
The National Archives, 1960.

802. _____ . The Territory of Florida, 1839-1845. The Ter-
      ritorial Papers of the United States. Vol. 26. Washington:
The National Archives, 1962.

803. Clarke, G. I. F. "A Letter of G. I. F. Clarke's Relating
      to Port St. Joseph, East Florida [1823], " F. H. Q. 5(1926):
50-53.

804. Covington, James W. "The Armed Occupation Act of 1842, "
      F. H. Q. 40(1961):41-52.

805. _____. "Federal Relations With the Apalachicola Indians, 1823-1838," F.H.Q. 42(1963):125-41.

806. _____. "Life at Fort Brooke, 1824-1836," F.H.Q. 36(1958):319-30.

807. _____. "A Petition From Some Latin-American Fishermen, 1838," Tequesta 14(1954):61-65.

808. Cushman, Joseph D., Jr. "The Indian River Settlement, 1842-1849," F.H.Q. 43(1964):21-35.

809. Davis, T. Frederick. "Pioneer Florida: Destruction of Fort Leon, 1843," F.H.Q. 24(1946):287-90.

810. _____. "Pioneer Florida: First Militia Organization," F.H.Q. 24(1946):290-92.

811. _____. "Pioneer Florida: The First Session of the Legislative Council of Florida," F.H.Q. 24(1946):207-09.

812. _____. "Pioneer Florida: Mexican Squadron Based at Key West, 1827," F.H.Q. 25(1946):64-75.

813. _____. "Pioneer Florida: The Wild Tallahassee of 1827," F.H.Q. 24(1946):292-94.

814. Dodd, Dorothy. "The Florida Census of 1825," F.H.Q. 22(1943):34-40.

815. _____. "Florida in 1845: Statistics--Economic Life--Social Life," F.H.Q. 24(1945):3-27.

816. _____. "Florida's Population in 1845," F.H.Q. 24(1945): 28-29.

817. _____. "Horse Racing in Middle Florida, 1820-1843," Apalachee 3(1948-50):20-29.

818. _____. "Letters From East Florida," F.H.Q. 15(1936): 51-64.

819. _____. "Locating the County Seat of Jackson County; the Difficulties of Pioneer Government: Chipola vs. Webbville vs. Marianna," F.H.Q. 26(1947):44-55.

820. Doherty, Herbert J., Jr. "Andrew Jackson's Cronies in Florida Territorial Politics," F.H.Q. 34(1955):3-29.

821. _____. "Political Factions in Territorial Florida [1823-45]," F.H.Q. 28(1949):131-42.

822. Downes, Alan J. "The Legendary Visit of Emerson to Tallahassee [1827]," F. H. Q. 34(1956):334-38.

823. Dunn, Hampton. "Cheers and Tears in Pensacola," Fla. Trend 12(1969):60-76.

824. Farris, Charles D. "The Courts of Territorial Florida," F. H. Q. 19(1941):346-67.

825. "The First Message of Gov. William P. Duval; to the Legislative Council Assembled in Tallahassee, Florida, 1824," F. H. Q. 1(1908):13-17.

826. "The First Session of the Legislative Council of Florida at Pensacola, July 22, 1822," F. H. Q. 11(1933):184-89.

827. Francois de la Porte, Comte de Castelnau. "Essay on Middle Florida, 1837-1838 (Essai sur la Floride du Milieu)." Translated by Arthur R. Seymour. F. H. Q. 26(1948):199-255, 300-24.

828. Gilpin, Henry Dilworth. A Statement of the Case of the Bonds and Guarantees Issued by the Territory of Florida, With the Grounds of the Claim of the Holders on the United States for Redress. Philadelphia: T. K. and P. G. Collins, Printers, 1847.

829. Glunt, James David. "Plantation and Frontier Records of East and Middle Florida, 1789-1868." Ph. D. dissertation, University of Michigan, 1930.

830. Griffin, Richard W. "The Cotton Mill Campaign in Florida, 1828-1863," F. H. Q. 40(1962):261-74.

831. Groene, Bertram H. "A Virginian's Cavalcade; Florida Territory Seemed a Promised Land to Captain Thomas Brown of Fauquier and his Fellow Pioneers," Va. Cavalcade 18(1968):15-21.

832. Hammond, E. A., ed. "Sanibel Island and its Vicinity, 1833, a Document," F. H. Q. 48(1970):392-411.

833. Hardaway, Sylvia Jean. "Capital Removal," F. H. Q. 36(1957):77-83.

834. Harper, Roland M. "Ante-bellum Census Enumerations in Florida," F. H. Q. 6(1927):42-52.

835. Haskew, Rev. Peter. "A St. Joseph Diary of 1839." Edited by F. W. Hoskins. F. H. Q. 17(1938):132-51.

836. Hastings, Donald Olin. "The East-West Controversy and the County Development During Territorial Florida." Master's thesis, University of Florida, 1952.

837.   Hering, Julia. "Plantation Economy in Leon County From
       1830-1840." Master's thesis, Florida State University, 1954.

838.   _____. "Plantation Economy in Leon County, 1830-1840,"
       F. H. Q. 33(1954):32-47.

839.   Hill, Dorothy E. "Joseph M. White, Florida's Territorial
       Delegate, 1825-1837." Master's thesis, University of Flori-
da,   1950.

840.   Keith, Rebecca. "The Humanitarian Movement in Florida,
       1821 to 1861." Master's thesis, University of Florida, 1951.

841.   Knauss, James O. "Education in Florida, 1821-1829," F. H.
       Q. 4(1923):22-35.

842.   _____. Territorial Florida Journalism. Florida Histori-
       cal Society Publication, #6. De Land: The Florida State
Historical Society, 1926.

843.   Lewis, Frank G. "Education in St. Augustine, 1821-1845,"
       F. H. Q. 30(1952):237-60.

844.   Lockey, Joseph B. "A Footnote to Captain Young's Itiner-
       aries; Four Letters of Jeremy Robinson With a Memorandum,"
       F. H. Q. 8(1935):224-35.

845.   McCord, Guyte, St. "A Glimpse at the Labors of the Court
       of Appeals of the Territory of Florida," Apalachee 4(1950-
56):87-93.

846.   Manucy, Albert C. "Some Military Affairs in Territorial
       Florida," F. H. Q. 25(1946):202-11.

847.   Marks, Henry S. "Proceedings of the First Florida Con-
       gressional Delegation," F. H. Q. 44(1966):205-11.

848.   Martin, Sidney Walter. Florida During the Territorial Days.
       Athens: The University of Georgia Press, 1944.

849.   _____. "The Proposed Division of the Territory of Flor-
       ida," F. H. Q. 20(1942):260-76.

850.   _____. "The Public Domain in Territorial Florida," J.
       S. Hist. 10(1944):174-87.

851.   _____. "Richard Keith Call, Florida Territorial Leader,"
       F. H. Q. 21(1943):332-51.

852.   _____. "The Territorial Period of Florida, 1819-1845."
       Ph. D. dissertation, North Carolina, 1942.

853.   Moore, John Hammond.   "A South Carolina Lawyer [Henry
       Summer] Visits St. Augustine--1837, " F. H. Q. 43(1965):361-
78.

854.   Phillips, Ulrich Bonnell and James David Glunt, eds.   Flori-
       da Plantation Records From the Papers of George Noble
Jones.   St. Louis: Missouri Historical Society, 1927.

855.   Portier, Michael.   "From Pensacola to St. Augustine in
       1827:   A Journey of the Rt. Rev. Michael Portier, " F. H. Q.
26(1947):135-66.

856.   Pyburn, Nita Katharine.   "Public Education in Territorial
       Florida (1821-45), " Fla. State Univ. Studies 9(1953):31-50.

857.   Rogers, William Warren.   "Newspaper Mottoes in Ante-
       bellum Florida, " F. H. Q. 42(1963):154-58.

858.   Shofner, Jerrell H. and Rogers William Warren.   "Sea Island
       Cotton in Ante-bellum Florida, " F. H. Q. 40(1962):373-80.

859.   Shores, Venilla Lovina.   "Canal Projects of Territorial
       Florida, " Tallahassee Historical Society Annual 2(1935):12-16.

860.   Stephens, Marcus Cicero.   "Letter of Marcus Cicero Stephens,
       Quincy, Florida, 1835, " F. H. Q. 8(1929):120-24.

861.   Sunderman, James F.   "Army Surgeon Reports on Lower
       East Coast, 1838, " Tequesta 10(1950):25-33.

862.   Thomas, David Yancey.   A History of Military Government
       in Newly Acquired Territory of the United States.   New York:
Columbia University Press, Macmillan Co. , agents, 1904.

863.   Thompson, Arthur W.   Jacksonian Democracy on the Florida
       Frontier.   Gainesville: University of Florida Press, 1961.

864.   Weidenbach, Nell L.   "Lieutenant John T. McLaughlin: Guilty
       or Innocent?" F. H. Q. 46(1967):46-52.

865.   Whitfield, James B.   "All Governors of Territorial Florida
       Had Been Members of Congress, " F. H. Q. 25(1947):277-78.

866.   Whitman, Alice.   "Transportation in Territorial Florida, "
       F. H. Q. 27(1938):25-53.

867.   Williams, John L.   The Territory of Florida.   Gainesville:
       University of Florida Press, 1962.

868.   Wilson, Osburn C.   "The Development of Florida Territory,
       1821-1845. "   Master's thesis, Vanderbilt, 1932.

869.   Wilson, Ruth Danenhower. "The Bulow Plantation, 1821-
       1835, " F. H. Q. 23(1945):227-40.

       B.   The Second and Third Seminole Wars

870.   Adams, George R. "The Caloosahatchee Massacre: Its Sig-
       nificance in the Second Seminole War, " F. H. Q. 48(1970):
368-80.

871.   Backus, Electus. "Diary of a Campaign in Florida in 1837-
       1838, " Hist. Mag. (1866):279-85.

872.   Barr, Captain James. A Correct and Authentic Narrative of
       the Indian War in Florida, With a Description of Maj. Dade's
Massacre, and an Account of the Extreme Suffering, for Want of
Provisions, of the Army--Having Been Obliged to Eat Horses' and
Dogs' Flesh, &c., &c. New York: J. Narine, 1836.

873.   Bemrose, John. "Bemrose's Medical Case Notes From the
       Second Seminole War. " Edited by E. A. Hammond.   F. H. Q.
47(1969):401-13.

874.   _____. Reminiscences of the Second Seminole War. Edi-
       ted by John K. Mahon. Gainesville: University of Florida
Press, 1966.

875.   Bittle, George C. "First Campaign of the Second Seminole
       War, " F. H. Q. 46(1967):39-45.

876.   _____. "The Florida Militia's Role in the Battle of With-
       lacoochee [1835 against Seminoles], " F. H. Q. 44(1966):303-11.

877.   Boyd, Mark Frederick. Florida Aflame: the Background and
       Onset of the Seminole War, 1835. Tallahassee: Distributed
by Florida Board of Parks and Historic Memorials, 1951.

878.   _____. "Horatio S. Dexter and Events Leading to the
       Treaty of Moultrie Creek With the Seminole Indians, " Fla.
Anthro. 11(1958):65-95.

879.   Buchanan, Robert Christie. "A Journal of Lt. Robert C.
       Buchanan During the Seminole War. " Edited by Frank F.
White, Jr. F. H. Q. 29(1950):132-51.

880.   Buker, George E. "Lieutenant Levin M. Powell, U. S. N.,
       Pioneer of Riverine Warfare, " F. H. Q. 47(1969):253-75.

881.   Canova, Andrew P. Life and Adventures in South Florida.
       Palatka, Fla.: 1885.

882.   Cardwell, Guy A., Jr. "William Henry Timrod, the Charles-
       ton Volunteers and the Defense of St. Augustine, " N. C. Hist.

Rev. 18(1941):27-37.

883.   Chandler, William. "A Tallahassee Alarm of 1836," F.H.Q.
        8(1930):197-99.

884.   Childs, Thomas. "General Childs, U.S.A.: Extracts From
        His Correspondence With His Family," Hist. Mag. 2(1873):
        299-304, 371-74; 3(1874):169-71, 280-84.

885.   Clausen, Carl J. "The Fort Pierce American Gold Find,"
        F.H.Q. 47(1968):51-58.

886.   Cobb, Samuel E. "The Florida Militia and the Affair at
        Withlacoochee," F.H.Q. 19(1940):128-39.

887.   _____. "The Spring Grove Guards," F.H.Q. 22(1944):
        208-16.

888.   Cohen, Myer M. Notices of Florida and the Campaigns.
        Introduction by O. Z. Tyler, Jr. Gainesville: University
        of Florida Press, 1964.

889.   Covington, James W. "Apalachicola Seminole Leadership:
        1820-1833," Fla. Anthol. 16(1963):57-62.

890.   _____. "Cuban Blood Hounds and the Seminoles," F.H.Q.
        33(1954):111-19.

891.   _____. "An Episode in the Third Seminole War [1855-
        58]," F.H.Q. 45(1966):45-59.

892.   _____. "Exploring the Ten Thousand Islands: 1838,"
        Tequesta 18(1958):7-13.

893.   _____. "Federal Relations With the Apalachicola Indians:
        1823-1838," F.H.Q. 42(1963):125-41.

894.   _____. "The Florida Seminoles in 1845," Tequesta
        24(1964):49-57.

895.   _____. "The Indian Scare of 1849," Tequesta 21(1961):
        53-63.

896.   Cubberly, Frederick. The Dade Massacre. Washington:
        Government Printing Office, 1921.

897.   Davis, T. Frederick. "The Seminole Council October 23-25,
        1834," F.H.Q. 7(1929):330-50.

898.   Doherty, Herbert J., Jr. "Richard K. Call vs. the Federal
        Government on the Seminole War," F.H.Q. 31(1953):163-80.

899.   Eby, Cecil D., Jr.   "Memoir of a West Pointer [Alfred
        Beckley] in Florida: 1825, " F.H.Q.   41(1962):154-64.

900.   Flannery, Edmund F.   "Naval Operations During the Second
        Seminole War, 1835-1842. "   Master's thesis, University of
Florida, 1958.

901.   Florida.   Board of State Institutions.   Soldiers of Florida in
        the Seminole Indian, Civil and Spanish-American Wars. Live
Oak: Democrat Print, 1903.

902.   Foreman, Grant, ed.   "Report of the Cherokee Deputies in
        Florida, February 17, 1838, to John Ross, Esq., " Chron.
Okla. 9(1931):423-38.

903.   Forry, Samuel.   "Letters of Samuel Forry, Surgeon, U.S.
        Army, 1837-1838, " F.H.Q.   6(1928):133-48, 206-19; 7(1928):
88-105.

904.   Gadsden, James.   "Letter of Colonel James Gadsden [July 3,
        1839], " F.H.Q.   7(1929):350-56.

905.   Giddings, Joshua R.   The Exiles of Florida.   Introduction
        by Arthur W. Thompson.   Gainesville: University of Florida
Press, 1964.

906.   Gifford, John C.   Billy Bowlegs and the Seminole War....
        Coconut Grove: Triangle Company, 1925.

907.   "Glimpses of Life in Florida During the Seminole War, "
        The Knickerbocker 35(1851):214.

908.   Griswold, Oliver.   "William Selby Harney: Indian Fighter, "
        Tequesta 9(1949):73-80.

909.   Halbe, James McCrary.   Tales of the Seminole War [1835-
        42].   Okeechobee, Fla.:   Okeechobee News, 1950.

910.   Hamilton, Holman.   Zachary Taylor, Soldier of the Repub-
        lic.   New York: Bobbs-Merril Co., 1941.

911.   Hammond, E. Ashby, ed.   "Dr. Strobel Reports on South-
        east Florida, 1836, " Tequesta 21(1961):65-75.

912.   Hitchcock, Ethan Allen.   Fifty Years in Camp and Field--
        The Diary of Major General Ethan Allen Hitchcock.   Edited
by W. A. Croffut.   New York: G. P. Putnam Sons, 1909.

913.   Hoffman, Edna Pearl.   "The Problem of Seminole Indian
        Removal From Florida. "   Master's thesis, Florida State,
1935.

914.   Hollingsworth, Henry. "Tennessee Volunteers in the Semi-
        nole Campaign: The Diary of Henry Hollingsworth." Edited
by Stanley F. Horn. Tenn. Hist. Q. 1(1942):269-74, 344-66; 2(1943):
61-73, 163-78, 236-56.

915.   Hoyt, William D. "A Soldier's View of the Seminole War,
        1838-1839, " F. H. Q. 25(1947):356-62.

916.   Hunter, Nathaniel. "Captain Nathaniel Wyche Hunter and the
        Florida Indian Campaigns, 1837-1841." Edited by Reynold
M. Wik. F. H. Q. 39(1960):62-75.

917.   Huse, Harriet Pickney. "An Untold Story of the Florida
        War, " Harper's Mag. 83(1891):591-94.

918.   "Indian Murders, " F. H. Q. 8(1930):200-203.

919.   "Jackson Gives 'em the Old Hickory, " Month at Goodspeed's
        19(1948):147-49.

920.   "Jacksonville and the Seminole War, 1835-36, " F. H. Q.
        3(1925):10-14,15-21; 4(1926):22-30.

921.   Jarvis, Nathan S. "An Army Surgeon's Notes on Frontier
        Service, 1833-1848, " J. Military Service Institution (1906):
3-8, 275-86.

922.   Jelks, Edward. "Dr. Henry Perrine [killed at Indian Key by
        Indians 1840], " Jacksonville Historical Society Annual (1933-
34):69-75.

923.   Knotts, Tom. "History of the Blockhouse on the Withlacoo-
        chee, " F. H. Q. 49(1971):245-54.

924.   Laumer, Frank. "Encounter by the River, " F. H. Q. 46(1968):
        322-39.

925.   _____ . Massacre! Gainesville: University of Florida
        Press, 1968.

926.   McCall, George Archibald. Letters From the Frontiers.
        Philadelphia: L. B. Lippincott, 1868.

927.   McGaughy, Felix P. "The Squaw Kissing War: Bartholomew
        M. Lynch's Journal of the Second Seminole War, 1836-1839. "
Master's thesis, Florida State University, 1965.

928.   Mahon, John K. History of the Second Seminole War, 1835-
        1842. Gainesville: University of Florida Press, 1967.

929.   _____ . "Postscript to John Bemrose's Reminiscences, "
        F. H. Q. 47(1968):59-62.

930. _____. "Two Seminole Treaties: Payne's Landing, 1832, and Ft. Gibbon, 1833, " F.H.Q. 41(1962):1-21.

931. Meek, A. B. "The Journal of A. B. Meek and the Second Seminole War, 1836." Edited by John K. Mahon. F.H.Q. 38(1960):302-18.

932. Motte, Jacob Rhett. "Army Surgeon Reports on Lower East Coast, 1838." Edited by James F. Sunderman. Tequesta 10(1950):25-33.

933. _____. Journey Into Wilderness; an Army Surgeon's Account of Life in Camp and Field During the Creek and Seminole Wars, 1836-1838. Edited by James F. Sunderman. Gainesville: University of Florida Press, 1953.

934. _____. "Life in Camp and Field; the Journal of an Army Surgeon 1836-38 [with an introduction by James F. Sunderman]." Master's thesis, University of Florida, 1949.

935. "Old Tiger Tail Dead, " F.H.Q. 4(1926):192-94.

936. "Original Narratives of Indian Attacks in Florida, " F.H.Q. 8(1930):179-203.

937. Parker, H. H. "The Battle of Okeechobee [Dec. 25, 1837]." Am. Philatelist 61(1948):808-10.

938. Parrish, John Orlando. Battling the Seminoles, Featuring John Akins, Scout. Lakeland: Southern Printing Company, 1930.

939. Phelps, John W. "Letters of Lieutenant John W. Phelps, U.S.A., 1837-1838, " F.H.Q. 6(1927):67-84.

940. Pierce, Philip N. and Lewis Meyers. "The Seven Years War, " Marine Corps Gazette 32(1948):32-38.

941. Porter, Kenneth W. "Billy Bowlegs (Holata Micco) in the Seminole Wars, " F.H.Q. 45(1967):219-42, 391-401.

942. _____. "Seminole Flight From Fort Marion, " F.H.Q. 22(1944):113-33.

943. _____. "Tiger Tail, " F.H.Q. 24(1946):216-17.

944. Potter, Woodburne. War in Florida: Being an Exposition of its Causes and an Accurate History of the Campaigns of Generals Clinch, Gaines, and Scott. Baltimore: Lewis & Coleman, 1836.

945. Preble, George Henry. "A Canoe Expedition Into the Everglades, " Tequesta 5(1945):30-51.

946.   Quigg, Joyce E.   "Brevet Brigadier General Duncan Lamont
        Clinch and his Florida Service."   Master's thesis, Univer-
sity of Florida, 1963.

947.   Richards, Robert L.   "Indian Removal in Florida, 1835-
        1842: A Study of the Causes and Conduct of the Seminole
War."   Master's thesis, University of Kansas, 1951.

948.   Roberts, Albert Hubbard.   "The Dade Massacre," F.H.Q.
        5(1927):123-38.

949.   Schloenback, Helen Holden.   "The Seminole War, 1835-1842."
        Master's thesis, University of Georgia, 1940.

950.   Seley, Ray B., Jr.   "Lieutenant Hartsuff and the Banana
        Plants [Seminole War 1855]," Tequesta 23(1963):3-14.

951.   Sheldon, Jane Murray.   "Seminole Attacks Near New Smyrna,
        1835-1836," F.H.Q. 8(1930):188-96.

952.   Smith, Joseph R.   "Letters From the Second Seminole War."
        Edited by John K. Mahon.   F.H.Q. 36(1958):331-53.

953.   Smith, W. W.   Sketch of the Seminole War, and Sketches
        During a Campaign.   Charleston, S. C.: Dan J. Dowling,
1836.

954.   Sprague, John T.   "MaComb's Mission to the Seminoles:
        John T. Sprague's Journal Kept During April and May, 1839."
Edited by Frank F. White, Jr. F.H.Q. 35(1956):130-93.

955.   _____. The Origin, Progress, and Conclusion of the
        Florida War.   Introduction by John K. Mahon.   Gainesville:
University of Florida Press, 1964.

956.   Stafford, Robert Charles.   "The Bemrose Manuscript on the
        Seminole War," F.H.Q. 18(1940):285-92.

957.   Taylor, Elizabeth Oursler.   "Hostilities in Florida Arising
        From the Removal of the Seminole Indians."   Master's thesis,
Oklahoma A & M, 1934.

958.   Tebbel, John and Keith Jennison.   "The Second Seminole
        War."   In The American Indian Wars.   New York: Harper
and Brothers, 1960. pp. 209-19.

959.   Tillis, James Dallas.   "Original Narratives of Indian Attacks
        in Florida; an Indian Attack of 1856 on the Home of Willough-
by," F.H.Q. 8(1930):179-87.

960.   Tyler, Martha.   "Reminiscences of the Indian Uprising Near
        Fort Gatlin, Florida," F.H.Q. 3(1924):37-41.

961. VanNess, Major W. P. "An Incident of the Seminole War,"
      Journal of the Military Service Institute of the United States
      1(1912):267-71.

962. Walker, Hester Perrine. "Massacre at Indian Key, August
      7, 1840, and the Death of Doctor Henry Perrine. Narrative
      of Hester Perrine Walker, a Survivor," F.H.Q. 5(1926):18-42.

963. Webb, Alex S. "Campaigning in Florida in 1855," Journal
      of the Military Service Institute (1909):397-429.

964. White, Frank F., Jr. "A Scouting Expedition Along Lake
      Panasoffkee [1842]," F.H.Q. 31(1953):282-89.

965. Williams, Isabella M. "The Truth Regarding 'Tiger-Tail,'"
      F.H.Q. 4(1925):68-75.

966. Woodward, A. L. "Indian Massacre in Gadsden County,"
      F.H.Q. 1(1908):17-25.

967. Woodward, Sara Alice. "The Second Seminole War With Es-
      pecial Reference to the Attitude of Congress." Master's
      thesis, Columbia University, 1933.

968. Young, Rogers W. "Fort Marion During the Seminole War,
      1835-1842," F.H.Q. 13(1935):193-223.

      C. Second Seminole War: Osceola

969. Boyd, Mark F. "Asi-Yaholo or Osceola," F.H.Q. 33(1955):
      249-305.

970. "The Case of Osceola," Mag. Am. Hist. 5(1880):447-50.

971. Coe, Charles H. "The Parentage and Birthplace of Osceola,"
      F.H.Q. 17(1939):304-11.

972. _____. "The Parentage of Osceola," F.H.Q. 33(1955):
      202-05.

973. Duke, Seymour R. A Narrative of the Early Days and Re-
      membrances of Oceola Nikkanochee, Prince of Econchatti, a
      Young Seminole Indian; Son of Econchatti-Mico, King of the Red
      Hills, in Florida; With a Brief History of His Nation, and His Re-
      nowned Uncle, Oceola, and His Parents: and Amusing Tales, Il-
      lustrative of Indian Life in Florida. London: Hatchard and Son,
      Piccadilly, 1841.

974. Goggin, John M. "Osceola: Portraits, Features, and
      Dress," F.H.Q. 33(1955):161-92.

975. McCarthy, Joseph E. "Portraits of Osceola and the Artists
      Who Painted Them, " Papers of the Jacksonville Historical
Society 2(1949):23-44.

976. Neill, Wilfred T. "The Site of Osceola's Village in Marion
      County, Florida [1837], " F. H. Q. 33(1955):240-46.

977. Porter, Kenneth W. "The Episode of Osceola's Wife: Fact
      or Fiction?" F. H. Q. 26(1947):92-98.

978. _____. "Osceola and the Negroes, " F. H. Q. 33(1955):235-
      39.

979. Simms, W. C. Osceola; or, Fact and Fiction: A Tale of
      the Seminole War. New York: Harper and Brothers, 1838.

980. Sturtevant, William C. "Notes on Modern Seminole Tradi-
      tions of Osceola [died 1838], " F. H. Q. 33(1955):206-17.

981. _____. "Osceola's Coats?" F. H. Q. 34(1956):315-28.

982. Tebbel, John. The Compact History of the Indian Wars.
      New York: Hawthorne Books, 1966.

983. Ward, May McNeer. "The Disappearance of the Head of
      Osceola, " F. H. Q. 33(1955):193-201.

984. Wells, W. Alva. "Osceola and the Second Seminole War. "
      Master's thesis, University of Oklahoma, 1936.

985. "The White Flag, " F. H. Q. 33(1955):218-234.

986. Wilson, Minnie Moore. Osceola; Florida's Seminole War
      Chieftan. Palm Beach: Davies Publishing Company, 1931.

      D. Negroes in the Seminole Wars

987. Brawley, Benjamin. A Social History of the American Ne-
      gro. New York: Macmillan, 1921. pp. 91-115.

988. Covington, James W. "An Episode in the Third Seminole
      War, " F. H. Q. 45(1966):45-59.

989. "Negroes, &c., Captured From Indians in Florida, &c. 25th
      Congress, 3d Session, House of Representatives, War De-
partment. " Document Number 225. Washington: Thomas Allen
Printer, 1839. Pp. 1-126.

990. Porter, Kenneth W. "Abraham, " Phylon 2(1941):107-116.

991. _____. "The Early Life of Luis Pacheco, nee Fatio, "
      Neg. Hist. Bull. 7(1943):52.

992. _____. "Florida Slaves and Free Negroes in the Semi-nole War, 1835-1842," J. Neg. Hist. 38(1943):390-421.

993. _____. "John Caesar: A Forgotten Hero of the Semi-nole War," J. Neg. Hist. 28(1943):53-65.

994. _____. "John Caesar: Seminole Negro Partisan," J. Neg. Hist. 31(1946):190-207.

995. _____. "Louis Pacheco: The Man and the Myth," J. Neg. Hist. 28(1943):65-72.

996. _____. "The Negro Abraham," F. H. Q. 25(1946):1-43.

997. _____. "Negro Guides and Interpreters in the Early Stages of the Seminole War, December 28, 1835-March 6, 1837," J. Neg. Hist. 35(1950):174-82.

998. _____. "Negroes and the Seminole War, 1817-1818," J. Neg. Hist. 36(1951):249-80.

999. _____. "Negroes and the Seminole War, 1835-1842," J. S. Hist. 30(1964):427-50.

XI. A NEW STATE, 1845-1861

1000. Clark, Patricia, ed. " 'A Tale to Tell From Paradise It-self' George Bancroft's Letters from Florida, March 1855," F. H. Q. 48(1970):264-78.

1001. "Contemporaneous Reactions to Statehood," F. H. Q. 23(1945):202-11.

1002. Davis, T. Frederick. "Pioneer Florida: Admission to Statehood, 1845," F. H. Q. 22(1944):134-39.

1003. DeGrove, John Melvin. "The Administration of Internal Improvement Problems in Florida, 1845-1869." Master's thesis, Emory, 1954.

1004. Dodd, Dorothy, ed. Florida Becomes a State. Foreword: Social Life in Florida in 1845, by W. T. Cash. Tallahas-see: Florida Centennial Commission, 1945.

1005. Doherty, Herbert J., Jr. "Florida and the Crisis of 1850," J. S. Hist. 19(1953):32-47.

1006. _____. "The Florida Whigs." Master's thesis, University of Florida, 1949.

1007. _____. "Union Nationalism in Florida, " F. H. Q. 29(1950): 83-95.

1008. _____. The Whigs of Florida, 1845-1854. Gainesville: University of Florida Press, 1959.

1009. _____. "Florida in 1856, " F. H. Q. 35(1956):60-70.

1010. Doty, Franklin A. "Florida, Iowa and the National 'Balance of Power, ' " F. H. Q. 35(1956):30-59.

1011. Graham, Thomas S. "Florida Politics and the Tallahassee Press, 1845-1861, " F. H. Q. 46(1968):234-42.

1012. Hodgson, Mabel. "The Relation of Legislative Action to the Development of Florida, 1845-1861. " Master's thesis, Florida State University, 1942.

1013. Jordan, Weymouth T. " 'The Florida Plan': An Ante-Bellum Effort to Control Cotton Sales, " F. H. Q. 35(1957): 205-18.

1014. Meador, John A. "Florida and the Compromise of 1850, " F. H. Q. 39(1960):16-33.

1015. _____. "Florida Political Parties, 1855-1877. " Ph. D. dissertation, University of Florida, 1964.

1016. Mool, J. B. "Florida in Federal Politics, Statehood to Secession. " Master's thesis, Duke University, 1940.

1017. Moseley, William D. "Inaugural Address of Governor Moseley, " F. H. Q. 23(1945):212-19.

1018. Norwood, Olin, ed. "Letters From Florida in 1851, " F. H. Q. 29(1951):261-83.

1019. Parker, Daisy. "The Inauguration of the First Governor of the State of Florida, " Apalachee 2(1946):59-67.

1020. Phillips, Rebecca. "The Diary of Jesse Talbot Bernard; Newmansville and Tallahassee, " F. H. Q. 18(1939):115-26.

1021. Porter, Emily Mary. "The Movement for the Admission of Florida into the Union, 1819-1845. " Master's thesis, Florida State University, 1938.

1022. Russell, Robert R. "Economic Aspects of Southern Sectionalism, 1840-1860. " Ph. D. dissertation, University of Illinois, 1922.

1023. Smith, Julia Frances. "The Plantation Belt in Middle Florida, 1850-1860. " Ph. D. dissertation, Florida State University, 1964.

1024.   Thompson, Arthur W.   "Political Nativism in Florida, 1848-
        1860:   a Phase of Anti-Secessionism, " J. S. Hist. 15(1949):
        39-65.

1025.   Williams, Edwin L., Jr.   "Florida in the Union, 1845-
        1861. "   Ph. D. dissertation, University of North Carolina,
        1951.

XII.   SECESSION

1026.   Davis, R. W.   "Florida in the Days of Secession, " Fla.
        Mag. 5(1902):5-8.

1027.   "Documents Relating to Secession in Florida, " F. H. Q.
        4(1926):183-85.

1028.   Dodd, Dorothy.   "The Secession Movement in Florida, 1850-
        1861, " F. H. Q. 12(1933):3-24, 45-66.

1029.   _____.   "Some Florida Secession History, " Tallahassee
        Historical Society Annual 3(1937):1-7.

1030.   Hadd, Donald R.   "The Irony of Secession, " F. H. Q.
        41(1962):22-28.

1031.   _____.   "Secession Movement in Florida, 1850-1861. "
        Master's thesis, Florida State University, 1960.

1032.   McGehee, John C.   "Address of John C. McGehee Before
        the Southern Rights Association of Madison County, June 7,
        1851, " F. H. Q. 5(1926):67-87.

1033.   Meredith, Evelyn T.   "The Secession Movement in Florida. "
        Master's thesis, Duke University, 1940.

1034.   "Notes On Secession in Tallahassee and Leon County, " F. H.
        Q. 4(1925):61-67.

1035.   Proctor, Samuel, ed.   "The Call to Arms: Secession From
        a Feminine Point of View, " F. H. Q. 35(1957):266-77.

1036.   Reiger, John F.   "Secession of Florida From the Union--A
        Minority Decision?" F. H. Q. 46(1968):358-68.

1037.   Rogers, William Warren, ed.   "Florida On the Eve of the
        Civil War as Seen by a Southern Reporter, " F. H. Q.
        39(1960):145-58.

1038.   Ruffin, Edmund. "Edmund Ruffin's Account of the Florida Secession Convention, 1861, " F. H. Q. 12(1933):67-76.

1039.   Weinberg, Sydney Jay. "Slavery and Secession in Florida, 1845-1861." Master's thesis, University of Florida, 1940.

1040.   Wooster, Ralph A. "The Florida Secession Convention, " F. H. Q. 36(1958):373-85.

1041.   _____. The People in Power: Courthouse and State-house in the Lower South, 1850-1860. Knoxville: The University of Tennessee Press, 1969.

1042.   _____. The Secession Convention of the South. Princeton, New Jersey: Princeton University Press, 1962.

1043.   Yulee, David L. "Two Letters of David L. Yulee: His Opinion on Secession in 1860 [and a Letter on Duty], " F. H. Q. 29(1950):125-31.

XIII.   THE WAR BETWEEN THE STATES

    A.   General Studies

1044.   Bickel, Karl A. "Robert E. Lee in Florida, " F. H. Q. 27(1948):59-66.

1045.   Bingham, Millicent Todd, ed. "Key West in the Summer of 1864 [letters of Union Capt. John Wilder], " F. H. Q. 43(1965):262-65.

1046.   Clarke, Robert L. "The Florida Railroad Company in the Civil War, " J. S. Hist. 19(1953):180-92.

1047.   Cortada, James W. "Florida Observes the Civil War Centennial: 1859-1959, " Apalachee 7(1968-70):106-19.

1048.   Davis, Fred H. "Leon County During the Civil War, " Tallahassee Historical Society Annual 3(1937):27-34.

1049.   Davis, William Watson. The Civil War and Reconstruction in Florida. New York: Columbia University Press, 1913, reprinted with an introduction by Fletcher M. Green. Gainesville: University of Florida Press, 1964.

1050.   _____. "A Review of A. J. Hanna's Flight Into Oblivion, " F. H. Q. 17(1939):227-36.

1051. Dibble, Ernest F. "War Averters: Seward, Mallory, and Fort Pickens, " F. H. Q. 49(1971):232-44.

1052. Dickison, Col. J. J. Military History of Florida. Atlanta: Confederate Publishing Company, 1899.

1053. Dickison, Mary E. Dickison and his Men: Reminiscences of the War in Florida. Louisville: Courier Journal Job Printing Company, 1890.

1054. East, Omega G. "St. Augustine During the Civil War, " F. H. Q. 31(1952):75-91.

1055. Ferrel, Sidney Scaife. "Public Opinion in Confederate Florida." Master's thesis, University of Florida, 1950.

1056. Florida Civil War Centennial Commission. A Hundred Years Ago. Coral Gables: University of Miami Press, 1960-65.

1057. Futch, Ovid L. "Salmon P. Chase and Civil War Politics in Florida, " F. H. Q. 32(1954):163-88.

1058. _____. "Salmon P. Chase and Radical Politics in Florida, 1862-1865." Master's thesis, University of Florida, 1952.

1059. Hall, Wade H. Reflections of the Civil War in Southern Humor. University of Florida Monographs--Humanities, #10. Gainesville: University of Florida Press, 1962.

1060. Hanna, Alfred J. Flight Into Oblivion. Richmond, Va.: Johnson Publishing Company, 1938.

1061. Havard, William C. "The Florida Executive Council: An Experiment in Civil War Administration [1862], " F. H. Q. 33(1954):77-96.

1062. Johns, John E. Florida During the Civil War. Gainesville: University of Florida Press, 1963.

1063. _____. "Florida in the Confederacy, " Ph. D. dissertation, University of North Carolina, 1959.

1064. Jones, James Pickett. "John L. Worden and the Fort Pickens Mission: The Confederacy's First Prisoner of War, " Ala. Rev. 21(1968):113-32.

1065. _____, ed. "Lincoln's Courier: John L. Worden's Mission to Fort Pickens, " F. H. Q. 41(1962):145-53.

1066. Keen, Mary W. "Some Phases of Life in Leon County During the Civil War, " Tallahassee Historical Society Annual

4(1939):20-47.

1067.   Nolan, Terrance H. "Florida's Reaction to the 'Military
        Bill,' " Apalachee 7(1968-70):99-105.

1068.   Norton, Herman. Rebel Religion: The Story of the Con-
        federate Chaplains. St. Louis: The Bethany Press, 1961.

1069.   Proctor, Samuel. Florida Commemorates the Civil War
        Centennial, 1961-1965; a Manual for the Observance of the
Civil War in the Counties and Cities of the State of Florida. Coral
Gables: Florida Civil War Centennial Commission, 1962.

1070.   _____ . "Jacksonville During the Civil War," F.H.Q.
        41(1963):343-55.

1071.   Reiger, John Franklin. "Anti-war and Pro-union Sentiment
        in Confederate Florida." Master's thesis, University of
Florida, 1966.

1072.   _____ . "Deprivation, Disaffection, and Desertion in Con-
        federate Florida," F. H. Q. 48(1970):279-98.

1073.   Roberts, Albert H. "Tallahassee Rejoins the Union," Apa-
        lachee 1(1944):74-80.

1074.   Sanford, Robert Meriwether. "The Literary Elements of the
        Florida Newspapers of the Civil War Period." Master's
thesis, University of Florida, 1936.

1075.   Shofner, Jerrell H. and William W. Rogers. "Confederate
        Railroad Construction: The Live Oak to Lawton Connector,"
F.H.Q. 43(1965):217-28.

1076.   Skinner, W. B. "Pensacola's Exiled Government [1862+], "
        F.H.Q. 39(1961):270-76.

1077.   Sweet, Zelia Wilson, comp. New Smyrna, Florida, in the
        Civil War. . . . Daytona Beach: Volusia County Historical
Commission, 1963.

1078.   Thomas, David Y. "Florida Finance in the Civil War,"
        Yale Rev. 16(1907):311.

1079.   Thompson, Arthur W. "Confederate Finance: A Documen-
        tary Study of a Proposal of David L. Yulee," F. H. Q.
30(1951):193-202.

1080.   Yonge, Julien C. "Pensacola in the War for Southern In-
        dependence," F. H. Q. 37(1959):357-71.

1081.   Zornow, William F. "State Aid for Indigent Soldiers and
        Their Families in Florida, 1861-65, " F. H. Q. 34(1956):

259-65.

B. Diaries, Letters, and Regimental Histories

1082. Adamson, Augustus Pitt. Brief History of the Thirtieth Georgia Regiment. Griffin, Ga.: Mills Printing Co., 1912.

1083. Amory, Charles Bean. A Brief Record of the Army Life of Charles B. Amory; Written for His Children. Boston: Privately Printed, 1902.

1084. Bittle, George C. "Fighting Men View the Western War, 1862-1864," F. H. Q. 47(1968):25-33.

1085. Bogg, William Robertson. ...Military Reminiscences of General William R. Boggs, C. S. A. Introduction by William K. Boyd. Durham, N. C.: Seeman Printer, 1913.

1086. Caldwell, Charles K. The Old Sixth Regiment, Its War Record, 1861-5. New Haven: Tuttle, Morehouse & Taylor, 1875.

1087. Chamberlain, Captain V. "A Letter of Captain V. Chamberlain 7th Connecticut Volunteers," F. H. Q. 15(1936):85-95.

1088. Clark, James H. The Iron Hearted Regiment: Being an Account of the Battles, Marches and Gallant Deeds Performed by the 115th Regiment N. Y. Volunteers. Albany, 1865.

1089. Copp, Elbridge J. Reminiscences of the War of the Rebellion, 1861-1865. Nashua, N. H.: Printed by the Telegraph Publishing Company, 1911.

1090. Croom, Wendell D. The War-history of Company "C", (Beauregard Volunteers) Sixth Georgia Regiment, (Infantry) With a Graphic Account of Each Member. Fort Valley, Ga.: Printed at the "Advertiser" Office, 1879.

1091. Dancy, James M. "Reminiscences of the Civil War," F. H. Q. 37(1958):66-89.

1092. Doty, Franklin A., ed. "The Civil War Letters of Augustus Henry Mathers, Assistant Surgeon, Fourth Florida Regiment, C. S. A.," F. H. Q. 36(1957):94-124.

1093. Duren, C. M. "The Occupation of Jacksonville, February 1864 and the Battle of Olustee; Letters of Lt. C. M. Duren, 54th Massachusetts Regiment, U. S. A.," F. H. Q. 32(1954):262-87.

1094. Egan, Patrick. The Florida Campaign With Light Battery C, Third Rhode Island Heavy Artillery. Providence, R. I.:

The Society, 1905.

1095.   Fleming, Francis P. Memoir of Captain C. Seton Fleming
        of the Second Florida Infantry, C. S. A. Illustrative of the
History of the Florida Troops in Virginia During the War Between
the States. With Appendix of the Casulties. Jacksonville: Times-
Union Publishing House, 1884.

1096.   Groene, Bertram H., ed. "A Letter From Occupied Talla-
        hassee," F. H. Q. 48(1969):70-75.

1097.   Hanna, Alfred J. "The Confederate Baggage and Treasure
        Train Ends Its Flight in Florida. A Diary of Tench Fran-
cis Tilghman," F. H. Q. 12(1939):159-80.

1098.   Higginson, Thomas Wentworth. Army Life in a Black Regi-
        ment. Boston: Fields, Osgood and Company, 1870.

1099.   _____. "Up the St. Johns," Atl. M. 16(1865):311-25.

1100.   _____. "Up the St. Mary's," Atl. M. 15(1865):422-36.

1101.   Jackson, J. Adrian. "Perry's Brigade of Florida's Fighting
        Rebels," Apalachee 7(1968-70):61-79.

1102.   Jones, Charles Colcock. Historical Sketch of the Chatham
        Artillery During the Confederate Struggle for Independence.
Albany: Joel Munsell, 1867.

1103.   Jones, Sarah L. "Governor Milton and His Family: a Con-
        temporary Picture of Life in Florida During the War, by an
English Tutor," F. H. Q. 2(1909):42-50.

1104.   Kinsman, Oliver D. ...A Loyal Man in Florida, 1858-1861.
        Prepared by companion Brevet Lieutenant Colonel Oliver K.
Kinsman...and read at the stated meeting of May 4, 1910. Washington: 1910.

1105.   Le Diable, Captain, pseud. Historical Sketch of the Third
        Annual Conquest of Florida. Port Royal, S. C.: 1864.

1106.   McMorries, Edward Young. ...History of the First Regi-
        ment, Alabama Volunteer Infantry, C. S. A. Montgomery,
Ala.: The Brown Printing Company, 1904.

1107.   Mellon, Knox, Jr., ed. "A Florida Soldier in the Army of
        Northern Virginia: The Hosford Letters," F. H. Q. 46(1968):
243-71.

1108.   Mudd, Nettie, ed. The Life of Dr. Samuel A. Mudd; Con-
        taining His Letters From Fort Jefferson, Dry Tortugas Is-
land Where He Was Imprisoned Four Years for Alleged Complicity

in the Assassination of Abraham Lincoln. New York: Neale Publishing Company, 1906.

1109. Nichols, James Moses. Perry's Saints; or, The Fighting Parson's Regiment in the War of the Rebellion. Boston: D. Lothrop and Company, 1886.

1110. Norton, Oliver Willcox. Army Letters, 1861-1865. Being Extracts From Private Letters to Relatives and Friends From a Soldier in the Field During the Late Civil War, With an Appendix Containing Copies of Some Official Documents, Papers and Addresses of a Later Date. Chicago: Printed by O. L. Deming, 1903.

1111. Palmer, Abraham John. The History of the Forty-eighth Regiment New York State Volunteers in the War for the Union, 1861-1865. Brooklyn: Published by the Veteran Association of the Regiment, 1885.

1112. Porter, David Dixon. Incidents and Anecdotes of the Civil War. New York: D. Appleton and Company, 1885.

1113. Reaver, J. Russell, ed. "Letters of Joel C. Blake [1862-63]," Apalachee 5(1957-62):5-25.

1114. Scott, Robert M., ed. The War of the Rebellion; a Compilation of the Official Records of the Union and Confederate Armies. Washington: Government Printing Office, 1891+ .

1115. Smith, William B. On Wheels and How I Came There. A Real Story for Real Boys and Girls, Giving the Personal Experiences and Observations of a Fifteen-year-old Yankee Boy as Soldier and Prisoner in the American Civil War. Edited by Rev. Joseph Gatch Bonnell. New York: Hunt & Eaton, 1893.

1116. Staudenraus, P. J., ed. "A [Union] War Correspondent's [Noah Brook's] View of St. Augustine and Fernandina, 1863," F. H. Q. 61(1962):60-65.

1117. Sterkx, Henry E. and Brooks Thompson, eds. "Letters of of a Teenage Confederate," F. H. Q. 38(1960):339-46.

1118. Swift, Lester L., ed. "Capt. Dana in Florida: A Narrative of the Seymour Expedition," Civil War Hist. 11(1965): 245-56.

1119. A Voice From Rebel Prisons: Giving an Account of Some of the Horrors of the Stockades at Andersonville, Milan [Millen], and Other Prisons. Boston: Press of George C. Rand & Avery, 1865.

1120. Williamson, Edward C., ed. "Francis P. Fleming in the War for Southern Independence; Soldiering With the 2nd

Florida Regiment, " F. H. Q. 28(1949):38-52, 143-55, 205-10.

1121. Woodford, Milton M. "A Connecticut Yankee Fights at
        Olustee: Letters From the Front. " Edited by Vaughn D.
Bornet.   F. H. Q. 27(1949):237-59, 385-403.

1122. Wright, Gilbert, ed. "Some Letters to His Parents by a
        Floridian in the Confederate Army, " F. H. Q. 36(1958):353-
72.

        C.   Ground Action

1123. Baltzell, George F. "The Battle of Olustee (Ocean Pond),
        Florida, " F. H. Q. 9(1931):199-223.

1124. Bearss, Edwin C. "Asboth's Expedition up the Alabama
        and Florida Railroad, " F. H. Q. 39(1960):159-66.

1125. _____. "Civil War Operations in and Around Pensacola,"
        F. H. Q. 36(1957):125-65; 39(1961):231-55,330-53.

1126. _____. "Federal Expedition Against Saint Marks Ends at
        Natural Bridge, " F. H. Q. 45(1967):369-90.

1127. _____. "Military Operations on the St. Johns, Septem-
        ber-October, 1862, " F. H. Q. 42(1964):232-47, 331-50.

1128. Boyd, Mark F. "The Battle of Marianna [Sept. 27, 1864], "
        F. H. Q. 29(1951):225-42.

1129. _____. "The Federal Campaign of 1864 in East Florida:
        a Study for the Florida State Board of Parks and Historic
Monuments, " F. H. Q. 29(1950):3-37.

1130. _____. "The Joint Operations of the Federal Army and
        Navy Near St. Marks, Florida, March 1865, " F. H. Q.
29(1950):96-124.

1131. Breeze, Lawrence E. "The Battle of Olustee [1864]: Its
        Meaning for the British, " F. H. Q. 43(1965):207-16.

1132. Burdett, Susan E. "The Military Career of Brigadier Gen-
        eral Joseph Finegan of Florida. " Master's thesis, Colum-
bia, 1930.

1133. Cash, W. T. "Taylor County History and Civil War De-
        serters, " F. H. Q. 27(1948):28-58.

1134. Clarke, Robert L. "Northern Plans for the Economic In-
        vasion of Florida, 1862-1865, " F. H. Q. 28(1950):262-70.

1135.   Cole, Ruth H.   The Battle of Olustee: A Description of
        Florida's Major Battle in the War Between the States.   St.
Augustine: United Daughters of the Confederacy, 1929.

1136.   Davis, T. Frederick.   "Engagements at St. Johns Bluff St.
        Johns River, Florida, September-October, 1862, " F. H. Q.
15(1936):77-84.

1137.   "Federal Raid on Tampa Bay, " F. H. Q.   4(1926):130-39.

1138.   Jones, Allen W.   "Military Events in Florida During the
        Civil War, 1861-1865, " F. H. Q.   39(1960):42-45.

1139.   Jones, James P. and William Warren Rogers.   "The Sur-
        render of Tallahassee, " Apalachee 6(1963-67):103-10.

1140.   Jones, Samuel.   "The Battle of Olustee, or Ocean Pond
        Florida. " In Battles and Leaders of the Civil War, edited
by Robert U. Johnson and Clarence C. Buell.   Vol. 1.   New York:
1888.   pp. 76-79.

1141.   Miller, William.   "The Battle of Natural Bridge, " Apala-
        chee 4(1950-56):76-86.

1142.   Olsen, Stanley J.   "Artillery Projectiles From the Civil
        War Engagement at Newport, Florida [Natural Bridge, 1865],"
Fla. Anthro. 15(1962):21-26.

1143.   Parker, Daisy.   "Battle Flags of Florida Troops in Con-
        federate Service, " Apalchee 3(1948-50):1-10.

1144.   Prentice, W. R.   "On the Dry Tortugas [1865], " McClure
        18(1901-2):564-70.

1145.   Welles, Gideon.   "Fort Pickens, Facts in Relation to the
        Reinforcement of Fort Pickens in the Spring of 1861, "
Galaxy 11(1871):92-107.

1146.   Williams, Ames W.   "Stronghold of the Straits: A Short
        History of Fort Zachary Taylor, " Tequesta 14(1954):3-24.

        D.   Naval Operations

1147.   Boykin, Edward Carrington.   Sea Devil of the Confederacy;
        the Story of the Florida and Her Captain, John Newland
Maffitt.   New York: Funk & Wagnalls, 1959.

1148.   Boynton, Charles B.   The History of the Navy During the
        Rebellion.   New York: D. Appleton and Company, 1867-68.

1149.   Camp, Vaughan, Jr.   "Captain Brannan's Dilemma: Key
        West 1861, " Tequesta 20(1960):31-43.

1150.   Cushman, Joseph D., Jr.   "The Blockade and Fall of
        Apalachicola, 1861-1862," F. H. Q. 61(1862):38-46.

1151.   Heffernan, John B.   "The Blockade of the Southern Confede-
        racy: 1861-1865," Smithsonian J. Hist. (1968):23-44.

1152.   Itkin, Stanley L.   "Operations of the East Gulf Blockade
        Squadron in the Blockade of Florida 1862-1865."   Master's
thesis, Florida State University, 1962.

1153.   Falero, Frank, Jr.   "Naval Engagements in Tampa Bay,
        1862," F. H. Q. 46(1967):134-40.

1154.   Larkin, J. L.   "Battle of Santa Rosa Island," F. H. Q.
        37(1959):372-76.

1155.   Lonn, Ella.   "The Extent and Importance of Federal Naval
        Raids on Salt-making in Florida, 1862-1865," F. H. Q.
10(1932):167-84.

1156.   Peters, Thelma.   "Blockade Running in the Bahama's Dur-
        ing the Civil War," Tequesta 5(1945):16-29.

1157.   Price, Marcus W.   "Ships That Tested the Blockade of the
        Georgia and East Florida Ports, 1861-1865," Am. Neptune
15(1955):97-132.

1158.   Schellings, William J., ed.   "On Blockade Duty in Florida
        Waters: Excerpts From a Union Naval Officer's Diary,"
Tequesta 15(1955):55-72.

1159.   Strickland, Alice.   "Blockade Runners," F. H. Q. 36(1957):
        85-93.

1160.   "Yellow Fever on the Blockade of Indian River; a Tragedy
        of 1864," F. H. Q. 21(1943):352-57.

XIV.   RECONSTRUCTION

1161.   Ackerman, Philip D., Jr.   "Florida Reconstruction From
        Walker Through Reed, 1865-1873."   Master's thesis, Uni-
versity of Florida, 1948.

1162.   Bentley, George R.   "The Political Activity of the Freed-
        men's Bureau in Florida [1865-70]," F. H. Q. 28(1949):
        28-37.

1163.   Cahill, Majorie.   "The Negro in Florida During Reconstruc-
        tion, 1865-1877."   Master's thesis, University of Florida,
        1954.

Reconstruction

1164. Clendenen, Clarence C. "President Hayes' 'Withdrawal' of Troops [from the South, 1877]--An Enduring Myth," S. C. Hist. Mag. 70(1969):240-50.

1165. Conrad, Mary Donthit. "Homesteading in Florida During the 1890's," Tequesta 17(1957):3-30.

1166. Cox, John and LaWanda. "General O. O. Howard and the 'Misrepresented Bureau,'" J. S. Hist. 19(1953):41-56.

1167. Cox, Merlin G. "Military Reconstruction in Florida," F. H. Q. 46(1968):219-33.

1168. Davis, T. Frederick. "The Disston Land Purchase," F. H. Q. 17(1939):200-10.

1169. Eckert, Edward K. "Contract Labor in Florida During Reconstruction," F. H. Q. 47(1968):34-50.

1170. Ewing, Cortez A. M. "Florida Reconstruction Impeachments," F. H. Q. 36(1958):299-318.

1171. Gleason, William H. "Florida's First Reconstruction Legislature [1868]." Edited by Edward C. Williamson. F. H. Q. 32(1953):41-43.

1172. Hayden, Clara Ryder. "Confederate Postwar Organizations and History of Anna Jackson Chapter, U. D. C. [Tallahassee, 1896-1947]," Apalachee 3(1948-50):71-79.

1173. Hill, Erastus G. "A Florida Settler of 1877: the Diary of Erastus G. Hill," F. H. Q. 28(1950):271-94.

1174. Huston, L. D. "A Political Rally of 1884 in Daytona," F. H. Q. 29(1951):206-09.

1175. Johnson, Kenneth Ray. "The Administration of William Dunnington Bloxham, 1881-1885." Master's thesis, Florida State University, 1959.

1176. Jones, James P., ed. "Grant Forecasts the Future of Florida," F. H. Q. 39(1960):52-54.

1177. McKelvey, Blake. "Penal Slavery and Southern Reconstruction," J. Neg. Hist. 20(1935):153-79.

1178. Osborn, George C., ed. "Letters of a Carpetbagger in Florida, 1866-1869," F. H. Q. 31(1958):239-85.

1179. Parks, Albert Stanley. "The Negro in the Reconstruction of Florida," Q. J. Fla. A. M. Col. 5(1936):35-61.

1180. Peek, Ralph L. "Aftermath of Military Reconstruction, 1868-69, " F. H. Q. 43(1964):123-41.

1181. _____. "Curbing of Voter Intimidation in Florida, 1871," F. H. Q. 43(1965):333-48.

1182. _____. "Election of 1870 and the End of Reconstruction in Florida, " F. H. Q. 45(1967):352-68.

1183. _____. "Lawlessness and the Restoration of Order in Florida, 1868-1871. " Ph. D. dissertation, University of Florida, 1964.

1184. _____. "Military Reconstruction and the Growth of Anti-Negro Sentiment in Florida, 1867, " F. H. Q. 47(1969):380-400.

1185. Proctor, Samuel. "Reminiscences of a Florida Pioneer: John M. McIntosh, " F. H. Q. 38(1959):67-70.

1186. Richardson, Joe M. "An Evaluation of the Freedmen's Bureau in Florida, " F. H. Q. 41(1963):223-38.

1187. _____. "Florida Black Codes, " F. H. Q. 47(1969):365-79.

1188. _____. "The Freedmen's Bureau and Negro Education in Florida, " J. Neg. Ed. 31(1962):460-67.

1189. _____. "The Freedmen's Bureau and Negro Labor in Florida, " F. H. Q. 39(1960):167-74.

1190. _____. "The Freedmen's Bureau in Florida, " Apalachee 6(1963-67):95-102.

1191. _____. "The Freedmen's Bureau in Florida. " Master's thesis, Florida State University, 1959.

1192. _____. "Jonathan C. Gibbs: Florida's Only Negro Cabinet Member, " F. H. Q. 42(1964):363-68.

1193. _____. "The Negro in the Reconstruction of Florida. " Ph. D. dissertation, Florida State University, 1963.

1194. _____. The Negro in the Reconstruction of Florida, 1865-1877. Tallahassee: Florida State University, 1965.

1195. _____, ed. "A Northerner [A. E. Kinne] Reports on [East Florida]: 1866, " F. H. Q. 40(1962):381-90.

1196. Roberts, Albert Hubbard. "Florida and Leon County in the Election of 1876, " Tallahassee Historical Society Annual 4(1939):88-96.

1197.   Roberts, Derrell.   "Joseph E. Brown and the Florida Elec-
        tion of 1876," F. H. Q. 40(1962):217-25.

1198.   _____.   "Social Legislation in Reconstruction Florida,"
        F. H. Q. 43(1965):349-60.

1199.   Rosen, F. Bruce.   "A Plan to Homestead Freedmen in
        Florida in 1866," F. H. Q. 43(1965):379-84.

1200.   Russ, William A., Jr.   "Disfranchisement in Florida Dur-
        ing Radical Reconstruction," Susquehanna U. Studies 4(1950):
162-81.

1201.   Scroggs, Jack B.   "Carpetbagger Constitutional Reform in
        the South Atlantic States, 1867-1868," J. S. Hist. 27(1961):
475-93.

1202.   Shofner, Jerrell H.   "Florida's Political Reconstruction and
        the Presidential Election of 1876." Ph. D. dissertation,
Florida State University, 1963.

1203.   _____.   "Political Reconstruction in Florida," F. H. Q.
        45(1966):145-70.

1204.   Sims, Leonard Henderson, Jr.   "A Study of the Florida
        Press During the Reconstruction Years, 1865-1870." Mas-
ter's thesis, University of Florida, 1958.

1205.   Smith, George Winston.   "Carpetbag Imperialism in Florida,
        1862-1868," F. H. Q. 27(1948):99-130; (1949):269-99.

1206.   Vance, Maurice M.   "Northerners in Late Nineteenth Cen-
        tury Florida: Carpetbaggers or Settlers?" F. H. Q.
38(1959):1-14.

1207.   Wallace, John.   Carpet Bag Rule in Florida.   The Inside
        Workings of the Reconstruction of Civil Government in Flor-
ida After the Close of the Civil War.   Jacksonville: Da Costa
Printing and Publishing House, 1888.

1208.   Williams, Emma Rochelle.   "Notes on Reconstruction in
        Tallahassee and Leon County, 1866-1876," F. H. Q. 5(1927):
153-58.

1209.   Woodman, Cyrus.   "Teaching Freedmen in the Post-war
        South."   Edited by Larry Gara. J. Neg. Hist. 40(1955):
274-76.

XV. THE SPANISH AMERICAN WAR, 1898

1210. Belknap, Reginald. "The Naval Base at Key West 1898,"
       Proc. U. S. Naval Institute 41(1915):1443-73.

1211. Carson, Ruby Leach. "Florida, Promoter of Cuban Liber-
       ty," F. H. Q. 19(1941):270-92.

1212. Gatewood, Willard B., Jr. "Negro Troops in Florida,
       1898," F. H. Q. 49(1970):1-15.

1213. Oppel, J. C. "The Unionization of Florida Cigar Makers
       and the Coming of the War With Spain," Hisp. Am. Hist.
Rev. 36(1956):38-49.

1214. Post, Charles Johnson. The Little War of Private Post.
       Boston: Little, Brown and Company, 1960.

1215. Proctor, Samuel. "Filibustering Aboard the Three Friends,"
       Mid-America 38(1956):84-100.

1216. Rickenbach, Richard V. "Filibustering With the Dauntless,"
       F. H. Q. 28(1950):231-53.

1217. _____. "History of Filibustering, Florida to Cuba, 1895-
       1898." Master's thesis, University of Florida, 1948.

1218. Schellings, William J. "The Advent of the Spanish-Ameri-
       can War in Florida, 1898," F. H. Q. 39(1961):311-29.

1219. _____. "Florida and the Cuban Revolution, 1895-1898,"
       F. H. Q. 39(1960):175-86.

1220. _____. "Florida Volunteers in the War With Spain,
       1898," F. H. Q. 41(1962):47-59.

1221. _____. "Key West and the Spanish American War," Te-
       questa 20(1960):19-29.

1222. _____. "The Role of Florida in the Spanish American
       War, 1898." Ph. D. dissertation, University of Florida,
1958.

1223. _____. "Soldiers in Miami, 1898," Tequesta 17(1957):
       69-76.

1224. _____. "Tampa, Florida: Its Role in the Spanish Amer-
       ican War, 1898." Master's thesis, University of Miami,
1954.

1225. Wellborn, Charles Griffis, Jr. "Treatment of the Spanish-
       American War by Selected Florida Newspapers." Master's

thesis, University of Florida, 1958.

XVI. TRAVEL AND DESCRIPTION

A.   16th, 17th, and 18th Centuries

1226. Andrews, Charles M. "God's Protecting Providence: A
       Journal by Jonathan Dickinson, " F. H. Q. 21(1942):107-26.

1227. Bartram, John. An Account of East Florida, With a Jour-
       nal Kept by John Bartram of Philadelphia, Botanist to His
Majesty for the Floridas; Upon a Journey From St. Augustine up
the River St. John's. London: Sold by W. Nicoll and G. Woodfall, 1766.

1228. _____. "Diary of a Journey Through the Carolinas,
       Georgia, and Florida From July 1, 1765, to April 10,
1766." Edited by Francis Harper. Transactions of the American
Philosophical Society 33(1942).

1229. Cabeza de Vaca, Alvar Nuñez. La Relacion Que Dio Aluar
       Nuñez Cabeza de Vaca de lo Acaescido En las Indias, En la
Armada Donde Yua por Gouernador Paphilo de Narbaez, Desde el
Año de Veynte y Siete Hasta el Año de Treynta y Ses.... Zamora,
1942.

1230. Catesby, Mark. The Natural History of Carolina, Florida,
       and the Bahama Islands: Containing the Figures of Birds,
Beasts, Fishes, Serpents, Insects, and Plants, Together With Their
Descriptions in English and French.... London, 1734.

1231. Coxe, Daniel. A Description of the English Province of
       Carolina, by the Spaniards Call'd Florida, and by the French
La Louisiane. As Also of the Great and Famous River Meschacebe
or Mississippi, the Five Vast Navigable Lakes of Fresh Water, and
the Parts Adjacent. London: Printed for A. Betteseorth, 1722.

1232. Dickinson, Jonathan. Journal; or, God's Protecting Provi-
       dence, Being the Narrative of a Journey From Port Royal
in Jamaica to Philadelphia, Between August 23, 1696 and April 1,
1697. 1699. Edited by Evangeline Walker Andrews and Charles
McLean Andrews with a foreword and new introduction by Leonard
W. Labaree. New Haven, Conn.: Printed for the Yale University
Press, 1961.

1233. Dubois-Fontanelle, Jean Gaspard. Naufrage et Aventures
       de Monsieur Pierre Viaud, Natif de Bordeaux, Captaine de
Navire; Histoire Veritable, Vérifiée Sur l'Attestation de Mr. Sevet-

tenham, Commandant du Fort St. Marc, des Appalaches.... Bordeaux: F. J. Desoer, 1770.

1234.   Elvas, Gentleman of.   True Relation of the Hardships Suffered by Governor Fernando de Soto and Certain Portuguese Gentlemen During the Discovery of the Province of Florida.   1557. 2 vols.   Translated and edited by James A. Robertson.   De Land: Florida State Historical Society, 1933.

1235.   Garcilaso de la Vega, el Inca.   The Florida of the Inca.... 1605.   Translated and edited by John Grier Varner and Jeannette Johnson Varner.   Austin: University of Texas Press, 1951.

1236.   Gauld, George.   An Account of the Surveys of Florida, etc. With Directions for Sailing From Jamaica or the West Indies, by the West End of Cuba and Through the Gulf of Florida. London: W. Faden, 1790.

1237.   Hawkins, Sir John.   A True Declaration of the Troublesome Voyage of M. John Haukins to the Parties of Guynea and the West Indies, in the Yeares of Our Lord 1567 and 1568.   Imprinted at London in Poules Churchyarde, by Thomas Purfoote for Lucus Harrison, 1569.

1238.   Hutchins, Thomas.   An Historical Narrative and Topographical Description of Louisiana and West-Florida.   1784.   Edited by Joseph C. Tregle, Jr.   Gainesville: University of Florida Press, 1968.

1239.   Laudonniere, Rene Goulaine De.   A Notable Historie, Containing Foure Voyages Made by Certayne French Captaynes Vnto Florida; Wherein the Great Riches and Fruitfulness of the Countrey With the Maners of the People, Hitherto Concealed, Are Brought to Light....   Translated by R. H. London, 1587.

1240.   Le Challeux, Nicolas.   Discovrs de l'histoire de la Floride Contenant la Trahison des Espagnois, Contre les Subiets du Roy...Redigé au Vray par Ceux Qui en Sont Restez.   Chose Autant Lamentable à Ouir qu'elle a Esté Proditoirement & Cruellement Executee par les Dits Espagnols....   Dieppe: Pour Lessé le Sellier, 1566.

1241.   Linschoten, John Huyghen Van.   His Discours of Voyages Into ye Easte and West Indies.   London, 1598.

1242.   Mattfield, Mary S.   "Journey to the Wilderness: Two Travellers in Florida, 1696-1774," F. H. Q. 45(1967):327-51.

1243.   Oré, Luis Gerónimo de.   Relacion de los Mártires Que ha Habida en las Provincias de la Florida.   Madrid, 1617.

1244. Ribaut, Jean. The Whole & True Discouerye of Terra Flor-
       ida. 1563. A transcript of an English version in the Brit-
ish Museum with notes by H. P. Biggar, and a biography by Jeannette Thurber Connor. A facsimile reproduction with introduction
by David L. Dowd. Gainesville: University of Florida Press,
1964.

1245. Roberts, William. An Account of the First Discovery, and
       Natural History of Florida. With a Particular Detail of the
Several Expeditions and Descents Made on That Coast. London:
Printed for T. Jefferys, 1763.

1246. Romans, Bernard. A Concise Natural History of East and
       West Florida; Containing an Account of the Natural Produce
of All the Southern Part of British America, in the Three Kingdoms
of Nature, Particularly the Animal and Vegetable.... New York:
Printed for the author, 1775.

1247. Schöpf, Johann David. Reise Durch Einige Der Mittlern
       Und Sudlichen Vereinigten Nordamerikanischen Staaten Nach
Ost-Florida Und Den Bahama-Inseln Unternommen in Den Jahren
1783 Und 1784. 2 Vols. Erlangen: J. J. Palm, 1788.

1248. Stork, William. Account of East Florida. With Remarks
       on Its Future Importance to Trade and Commerce. London:
Printed for G. Woodfall, 1766.

       B. 19th Century

1249. Arnold, William E., comp. Florida; or, Summer in the
       Winter Time. Savannah: Ocean Steamship Company, 1891-
1892.

1250. Audubon, John James. "Three Florida Episodes," Teques-
       ta 5(1945):52-68.

1251. Barbour, George M. Florida for Tourists, Invalids, and
       Settlers: Containing Practical Information Regarding Cli-
mate, Soil, and Productions; Cities, Towns, and People; the Culture of the Orange and Other Tropical Fruits; Farming and Garden-
ing; Scenery and Resorts; Sport; Routes of Travel.... New York:
D. Appleton and Company, 1882.

1252. Bartholf, J. F. and F. C. M. Boggess. South Florida,
       the Italy of America, Its Climate, Soil and Productions....
Jacksonville: Ashmeade Brothers, 1881.

1253. Beecher, Eunice White Bullard. Letters From Florida.
       New York: D. Appleton and Company, 1879.

1254. Bentley, George R. "Colonel Thompson's 'Tour of Tropical
       Florida,' " Tequesta 10(1950):3-12.

1255. Gerquin-Duvallon. Travels in Louisiana and the Floridas,
       in the Year, 1802, Giving a Correct Picture of Those Coun-
tries. Translated by John Davis. New York: Printed by I. Riley
and Company, 1806.

1256. Bill, Ledyard. A Winter in Florida; or, Observations on
       the Soil, Climate, and Products of Our Semi-tropical State;
With Sketches of the Principal Towns and Cities in Eastern Florida.
New York: Wood & Holbrook, 1869.

1257. Birchard, Mary R. "A Trip to Florida, 1867; Three Let-
       ters of Mary R. Birchard." Edited by Watt P. Marchman.
F. H. Q. 33(1954):142-52.

1258. Bloomfield, Max. Bloomfield's Illustrated Historical Guide,
       Embracing an Account of the Antiquities of St. Augustine
Florida.... St. Augustine: Max Bloomfield, 1884.

1259. Brinton, Daniel Garrison. A Guide-book of Florida and the
       South, for Tourists, Invalids, and Emigrants. Philadelphia,
George Maclean; Jacksonville: C. Drew, 1869.

1260. Brooks, Abbie M. Petals Plucked From Sunny Climes.
       Nashville: Southern Methodist Publishing House, 1883.

1261. Bryant, William Cullen. "Letters of William Cullen Bry-
       ant." Edited by Charles I. Glicksberg. F. H. Q. 14(1936):
255-74.

1262. Campbell, Reau. Winter Cities in a Summer Land. A
       Tour Through Florida and the Winter Resorts of the South.
Cincinnati, New Orleans and Texas-Pacific Railway Company, 1883.

1263. Canova, Andrew P. Life and Adventures in South Florida.
       Palatka, Fla.: Southern Sun Publishing House, 1885.

1264. Castelnau, Francis, Comte de. Essai Sur la Floride du
       Milieu. Nouvelles Annales Des Voyage et Des Sciences.
Paris, 1843.

1265. Central Florida Land Agency. Florida: Its Climate, Soil,
       and Productions. Compiled by the Central Florida Land
Agency, for the Information of Immigrants, 1870.

1266. Cloyd, William C. Tourists' Invalids' and Immigrants'
       Guide to Florida. Jacksonville: Bowden, 1878.

1267. Coale, Edward J. (?) An Original Memoir, on the Flori-
       das, With a General Description, From the Best Authorities.
Baltimore: Printed for Edward J. Coale, by Richard J. Matchett,
1821.

1268. Cory, Charles Barney. Hunting and Fishing in Florida, Including a Key to the Water Birds Known to Occur in the State. Boston: Estes and Lauriat, 1896.

1269. _____. Southern Rambles. Florida. Boston: A. Williams and Company, 1881.

1270. Crosby, Oliver Marvin. Florida Facts Both Bright and Blue. A Guide Book to Intending Settlers, Tourists, and Investors, From a Northerner's Standpoint.... New York: Privately Published, 1887.

1271. Darby, William. Memoir on the Geography, and Natural and Civil History of Florida, Attended by a Map of That Country, Connected With the Adjacent Places.... Philadelphia: Printed by T. H. Palmer, 1821.

1272. Davidson, James Wood. The Florida of Today, a Guide for Tourists and Settlers. New York: D. Appleton and Company, 1889.

1273. Deland, Margaret Wade. Florida Days. Boston: Little, Brown and Company, 1889.

1274. Dennis, Alfred L. From the Hudson to the St. Johns. Newark, N. J.: Published for Private Distribution, 1874.

1275. Edwards, John L. Edwards' Guide to East Florida, Historical, Geographical, Descriptive, Climatic, etc. Jacksonville: Ashmund Brothers, 1881.

1276. "An 1870 Itinerary From St. Augustine to Miami, " F. H. Q. 18(1940):204-15.

1277. Emigration to North America. Prospectus of an English Colony Forming in the Province of East Florida by a Company of Proprietors. London, 1819.

1278. Florida. Bureau of Immigration. Florida: a Pamphlet Descriptive of Its History, Topography, Climate, Soil, Resources and Natural Advantages. Prepared by A. A. Robinson. Tallahassee: Printed at the Floridian Book and Job Office, 1882.

1279. Florida. Commissioner of Lands and Immigration. Florida: Its Climate, Soil and Productions, With a Sketch of Its History, Natural Features and Social Condition; a Manual of Reliable Information Concerning the Resources of the State and the Inducements to Settlers. New York: The Florida Improvement Company, 1869.

1280. _____. Florida: Its Climate, Soil and Productions, With a Sketch of Its History, Natural Features and Social

Condition.   A Manual of Reliable Information Concerning the Re-
sources of the State and the Inducements Which it Offers to Those
Seeking New Homes.   Published for the state by J. S. Adams.
New York: Printed by Fisher & Field, 1870.

1281. _____ .   The Florida Settler, or Immigrants' Guide; a
        Complete Manual of Information Concerning the Climate,
Soil, Products and Resources of the State.   Prepared by D. Eagan.
Tallahassee: Printed at the Office of the Floridian, 1873.

1282.   Florida: Beauties of the East Coast.   Text by Mrs. H. K. In-
        gram.   Buffalo, N.Y.:   The Matthews-Northrup Company, 1893.

1283.   Florida; Its Climate and Productions.   De Land; a Famous
        Resort and Educational Center.   The Home for the Invalid,
Pleasure Seeker, and Those Wishing to Escape the Rigors of a
Winter Climate.   Issued by the Florida Agriculturist.   1887-1888.
De Land: Agriculturist Job Print, 1887.

1284.   Florida.   Its Climate, Soil, and Productions; With a Sketch
        of Its History, Natural Features and Social Condition.   A
Manual of Reliable Information Concerning the Resources of the
State and the Inducements Which it Offers to Immigrants.   Jack-
sonville: L. F. Dewey and Company, 1868.

1285.   Florida: Past and Present, Together With Notes From Sunland,
        on the Manatee River, Gulf Coast, of South Florida; Its Climate,
Soil and Productions.   Jacksonville: Ashmead Brothers, 1883.

1286.   The Florida Railway and Navigation Company.   The Key
        Line Comprising the Gulf Coast Route From the Sea to the
Gulf.   New York: The South Publishing Company, 1884.

1287.   Florida, the Italy of America.   The Winter Garden of the
        North.   The World's Sanitarium, Hernando the Richest,
Most Attractive and Picturesque County in South Florida, and the
Famous Annuttaliga Hammock, the Richest and Most Productive
Land in Hernando County.   Palatka: Southern Sun Publishing Com-
pany, 1885.

1288.   Forbes, James Grant.   Sketches, Historical and Topograph-
        ical, of the Floridas; More Particularly of East Florida.
New York: C. S. Van Winkle, 1821.

1289.   Foss, James H.   Florida: Its Climate, Soil, Productions,
        and Agricultural Capabilities.   Washington: Government
Printing Office, 1882.

1290.   French, Seth.   Semi-tropical Florida; Its Climate, Soil and
        Productions, With a Sketch of Its History, Natural Features
and Social Condition, Being a Manual of Reliable Information Concerning the Resources of the State, and the Inducements Which it
Offers to Persons Seeking New Homes and Profitable Investment.
Chicago: Rand, McNally and Company, 1879.

1291. Garden Spots of the South. Short Descriptions of the Re-
       sources and Character of the Soil of That Portion of Ken-
tucky, Tennessee, Alabama, West Florida, and Southern Mississippi Traversed by the Louisville and Nashville Railroad by Counties
in Detail. Louisville: Passenger Department of the Louisville and
Nashville Railroad Company, 1891.

1292. Gardiner, R. S. A Guide to Florida, "The Land of Flow-
       ers." Containing an Historical Sketch, ... and General In-
formation Invaluable to the Invalid, Tourist, or Emigrant. New
York: Cushing, 1872.

1293. Gate City Route. South Florida Railroad. New York:
       Southern Publishing Company, 1887.

1294. Gilpin, Mrs. John R. "Diary of a West Coast Sailing Ex-
       pedition, 1885," Tequesta 7(1947):44-64.

1295. _____. "To Miami, 1890 Style," Tequesta 1(1941):89-
       106.

1296. Glicksberg, Charles I. "Letters of William Cullen Bryant
       From Florida," F. H. Q. 14(1936):253-74.

1297. Gottschall, Amos H. Travels From Ocean to Ocean, and
       From the Lakes to the Gulf; Being the Narrative of a Twelve
Years' Ramble, and What Was Seen and Experienced: Embracing
Journeys East, West, North, South. ... Harrisburg, Pa.: Amos
H. Gottschall, 1882.

1298. Goulding, Francis Robert. Les Jeunes Adventuriers de la
       Floride d'après Goulding. Translated by J. F. Brunet.
Paris: Bibliothèque d'éducation et de récréation, J. Hetzel et cie.,
1890.

1299. Great Southern Railway, a Trunk Line, Between the North
       and the Tropics, to Within Ninety Miles of Havana, Con-
necting at the Nearest Possible Point With the West Indies, Central and South America. New York: William P. Hickok, Printer,
1878.

1300. Griffing, Jane R. Letters From Florida on the Scenery,
       Climate, Social and Material Conditions, and Practical Ad-
vantages of the "Land of Flowers." Lancaster, N. H.: The Republican Office, 1883.

1301. Hallock, Charles, ed. Camp Life in Florida; a Handbook
       for Sportsmen and Settlers. New York: Forest and Stream
Publishing Company, 1876.

1302. Handy Guide to the Southeastern States; Including Florida,
       Georgia, and the Carolinas, and the Gulf Coast. Chicago
and New York: Rand, McNally and Company, 1896.

114   Florida History

1303. Hardy, Iza Duffus. Oranges and Alligators: Sketches of
       South Florida Life. London: Ward and Downey, 1886.

1304. Hawks, John Milton. The East Coast of Florida, a Descrip-
       tive Narrative. Lynn, Mass.: Lewis and Winship, 1887.

1305. _____. The Florida Gazetteer, Containing a Guide
       Through the State: Complete Official and Business Direc-
tory; State and National Statistics. New Orleans: Bronze Pen
Steam Book and Job Office, 1871.

1306. Heilprin, Angelo. Explorations of the West Coast of Flori-
       da and the Okeechobee Wilderness With Special Reference to
the Geology and Zoology of the Floridian Peninsula, a Narrative of
Researches Undertaken Under the Auspices of the Wagner Free Institute of Science of Philadelphia. Philadelphia: Wagner Free Institute of Science, 1886.

1307. Henshall, James Alexander. Camping and Cruising in Flor-
       ida. Cincinnati: Robert Clarke and Company, 1884.

1308. _____. Notes on Fishes Collected in Florida, 1892.
       Washington, D. C.: Government Printing Office, 1895.

1309. _____. Report Upon Collection of Fishes Made in
       Southern Florida During 1889. Washington, D. C.: Govern-
ment Printing Office, 1889.

1310. Hine, C. Vickerstaff. On the Indian River. Chicago:
       Charles H. Sergel and Company, 1891.

1311. Howgate, Henry W. Notes on Florida, Prepared With Spe-
       cial Reference to the Howgate Grant, on Lake George. New
York: B. H. Tyrrel, Printer, 1881.

1312. Ingram, Helen K. Tourists' and Settlers' Guide to Florida.
       Jacksonville: Dacosta, 1895-1896.

1313. Jacques, Daniel Harrison. Florida as a Permanent Home:
       Embracing a Description of the Climate, Soil and Produc-
tions of the State, Together With Hints to New-comers and Prospective Settlers. Jacksonville: Charles W. Blew, 1877.

1314. Jenks, John Whipple Potter. Hunting in Florida in 1874.
       Providence: By the Author, 1884.

1315. Keasbey, Anthony Quinton. From the Hudson to the St.
       Johns. Newark: Daily Advertiser for Private Distribution,
1874.

1316. Ker, Henry. "An Early Nineteenth Century Traveler in
       Pensacola, " F. H. Q. 10(1932):162-63.

1317. Knapp, J. G. Only One Florida. Considered From Every
       Point of View. Jacksonville: W. T. Forbes and Company,
1886.

1318. Lanier, Sidney. Florida: Its Scenery, Climate, and His-
       tory. With an Account of Charleston, Savannah, Augusta,
and Aiken; and a Chapter for Consumptives; Being a Complete
Hand-book and Guide. Philadelphia: J. B. Lippincott, 1875.

1319. Large, John, Jr. "A Scientist [Jared Potter Kirteland]
       Observes Florida: 1870, " F. H. Q. 42(1963):48-54.

1320. Lee, Henry, ed. The Tourist's Guide of Florida. New
       York: Leve and Alden Printing Company, 1885.

1321. Legal Opinions on the Title of Richard S. Hackley, to Lands
       in East Florida: With Documents in Relation to the Climate
and Soil of Florida. New York: Peter A. Mesier, 1841.

1322. Lente, Frederick Divoux. The Constituents of Climate With
       Special Reference to the Climate of Florida. Louisville:
Richmond and Louisville Medical Journal Book and Job Steam Press,
1878.

1323. McDonald, J. A. Plain Talk About Florida, for Homes and
       Investments. Eustis: J. A. McDonald, Printer, 1883.

1324. McQuade, James. The Cruise of the Montauk to Bermuda,
       the West Indies and Florida. New York: Thomas R. Knox
and Company, 1885.

1325. Melish, John. A Description of East and West Florida and
       the Bahama Islands, a Military and Topographical Atlas of
the United States; Including the British Possessions and Florida. . . .
Philadelphia: Printed by G. Palmer, 1813.

1326. Munroe, Kirk. "A Lost 'Psyche': Kirk Munroe's Log of a
       1,600 Mile Canoe Cruise in Florida Water, 1881-1882. "
Edited by Irving A. Leonard. Tequesta 28(1968):63-89.

1327. Nichols, G. W. "Six Weeks in Florida, " Harper's Mag.
       41(1870):655-67.

1328. Norton, Charles Ledyard. A Handbook of Florida. New
       York: Longmans, Green and Company, 1891.

1329. Notes on Florida Prepared With Special Reference to the
       Howgate Grant on Lake George. New York: Benjamin H.
Tyrel, 1881.

1330. Ober, Frederick Albion. The Knockabout Club in the Ever-
       glades: the Adventures of the Club in Exploring Lake Okee-
chobee. Boston: Estes and Lauriat, 1887.

1331. Olney, George Washington. A Guide to Florida, "the Land
       of Flowers," Containing an Historical Sketch, Geographical,
Agricultural and Climatic Statistics, Routes of Travel by Land and
Sea, and General Information Invaluable to the Invalid, Tourist or
Emigrant.... New York: Cushing, Bardua and Company, Printers,
1872.

1332. An Original Memoir, on the Floridas, With a General De-
       scription, From the Best Authorities. By a gentleman of
the South. Baltimore: Printed for E. J. Coale, by R. J. Matchett, 1821.

1333. Perrine, Henry. "Random Records of Tropical Florida,"
       Tequesta 11(1951):51-62.

1334. Perry, W. L. Scenes in a Surveyor's Life; or, A Record
       of Hardships and Dangers Encountered...in the Operations
of a Party of Surveyors in South Florida. Jacksonville: Drew's,
1859.

1335. Rigby, T. C. Dr. Rigby's Papers on Florida, Giving a
       General View of Every Portion of the State, Its Climate,
Resources, Statistics, Society, Crops, Trade, &c. Cincinnati: E.
Mendenhall, 1876.

1336. Robin, Claude C. Voyages dans l'intérieur de la Louisiane,
       de la Floride Occidentale, et Dans les Isles de la Marti-
que et de Saint-Domingue, Pendant les Années 1802, 1803, 1804,
1805 et 1806.... 3 vols. Paris: F. Buisson, 1807.

1337. Robinson, Mrs. Albert A. The Resources and Natural Ad-
       vantages of Florida; Containing Special Papers Descriptive
of the Several Counties. Tallahassee: The Floridian Book and
Job Office, 1882.

1338. Rod & Gun on the West Coast of Florida, Published by
       Passenger Department of the Plant System. N. p., 1895.

1339. Rogers, Benjamin F. "Florida Seen Through the Eyes of
       Nineteenth Century Travellers," F. H. Q. 34(1955):177-89.

1340. Roosevelt, Robert Barnwell. Florida and the Game Water-
       birds of the Atlantic Coast and the Lakes of the United
States With a Full Account of the Sporting Along Our Seashores
and Inland Waters, and Remarks on Breech-loaders and Hammer-
less Guns. New York: Orange Judd and Company, 1884.

1341. Sargeant, Angelina M. Notes of Travel and Mementos of
       Friendship. Rochester, N. Y.: E. R. Andrews, Printer,
1894.

1342. Schroder, Hugo H. "Audubon in the Florida Wilderness
       [1831-31]," Mass. Audubon Soc. Bul. 35(1955):187-91.

1343.   A Series of Letters Comparing the Soil, Climate, and Pro-
        ductions of These States, Setting Forth Many Advantages
That East and South Florida Offers to Emigrants.   Ocala: Printed
at the "East Florida Banner" Office, by T. F. Smith, 1866.

1344.   Shoemaker, W. B.   Florida As It Is.   It Tells All About
        the Industries of the State, Its Climate and Resources.
Written in Common Sense Without Paint or Varnish.   Neville, Pa.:
Times Steam Plant, 1887.

1345.   Simpson, Frank.   A Trip Through Northern and Central
        Florida, During March and April, 1882.   East Orange, N.
J.:   East Orange Gazette, 1882.

1346.   Stimson, Melvin Oscar.   Guide to Florida.   New York:
        The American News Company, 1873.

1347.   Stowe, Harriet Beecher.   Palmetto Leaves.   1873.   Edited
        by Mary B. Graff and Edith Cowles.   Gainesville: Univer-
sity of Florida Press, 1968.

1348.   Stuart, Villiers.   Adventures Amidst the Equatorial Forests
        and Rivers of South America; Also in the West Indies and
the Wilds of Florida, to Which is Added "Jamaica Revisited."   London: John Murray, 1891.

1349.   Taylor, F. H. and Charles A. Choate.   From the St. Johns
        to the Apalachicola: or, Through the Uplands of Florida.
New York: Leve and Alden's Publication Department of the Florida
Central Railroad, 1882.

1350.   Thompson, Arthur W.   "A Massachusetts Mechanic in Flori-
        da and Mexico--1847," F. H. Q. 33(1954):130-41.

1351.   Torrey, Bradford.   A Florida Sketch-book.   New York:
        Houghton-Mifflin and Company, 1895.

1352.   Townshend, Frederick Trench.   Wild Life in Florida, With
        a Visit to Cuba.   London: Hurst and Blackett, 1875.

1353.   Tyler, Daniel F.   Where to go in Florida.   New York:
        Hopcraft and Company, 1880.

1354.   Volney, C. F. C., Comte de.   View of the Climate and
        Soil of the United States of America: to Which are Annexed
Some Accounts of Florida, the French Colony on the Scioto, Certain Canadian Colonies, and the Savages or Natives.   Translated
from the French.   London: Printed for J. Johnson, 1804.

1355.   Warner, Helen Garnie.   Home Life in Florida.   Louisville:
        John P. Morton and Company, 1889.

1356. Watteyne, Victor. Lettres de Floride. Bruxelles: Societe
      Belge de Libraitie, 1892.

1357. Webb, Wanton S., ed. Webb's Historical, Industrial and
      Biographical Florida. New York: Webb and Company, 1885.

1358. Webber, Charles Henry. The Eden of the South, Descrip-
      tive of the Orange Groves, Vegetable Farms, Strawberry
      Fields, Peach Orchards, Soil, Climate, Natural Peculiarities, and
      the People of Alachua County, Florida.... New York: Leve and
      Alden, 1883.

1359. Wells, George W. Facts for Immigrants. Comprising a
      Truthful Description of the Five Following Counties of South
      Florida, To-wit: Hernando, Hillsboro, Polk, Manatee, and Monroe.
      Jacksonville: Printed at the Press Office, 1877.

1360. White, Joseph W. White's Guide to Florida and Her Fa-
      mous Resorts. Jacksonville: Dacosta Printing and Pub-
      lishing House, 1890.

1361. Whiting, Henry. "Cursory Remarks Upon East Florida in
      1838," Am. J. Sci. & Arts 35(1839):47-64.

1362. Whitney, John P. Whitney's Florida Pathfinder. A Guide
      to Florida. Information for the Tourist, Traveler and In-
      valid...Season 1880-81. New York: Pathfinder Office, 1881.

1363. Wilkinson, R. A. The Gulf Coast. Letters Written for the
      New Orleans Times-Democrat. Louisville: Louisville and
      Nashville Railroad Passenger Department, 1886.

1364. Williams, John Lee. The Territory of Florida: or, Sketches
      of the Topography, Civil and Natural History, of the Coun-
      try, the Climate, and the Indian Tribes, From the First Discovery
      to the Present Time.... New York: A. T. Goodrich, 1837.

1365. _____. A View of West Florida, Embracing Its Geogra-
      phy, Topography, &c. With an Appendix, Treating of Its
      Antiquities, Land Titles, and Canals.... Philadelphia: Printed
      for H. S. Tanner and the author, L. R. Bailey, Printer, 1827.

1366. Willoughby, Hugh Laussat. Across the Everglades; a Canoe
      Journey of Exploration. Philadelphia: J. B. Lippincott
      Company, 1898.

1367. Wilson, F. Page. "We Choose the Subtropics," Tequesta
      12(1952):19-45.

C.   20th Century

1368. Adams, Benjamin Franklin. An Adventure on the Oklawaha River, Florida, With Illustrations From Photographs. Jacksonville: Adams Printing and Publishing Company, 1926.

1369. Adams, S. H. "Sack of Snakes: Florida Snake Collector," New Yorker 27(1941):30-34.

1370. Aflalo, Frederich George. Sunshine and Sport in Florida and the West Indies. Philadelphia: Jacobs and Company, 1907.

1371. Agassiz, Garnault. Florida in Tomorrow's Sun. New York: L. H. Bigelow and Company, 1925.

1372. Alberton, Edwin. The Florida Wilds. New York: Neale Publishing Company, 1906.

1373. Allyn, Rubert Royce. Outdoors Afloat. St. Petersburg: Great Outdoors Association, 1957.

1374. Ames, Fisher, Jr. By Reef and Trail--Bob Leach's Adventures in Florida. New York: Scribners and Sons, 1910.

1375. Andrews, Allen H. A Yankee Pioneer in Florida. Recounting the Adventures of a City Chap Who Came to the Wilds of South Florida in the 1890's and Remained to Grow up With the Country. Jacksonville: The Press of the Douglas Printing Company, 1950.

1376. Austin, Guy K. Pilgrim Father; Being the Adventures of an English Family in America Through the Great Depression. London: Geofrey Bles, 1934.

1377. Barbour, Ralph Henry. Let's go to Florida! Information for Those Who Haven't Been, But Are Going, Those Who Have Been and Are Going Back, and Those Who Don't Expect to Go But Will. New York: Dodd, Mead, and Company, 1926.

1378. Blanding, Don. Floridays. New York: Dodd, Mead and Company, 1941.

1379. Blatchley, Willis Stanley. In Days Agone; Notes on the Fauna and Flora of Subtropical Florida in the Days When Most of Its Area Was a Primeval Wilderness. Indianapolis: The Nature Publishing Company, 1932.

1380. Bulske, Max E. Florida Isn't Heaven. New York: Vantage Press, 1951.

1381. Cox, Merlin G. "Florida--a Land of Change and Progress," S. Observer 4(1956):34-41.

1382. Diettrich, Sigismond de R. "Florida's Climatic Extremes:
      Cold Spells and Freezes [1835-1940]," Econ. Geog.
25(1949):68-74.

1383. Dietrich, T. Stanton. "Florida's Changing Population [1940-
      50]," Fla. State Univ. Studies 10(1953):117-49.

1384. _____. Statistical Handbook No. 2: Fifty Years of Pop-
      ulation Growth, Florida, 1900-1950--Age, Sex, and Race
Characteristics for Urban and Rural Populations. Tallahassee:
Florida State University, 1954.

1385. Dusenbury, George. How to Retire to Florida. 4th ed.
      New York: Harper, 1959.

1386. Easley, Philip Samuel. The "Low-down" on Florida.
      Statesville, N. C.: Brady Printing Company, 1926.

1387. Federal Writers' Project. Florida. Florida; a Guide to
      the Southernmost State. Compiled and written by the Fede-
ral Writers' Project of the Work Projects Administration for the
State of Florida. Sponsored by State of Florida Department of Public Instruction. New York: Oxford University Press, 1939.

1388. Florida. Bureau of Immigration. All Florida. Issued by
      the Bureau of Immigration, Department of Agriculture. Tal-
lahassee, Florida, June, 1926. St. Augustine: Printed by the
Record Company, 1926.

1389. _____. Florida's Progress in Thirty Years; a Short
      Resumé for Those Interested in the State's Future. Talla-
hassee, 1955. (Florida. State Dept. of Agriculture, Bulletin no.
160.)

1390. _____. Know Florida; a Narrative and Graphic Guide to
      the Sixty-seven Counties of the State. Tallahassee, 1944.

1391. _____. Opportunities in Florida, a Look at the Record.
      Tallahassee, 1947.

1392. Florida. Department of Agriculture. Florida: a Land of
      Homes. "Where Art and Nature Join Their Crafts in a
Kingdom by Southern Seas." Tallahassee: Florida State Department of Agriculture, 1934.

1393. _____. ...Florida. A Pamphlet Descriptive of its His-
      tory, Topography, Climate, Soil, Resources and Natural Ad-
vantages, in General and by Counties. Prepared by the Department
of Agriculture. Tallahassee: I. B. Hilson, State Printer, 1904.

1394. _____. Florida, an Advancing State, 1907-1917-1927.
      An industrial survey authorized by the legislature of 1927

and carried through under the direction of Nathan Mayo, Commissioner of Agriculture, Tallahassee, Fla. St. Petersburg: Lassing
Publishing Company, 1928.

1395. _____. Fun in the Sun in Florida. Tallahassee, 1957.

1396. _____. Why I Like Florida. A Compilation of Letters
       and Gems of Thought From Men and Women of Renown Who
Have Visited Florida or Become Citizens of the State. St. Augustine: The Record Company, 1923.

1397. Florida. Hotel Commission. Florida, Empire of the Sun;
       a Description of the Living Advantages of Florida Cities,
the Pleasures, Recreations and Resort Facilities Now Available to
Visitors and Prospective Residents. Tallahassee: Florida State
Hotel Commission, 1930.

1398. Florida. State Department of Education. Florida: Wealth
       or Waste? Florida State Department of Education, Talla-
hassee. Colin English, Superintendent. Tallahassee, 1947.

1399. Florida and Nassau in Sunlight Pictures. St. Augustine:
       Foster and Reynolds, 1901.

1400. Florida, Devoted to the Portrayal of the Marvelous Beauties,
       the Climatic Advantages, the Untold Resources and Endless
Possibilities of Florida. Philadelphia: F. A. Davis Company,
1905.

1401. The Florida Times-Union, Jacksonville, Fla. The Florida
       Times-Union's Special World's Fair Edition in Three Parts
.... Jacksonville, 1904.

1402. Florida Tourist Survey Project. The Florida Tourist. A
       Preliminary Report of the Florida Tourist Survey Project,
September, 1939. Prepared by Work Projects Administration of
Florida. Sponsored by the Florida Railroad Commission and the
Florida State Chamber of Commerce. Jacksonville, 1939.

1403. Fox, Charles Donald. The Truth About Florida. New
       York: Charles Renard Corporation, 1925.

1404. Francé, Annie. Florida, das Land des Überflusses; Mit
       Originalzeichnungen von R. H. Francé und Eigenen Aufna-
hmen der Verfasserin Und Einer Wirtschaftskarte. Berlin-Schöne-
berg: Oestergaard, 1931.

1405. Francé, Raoul Heinrich. Lebender Braunkohlenwald, Eine
       Reise Durch Die Heutige Urwelt. Stuttgart: Kosmos,
Gesellschaft der Naturfreunde, 1932.

1406. Gatewood, George W. On Florida's Coconut Coasts, ...
       Reminiscences, Character Sketches, Fishing Lore. Punta

Gorda: Punta Gorda Herald, 1944.

1407. Hammond, John Martin. Winter Journeys in the South.
       Pen and Camera Impressions of Men, Manners, Women,
and All Things All the Way From the Blue Gulf and New Orleans
Through Fashionable Florida Palms to the Pines of Virginia.
Philadelphia and London: J. B. Lippincott, 1916.

1408. Harvey, F. L. "State of Florida, " Am. Mercury 67(1948):
       326-33.

1409. Hepburn, Andrew. Florida. Boston: Houghton Mifflin,
       1956.

1410. Hill, Norman Alan, ed. Florida Cruise. Baltimore, Md.:
       George W. King Printing Company, 1945.

1411. Hill, Ralph Nading. Window in the Sea. New York: Rine-
       hart, 1956.

1412. Hines, Needham Christopher. The Truth About Florida.
       Miami: Florida Research Press, 1956.

1413. Johnson, Clifton. Highways and Byways of Florida; Human
       Interest Information for Travellers in Florida; and for Those
Other Travellers Who are Kept at Home by Chance or Necessity,
But Who Journey Far and Wide on the Wings of Fancy. New York:
Macmillan Company, 1918.

1414. Joseph, Richard. Florida. Prepared with the cooperation
       of the American Geographical Society. Garden City, N. Y.:
Doubleday, 1958.

1415. Lagergren, H. E. "From the Diary of an Old-timer."
       Edited by M. G. McMillan. Surveying and Mapping
14(1954):54-8.

1416. Morris, Allen. The Florida Handbook, 1949-1950. Talla-
       hassee: Peninsular Publishing Company, 1950.

1417. Muir, John. A Thousand-mile Walk to the Gulf. Edited
       by William Frederick Bode. Boston, New York: Houghton
Mifflin Company, the Riverside Press, 1916.

1418. Packard, Winthrop. Florida Trails as Seen From Jackson-
       ville to Key West and From November to April Inclusive.
Boston: Small, Mayard and Company, 1910.

1419. Rhodes, Harrison Garfield and Mary Wolfe Dumont. A
       Guide to Florida for Tourists, Sportsmen and Settlers. . . .
New York: Dodd, Mead and Company, 1912.

1420. Roberts, Kenneth Lewis. Florida. New York and London: Harper and Brothers, 1926.

1421. _____. Florida Loafing; an Investigation Into the Peculiar State of Affairs Which Leads Residents of 47 States to Encourage Spanish Architecture in the 48th. Indianapolis: The Bobbs-Merrill Company, 1925.

1422. _____. Sun Hunting; Adventures and Observations Among the Native and Migratory Tribes of Florida, Including the Stoical Time-killers of Palm Beach, the Gentle and Gregarious Tin-canners of the Remote Interior, and the Vivacious and Semi-violent Peoples of Miami and Its Purlieus. Indianapolis: The Bobbs-Merrill Company, 1922.

1423. Shelton, William Roy. Land of the Everglades, Tropical Southern Florida. Tallahassee: Department of Agriculture, 1957.

1424. Simpson, Charles Torrey. In Lower Florida Wilds; a Naturalist's Observations on the Life, Physical Geography, and Geology of the More Tropical Part of the State. New York and London: G. P. Putnam's Sons, 1920.

1425. Smith, Mary Ellen. Florida, a Way of Life. New York: Dutton, 1959.

1426. Stockbridge, Frank Parker and John Holiday Perry. Florida in the Making. With a foreword by the governor of Florida. New York, Jacksonville: The De Bower Publishing Company, 1925.

1427. Van Schaick, John, Jr. Cruising Cross Country; or, the Journeyings of an Editor. Boston and Chicago: Universalist Publishing House, 1926.

1428. Verrill, Alpheus Hyatt. Romantic and Historic Florida. New York: Dodd, Mead and Company, 1935.

1429. Waters, Don. Outboard Cruising. New York: L. Furman, Inc., 1939.

1430. Weigall, Theyre Hamilton. Boom in Florida. London: John Lane, 1931.

1431. Wickert, Erwin. Fata Morgana Uber den Strassen. Leipzig: Strauch, 1938.

1432. Winter, Nevin Otto. Florida, the Land of Enchantment; Including an Account of Its Romantic History From the Days of Ponce de Leon and the Other Early Explorers and Settlers, and the Story of Its Native Indians... a Comprehensive Review of the Florida of To-day... for Health and Pleasure Seekers, Nature

Lovers, Motorists and Sportsmen.   Boston: The Page Company,
1918.

1433.   Wirén, Gösta.   På Jakt Efter Jobb i U. S. A.   Mina Vaga-
        bondår i Amerika.   Stockholm: Wahlström, 1933.

PART TWO

XVII. THE CHURCH

A. Catholic

1434. Boyd, Mark Frederick, ed. "Further Consideration of the Apalachee Missions," Americas 9(1953):459-79.

1435. _____. "Mission Sites in Florida, an Attempt to Approximately Identify the Sites of Spanish Mission Settlements of the Seventeenth Century in Northern Florida," F. H. Q. 17(1939): 255-80. (Also in Tallahassee Historical Society Annual 4(1939):1-11.)

1436. _____, Hale G. Smith, and John W. Griffin. Here They Once Stood: The Tragic End of the Apalachee Missions. Gainesville: University of Florida Press, 1951.

1437. Burns, Thomas J. "The Catholic Church in West Florida, 1783-1850." Master's thesis, Florida State University, 1962.

1438. Calderon, Gabriel Diaz Vara. A 17th Century Letter of Gabriel... Calderon, Bishop of Cuba, Describing the Indians and Indian Missions of Florida. Washington, D. C.: Smithsonian Institution, 1936.

1439. Carroll, Mary Theresa Austin, Mother. A Catholic History of Alabama and the Floridas, by a Member of the Order of Mercy, Author of "The Life of Catherine McAuley." New York: P. J. Kennedy and Sons, 1908.

1440. Centennial of St. Johns Parish, Jacksonville, Florida, A. D. 1934. Compiled Under the Direction of the Centennial Committee. Jacksonville: Drew Press, 1934.

1441. Chatelain, Verne E. "Spanish Contributions in Florida to American Culture," F. H. Q. 19(1941):213-45.

1442. Chronicles, the Church of Bethesda-by-the-Sea, Palm Beach, Florida, 1889-1964. West Palm Beach: Distinctive Print, 1964.

1443.   Claureul, Henry Peter. Notes on the Catholic Church in
        Florida, 1565-1876. St. Leo, 1910.

1444.   Curley, Michael Joseph. "Church and State in the Spanish
        Floridas (1783-1822)." Ph. D. dissertation, Catholic Uni-
versity, 1940.

1445.   DePuy, Henry Farr. "An Early Account of the Establish-
        ment of Jesuit Missions in America," Proc. Am. Ant. Soc.
New Series 30, Part 1 (1920):62-80.

1446.   Dodd, Dorothy. " 'Bishop' Pearce and the Reconstruction
        of Leon County," Apalachee 2(1946):5-12.

1447.   Engelhardt, Zephyrin. "Florida's First Bishop, Rt. Rev.
        Juan Juares, OFM," Cath. Hist. Rev. 4(1919):479-85.

1448.   Evans, Jane B. "Irish Priests in Early Florida," Am.
        Irish Hist. Soc. J. 32(1941):74-8.

1449.   Gannon, Michael V. "Alter and Hearth: The Coming of
        Christianity, 1521-65," F. H. Q. 44(1965):17-44.

1450.   _____. The Cross in the Sand: The Early Catholic
        Church in Florida, 1513-1870. Gainesville: University of
Florida Press, 1965.

1451.   _____. Rebel Bishop: The Life and Era of Augustine
        Verot. Milwaukee: Bruce Publishing Company, 1964.

1452.   _____. "Sebastian Montero, Pioneer American Mission-
        ary, 1566-1572," Cath. Hist. Rev. 51(1965):335-53.

1453.   Geiger, Maynard J., Father. Biographical Dictionary of
        the Franciscans in Spanish Florida and Cuba (1528-1841).
Paterson, N. J.: St. Anthony Guild Press, 1940.

1454.   _____. The Early Franciscans in Florida and Their Re-
        lation to Spain's Colonial Effort. Paterson, N. J.: St.
Anthony Guild Press, 1936.

1455.   _____. The Franciscan Conquest of Florida (1573-1618).
        Washington, D. C.: The Catholic University of America,
1937.

1456.   Gold, Robert L. "The Departure of Spanish Catholicism
        From Florida, 1763-1765," Americas 22(1966):377-88.

1457.   Glodt, John T. "Our Florida Martyr Priests," Eccles.
        Rev. 69(1923):498-513, 614-31.

1458.   Griffin, John W. "Preliminary Report on the Site of the
        Mission of San Juan del Puerto, Fort George Island, Flori-

The Church 127

da, " Papers of the Tallahassee Historical Society 4(1960):63-66.

1459. Habig, Marion Alphonse. "The First Marian Shrine in the United States [St. Augustine, since ca. 1602], " Am. Eccles. Rev. 136(1957):81-89.

1460. Hilliard, Marion Pharo. "The Cradle of Catholic Faith and Art in the United States, " Acad. Christ. Art J. 1(1938):43-57.

1461. Hinnebusch, Frederick. "Friar Luis' Folly, " Dominicana 34(1949):107-14.

1462. Historical Records Survey. Florida. White Baptisms 1784-1792. Translation and Transcription of Church Archives of Florida; Roman Catholic Records. St. Augustine Parrish. Tallahassee: State Library Board, 1941.

1463. _____. White Baptisms 1792-1799. Translation and Transcription of Church Archives of Florida. Roman Catholic Records. St. Augustine Parrish. Tallahassee: State Library Board, 1941.

1464. _____. White Marriages 1784-1801. Translations from Records at The Catholic Bishop's Residence, St. Augustine, Florida. Jacksonville: Copy prepared by Historical Records Survey, 1937.

1465. Jerome, Father. Church and State in Florida in 1822. St. Leo: Abbey Press, 1963.

1466. _____. "The First Bishop of Florida, " F.H.Q. 40(1962): 295-300.

1467. _____. They Came and Remained. St. Leo: Abbey Press, 1964.

1468. Keegan, P. G. J. and L. Tormao Sanz. Experiencia Misionera en la Florida (Siglos 16 and 17). Instituto Santo Toribio de Mogrovejo. Consejo Superior de Investigaciones Cientificas. Biblioteca "Missionálica Hispánica, " Series B., Vol. 7. Madrid: Talleres Gráficos Jura, 1957.

1469. Kenny, Michael. Pedro Martinez, S. J. Martyr of Florida, 1566.... St. Leo: Abbey Press, 1939.

1470. _____. "What History Says of Florida's Beginnings, " Cath. World 162(1945):232-37.

1471. Leo Xavier, Sister. "Missionary Labors in East Florida, 1565-1700. " Master's thesis, University of Florida, 1945.

1472. Lipscomb, Oscar Hugh. The Administration of John Quintan, Second Bishop of Mobile, 1859-1883. Philadelphia: American Catholic Historical Society of Philadelphia, 1968.

1473. Lyon, Anne Bozeman. "The Early [Spanish] Missions of the South [Florida]," Gulf State Hist. Mag. 2(1903):186-93.

1474. McNulty, J. P. "Diocesan Priests in Florida's Beginnings; Reply to M. Kenny With Rejoinder," Cath. World 162(1946): 527-36.

1475. Mohr, Charles H. "St. Francis Barracks, St. Augustine; the Franciscans in Florida," F. H. Q. 7(1929):214-33.

1476. O'Daniel, Victor Francis. Dominicans in Early Florida. New York: The United States Catholic Historical Society, 1930.

1477. Omaechevarria, Ignacio. Sangre Vizcaina en los Pantanos de la Florida. Fr. Francisco de Berascola, D. F. M. (1564-1597), Martir, Natural de Gordejuela (Vizcaya). Vitoria: Edit. S. Catolica, 1948.

1478. Oré, Luis Jeronimo de, Bishop. The Martyrs of Florida (1513-1616). Translated with Biographical introduction by Maynard Geiger, O. F. M. Franciscan Studies, No. 18. New York: Joseph F. Wagner, Inc., 1936.

1479. Page, David P. "Bishop Michael J. Curley and Anti-Catholic Nativism in Florida," F. H. Q. 45(1966):101-17.

1480. Phinney, A. H. "Florida's Spanish Missions," F. H. Q. 4(1925):15-21.

1481. Pohltecamp, Diomede. "The Franciscans in Florida," St. Anthony Messenger 60(1933):483-92; 61(1933):323-28, 372-82.

1482. Ray, Samuel H. "Jesuit Martyrs in Florida," F. H. Q. 6(1928):182-86.

1483. Redlinger, Joseph. America's First Pioneers: Santa Maria Filipina Mission at Pensacola, Florida, 1559-1561. Pensacola: Pensacola Council, Knights of Columbus, 1954.

1484. Robertson, James A. "Notes on Early Church Government in Spanish Florida," Cath. Hist. Rev. 17(1931):151-74.

1485. Salazar, Pedro de Hita. "Enumeration of Florida Spanish Missions in 1675." With translations of documents, by Mark F. Boyd. F. H. Q. 27(1948):181-88.

1486. Scammon, E. P. "Recollections of Florida and the South," Cath. World 54(1892):691-711.

1487.   Shea, John G. The Catholic Church in Colonial Days, 1521-
        1763. New York: John G. Shea, 1886.

1488.   Siebert, Wilbur H. "Some Church History of St. Augustine
        During the Spanish Regime, " F. H. Q. 9(1930):117-23.

1489.   Silver Jubilee of Sacred Heart Church Parish, Saint Joseph,
        Pasco County, Florida, 1888-1913. St. Leo: Abbey Press,
1913.

1490.   Sisters of St. Joseph. Sheaves Gathered From the Mission-
        ary Fields of the Sisters of St. Joseph in Florida, 1866-
1936.   St. Augustine: Standard Printing Company, 1936.

1491.   Smith, Hale G. "Results of an Archaeological Investigation
        of a Spanish Mission Site in Jefferson County, Florida, "
Fla. Anthro. 1(1948):1-10.

1492.   Spellman, Charles W. "The 'Golden Age' of the Florida
        Missions, 1632-1674, " Cath. Hist. Rev. 51(1965): 354-72.

1493.   _____ . "The Spanish Missions of Florida, 1618-1763. "
        Master's thesis, University of California, 1947.

1494.   Van Brunt, Dorothy. "Father Hugon and the Early Catholic
        Church in Tallahassee, " Apalachee 1(1944):62-73.

1495.   Williams, Emma Rochelle. "The Society's Relics--I. The
        Bell of a Florida Spanish Mission, " F. H. Q. (1927):159-61.

1496.   Zubillaga, Felix. La Florida. La Mission Jesuitica (1566-
        1572) y la Colonizacion Española. Roma: Institutum His-
toricum, 1941.

B.   Episcopal

1497.   Carter, W. H. "History of St. John's Church, Tallahas-
        see. " In Semi-Centennial of the Diocese of Florida Held
in Tallahassee, 1888. Jacksonville: Printed by the Church Year
Publishing Company, 1889.

1498.   Cushman, Joseph D., Jr. "The Episcopal Church in Flori-
        da, 1821-1865. " Master's thesis, Florida State University,
1958.

1499.   _____ . "The Episcopal Church in Florida: 1821-1892. "
        Ph. D. dissertation, Florida State University, 1962.

1500.   _____ . "The Episcopal Church in Florida During the
        Civil War, " F. H. Q. 38(1960):294-301.

1501. _____ . A Goodly Heritage: The Episcopal Church in
        Florida, 1821-1892. Gainesville: University of Florida
Press, 1965.

1502. Daniel, James Jaquelin. "Historical Sketch of the [Episco-
        pal] Church in Florida." In Semi-Centennial of the Diocese
of Florida Held in Tallahassee, 1888. Jacksonville: Printed by
the Church Year Publishing Company, 1889.

1503. Fairbanks, George R. "The Early [Episcopal] Churchmen
        of Florida." In Semi-Centennial of the Diocese of Florida
Held in Tallahassee, 1888. Jacksonville: Printed by the Church
Year Publishing Company, 1889.

1504. Fowler, Andrew. A Short Account of the Rise and Progress
        of the Protestant Episcopal Church in the City of St. Augus-
tine. Charleston: Dan J. Dowling, 1835.

1505. Gearhart, Edward B. "St. Paul's Church [Episcopal] in
        Quincy, Florida, During the Territorial Period [1834-45],"
F. H. Q. 34(1956):339-65.

1506. Leonard, Paul Augustus, Jr. "The Growth of the Episcopal
        Church in South Florida 1892-1932." Master's thesis, Uni-
versity of Florida, 1951.

1507. Patton, Laura Conrad. "St. Andrew's Episcopal Church,
        Built and Forgotten," Tequesta 24(1964):21-40.

1508. Pennington, Edgar Legare. "The Episcopal Church in Flor-
        ida, 1763-1892," Hist. Mag. Prot. Episcopal Church
7(1938):1-77.

1509. _____ . "The Episcopal Church in South Florida, 1764-
        1892," Tequesta 1(1941):47-88.

1510. _____ . "John Forbes (d. 1783)," F. H. Q. 8(1930):164-68.

1511. _____ . "The Reverend James Seymour, S. P. G. Mis-
        sionary in Florida," F. H. Q. 5(1927):196-201.

1512. _____ . Soldier and Servant: John Freeman Young,
        Second Bishop of Florida. Hartford, Conn.: Church Mis-
sions Publishing Company, 1939.

1513. _____ . "Some Experiences of Bishop Young," F. H. Q.
        15(1936):35-50.

1514. Robinson, William M., Jr. The First Coming to America
        of the Book of Common Prayer, Florida, July 1565. Aus-
tin: The Church Historical Society, 1965.

C. Methodist

1515. Baker, Jesse L. The Gathering by the River; a History of
Sopchoppy Methodist Church, Sopchoppy, Florida, 1859-1966.
[n. p., 1966].

1516. _____. Where Cross the Crowded Ways; a History of
Crawfordsville Methodist Church, Crawfordsville, Florida,
1866-1966. [n. p., 1966].

1517. Breeze, Lawrence E. "The Lord First": A History of the
Arlington Methodist Church. [Jacksonville?: 1964.]

1518. Brooks, William E., ed. From Saddlebags to Satellites:
A History of Florida Methodism. Maitland: Florida Annual
Conference, United Methodist Church, 1969.

1519. Carswell, Elba Wilson. Holmes Valley, a West Florida
Cradle of Christianity. Bonifay: Central Press, 1969.

1520. Cash, W. T. "History of Trinity Methodist Church," Apalachee 2(1946):46-58.

1521. Foster, George. The Methodist Church in Ocala, Florida,
1844-1953. Ocala: Ocala Star Banner, 1953.

1522. Gainesville First Methodist Church. A Century of Methodism in Gainesville. Gainesville: First Methodist Church,
1957.

1523. Gatewood, George W. History of the Methodist Church of
Quincy, Florida. Quincy: Times Press, 1939.

1524. Guerry, Jean U. "The Matecumbe Methodist Church," Tequesta 30(1970):64-68.

1525. A History of the Synder Memorial Church, Formerly Trinity
Methodist Episcopal Church, Jacksonville, Florida, From
1870-1944. Jacksonville: Commercial Printing Company, 1944.

1526. Hoskins, F. W. The History of Methodism in Pensacola
Florida, Its Rise and Progress. Nashville: Publishing
House of the Methodist Episcopal Church, South, 1928.

1527. Jones, Robert Eugene. "The Methodist Circuit Rider in
Territorial East Florida." Master's thesis, University of
Florida, 1953.

1528. Kershaw, A. J. "Introduction of African Methodism in
West Florida." In Proceedings of the Quarto-Centennial
Conference of the African Methodist Episcopal Church, edited by
Benjamin W. Arnett. [N. p., 1890.] pp. 163-68.

1529. Lazenby, Marion Elias. History of Methodism in Alabama
       and West Florida. Nashville, 1960.

1530. Sawyer, J. J. "The Pioneer Workmen [of the African
       Methodist Church in Florida]." In Proceedings of the
Quarto-Centennial Conference of the African Methodist Episcopal
Church, edited by Benjamin W. Arnett. [N. p., 1890.]

1531. Scott, John R. "Introduction of African Methodism Into
       East Florida." In Proceedings of the Quarto-Centennial
Conference of the African Methodist Episcopal Church, edited by
Benjamin W. Arnett. [N. p., 1890.]

1532. Smith, M. E. C. "Pioneer Women of East Florida [Afri-
       can Methodist Church]." In Proceedings of the Quarto-Cen-
tennial Conference of the African Methodist Episcopal Church,
edited by Benjamin W. Arnett. [N. p., 1890.]

1533. Thrift, Charles Tinsley, Jr. The Trail of the Florida Cir-
       cuit Rider, an Introduction to the Rise of Methodism in
Middle and East Florida. Lakeland: Florida Southern College
Press, 1944.

       D. Presbyterian

1534. Centennial Booklet of the First Presbyterian Church, Jack-
       sonville, 1840-1940. [Jacksonville: Tutweiler Press,
1941?]

1535. Gainesville, Florida First Presbyterian Church. History of
       the First Presbyterian Church 1867 to 1957. Gainesville,
1957.

1536. A House Not Made With Hands. Bradenton: Bradenton
       Herald Job Department, 1964.

1537. Hoyt, Nathan. "A Religious Revival in Tallahassee in 1843."
       Edited by George C. Osborn. F. H. Q. 32(1954):288-94.

1538. Lee, Walter Howard. The Flagler Story and Memorial
       Church. St. Augustine: Memorial Presbyterian Church
Society, 1949.

1539. Presbyterian Church in the U. S. "The Synod of Florida
       [and Its Forerunners, 1824-1955]," Presbyterian Survey
45(1955):36-38, 61.

1540. Redding, David A. Flagler and His Church. Jacksonville:
       Paramount Press, 1970.

E. Baptist

1541. Browning, Edwin B. The Early History of Concord Mis-
       sionary Baptist Church [Madison County], 1841-1868. [N.p.,
1947.]

1542. Dalton, Jack. "A History of Florida Baptists." Ph.D.
       dissertation, University of Florida, 1952.

1543. Nelson, P. V. Forty Fruitful Years; History of Lake
       County Association of Baptist Churches, 1924-1964. [N.p.,
1965?]

1544. Osborn, George C. and Jack P. Dalton. "The South Flori-
       da Baptist Association," Tequesta 14(1954):51-60.

1545. _____. The First Baptist Church, Gainesville, Florida,
       1870-1970. Gainesville: Storter Printing Company, 1970.

1546. Pensacola First Baptist Church, Centennial Celebration,
       1847-1947. Pensacola: Pfeiffer Printing Company, 1947.

1547. Rosser, John Leonidas. A History of Florida Baptists
       [1821-1946]. Nashville: Broadman Press, 1949.

1548. Spain, Rufus B. At Ease in Zion: A Social History of
       Southern Baptists, 1865-1900. Nashville: Vanderbilt Uni-
versity Press, 1967.

F. Others

1549. Abercrombie, Lelia. "Early Churches of Pensacola,"
       F.H.Q. 37(1959):446-62.

1550. Aldrich, Guy V. Seven Miles Out; the Story of Pasadena
       Community Church, St. Petersburg, Florida, 1924-1960.
[Tampa, 1965?]

1551. Historical Records Survey. Florida. A Preliminary List
       of Religious Bodies in Florida. Prepared by the Historical
Records Survey, Division of Professional and Service Projects,
Works Progress Administration. Jacksonville: Historical Records
Survey, 1939.

1552. King, Elisha Alonzo. Planting a Church in a National Play-
       ground, Miami Beach, Florida, 1920-41. Miami: The
Personal Help Library, 1942.

1553. Nance, Ellwood C. Florida Christians, Disciples of Christ.
       Winter Park: Rollins College Press, 1941.

1554. Prince, John Conger. Olds Hall, a Residence for Retired
       Ministers and Missionaries. Nashville: Parthenon Press,
1955.

XVIII. EDUCATION

A. General Studies

1555. Ballas, Parascho P. "A Study of the Organization and Ad-
       ministration of the Florida State Department of Education."
Master's thesis, Florida State University, Government Department,
1959.

1556. Black, Marian Watkins. "Battle Over Uniformity of Text-
       books in Florida, 1868-1963," Hist. Ed. Q. 4(1964):106-18.

1557. Bush, George G. History of Education in Florida. Con-
       tributions to American Educational History, No. 6. Wash-
ington, D. C.: Government Printing Office, 1889.

1558. Cochran, Thomas Everette. History of the Public-School
       Education in Florida. Lancaster, Pa.: Press of the New
Era Printing Company, 1921.

1559. Cook, Denton L. "Some State and Local Trends in Florida
       School Expenditures Affecting Negro Education." Ph. D.
dissertation, Colorado State College of Education, 1952.

1560. Copeland, Richard Watson, Jr. "Public School Indebtedness
       in Florida [1885-1950]." Ph. D. dissertation, University of
Florida, 1952.

1561. Dean, Harris W. "The School Board in Florida." In Edu-
       cation in Florida Past and Present, edited by the Florida
State Research Council. Tallahassee: Florida State University,
1954. pp. 87-93.

1562. Eason, H. H. "Adult Education Program; Its First Year,"
       Wilson Lib. Bull. 29(1954):302-05.

1563. Florida. Citizens Committee on Education. Education and
       the Future of Florida, a Report of the Comprehensive Study
of Education in Florida. Tallahassee, 1947.

1564. Goulding, R. L. "Development of Teacher Training in
       Florida." Ph. D. dissertation, George Peabody College for
Teachers, Nashville, Tennessee, 1933.

1565. Hand, S. E. "Florida State Board of Education; a Study of Its Minutes From 1871-1895." In Education in Florida Past and Present, edited by the Florida State University Research Council. Tallahassee: Florida State University, 1954. pp. 21-28.

1566. History of the Florida Education Association; 1886-87 to 1956-57. Tallahassee: Florida Education Association, 1958.

1567. Lockey, Joseph B. "Public Education in Spanish St. Augustine," F. H. Q. 15(1937):147-68.

1568. McClellan, James E. "English School in Spanish St. Augustine, Florida, 1805." In Education in Florida Past and Present, edited by the Florida State University Research Council. Tallahassee: Florida State University, 1954. pp. 1-5.

1569. McGoldrick, Sister Thomas Joseph. "The Contributions of the Sisters of St. Joseph of Augustine to Education 1866-1960." Master's thesis, University of Florida, 1961.

1570. Moore, M. M. "Rise and Progress of Our Educational Work in Florida [African Methodist Church]." In Proceedings of the Quarto-Centennial Conference of the African Methodist Episcopal Church, edited by Benjamin W. Arnett. [N. p., 1890.]

1571. National Congress of Parents and Teachers. Florida Branch. Lest We Forget: Silver Anniversary History of the Florida Congress of Parents and Teachers, 1923-1948. Orlando, 1949.

1572. Pyburn, Nita Katharine. Documentary History of Education in Florida, 1822-1860. Tallahassee: Florida State University, 1951.

1573. _____. "An Early Proposal for the Development of the State System of Education: Footnote Annotations on the First Report of Superintendent of the Schools for Florida, 1850." In Education in Florida Past and Present, edited by the Florida State University Research Council. Tallahassee: Florida State University, 1954. pp. 7-20.

1574. _____. The History of the Development of a Single System of Education in Florida, 1822-1903. Tallahassee: Florida State University, 1954.

1575. Sellars, E. H. "Florida's Educational System," Outlook 80(1905):840-41.

1576. Tomberlin, Joseph Aaron. "Integration and Education in Florida: The First Decade, 1954-1964." Master's thesis, Florida State University, 1964.

1577.   Verner, Coolie.   "A Preliminary History of Adult Education
        in Florida."   In Education in Florida Past and Present,
edited by the Florida State University Research Council.   Tallahassee: Florida State University, 1954.   pp. 29-40.

1578.   Whitaker, Mary Ann.   "Henry Prather Fletcher: His Years
        of Apprenticeship."   Master's thesis, Florida State Univer-
sity, 1963.

        B.   Elementary and Secondary

1579.   Alberta, Sister Mary.   "A Study of the Schools Conducted
        by the Sisters of St. Joseph of the Diocese of St. Augustine,
Florida, 1866-1940."   Master's thesis, University of Florida, 1940.

1580.   Cuthbert, Norma B.   "Yankee Preacher-teacher in Florida,
        1838, "   Hunt. Lib. Q.   7(1944):95-104.

1581.   Davis, T. Frederick.   "Pioneer Florida: A Free Public
        School in St. Augustine, 1832, "   F. H. Q.   12(1944):200-07.

1582.   Ezell, Boyce Fowler.   The Development of Secondary Edu-
        cation in Florida, With Special Reference to the Public
White High School.   De Land, 1932.

1583.   Florida.   Legislative Reference Bureau.   Seven Years of
        the Minimum Foundation Program [1947-54]:   A Report to
the Florida Legislative Council by the Select Committee on Education.   Tallahassee, 1955.

1584.   Fry, Alice.   "Recollections of a Florida Schoolteacher, "
        F. H. Q.   43(1965):270-75.

1585.   Hammond, Sarah Lou.   "Anna E. Chaires and Kindergarten
        Education in Florida."   In Florida Educators, edited by the
Florida State University Research Council.   Tallahassee: Florida
State University, 1959.

1586.   _____.   "Historical Development of Schools for Young
        Children in Florida."   In Education in Florida Past and
Present, edited by the Florida State University Research Council.
Tallahassee: Florida State University, 1954.   pp. 41-75.

1587.   _____.   "An Inquiry Into the Development and Present
        Status of Education for Young Children in Florida [1875-
1952]."   Ph.D. dissertation, University of Florida, 1953.

1588.   Henry, Erma.   "A History of the Development of the Pub-
        lic Schools in Dade County, Florida."   Master's thesis,
University of Miami, 1945.

1589.   Hurt, Ashley Davis.   "An Educator Looks at Florida in
        1884."   Edited by Samuel Proctor.   F. H. Q. 31(1953):208-
13.

1590.   Proctor, Samuel.   "Yankee Schoolmarms in Postwar Flori-
        da," J. Neg. Hist. 44(1959):275-77.

1591.   Rhodes, Francis A.   "A History of Education in Leon Coun-
        ty, Florida." Master's thesis, University of Florida, 1946.

1592.   Rosen, Frederic Bruce.   "The Development of Public School
        Education in Bradford County, Florida."   Master's thesis,
University of Florida, 1961.

        C.   Higher

1593.   Barrow, Mark V.   "A Short History of the University of
        Florida College of Medicine to 1960," J. Fla. Med. Assn.
55(1968):757-64.

1594.   Bridges, J. H.   "The Florida Agricultural College,"   Fla.
        Mag. 5(1902):71-84.

1595.   Bristol, L. M.   Three Focal Points in the Development of
        Florida's State System of Higher Education.   Gainesville:
University of Florida Bookstore, 1952.

1596.   Campbell, Doak S.   A University in Transition: Florida
        State College for Women and Florida State University, 1941-
1957.   Florida State University Studies, No. 40.   Tallahassee:
Florida State University, 1964.

1597.   Cobb, Arthur.   Go Gators!   Official History; University of
        Florida Football: 1889-1967.   Pensacola: Sunshine Pub-
lishing Company, 1967.

1598.   Covington, James Warren and Carl Herbert Laub.   The
        Story of the University of Tampa: A Quarter Century of
Progress From 1930 to 1955.   Tampa: University of Tampa
Press, 1955.

1599.   Crow, C. L.   "East Florida Seminary--Micanopy," F. H. Q.
        14(1936):193-216.

1600.   _____.   "Florida University (1883)," F. H. Q. 15(1936):
        96-112.

1601.   Dodd, William G.   "Early Education in Tallahassee and the
        West Florida Seminary, Now Florida State University [1827-
60]," F. H. Q. 27(1948):1-27, 157-80.

138   Florida History

1602. Florida. University, Gainesville. Views of University of
       Florida, Gainesville. Gainesville: Pepper Publishing and
Printing Company, 1914.

1603. Garwood, Harry C. Stetson University and Florida Bap-
       tists: A Documentary History of Relations Between Stetson
University and the Florida Baptists. Edited by Edward A. Holmes,
Jr. De Land: Florida Baptist Historical Society, 1962.

1604. Hanna, A. J. "The Founding of Rollins College: A Record
       of the Conception, Formation and Establishment of Florida's
Oldest Institution of Higher Education, Presented as a Report of
the Observance of the Semi-Centennial Anniversary, 1885-1935, "
Rollins Coll. Bull. 31(1935):vii, 1-69.

1605. Miller, E. Morton. "A Brief History of the Botany and
       Zoology Department at University of Miami, Florida [1926-
48], " Bios 19(1948):86.

1606. Neyland, Leedell W. and John W. Riley. The History of
       Florida Agricultural and Mechanical University. Gaines-
ville: University of Florida Press, 1963.

1607. _____. "State-Supported Higher Education Among Ne-
       groes in the State of Florida, " F. H. Q. 43(1964):105-22.

1608. Proctor, Samuel. "The South Florida Military Institute
       (Bartow): A Parent of the University of Florida [1895-
1906], " F. H. Q. 32(1953):28-40.

1609. _____. "The University of Florida: Its Early Years,
       1853-1906. " Ph. D. dissertation, University of Florida,
1958.

1610. _____. "The University of Florida, One Hundred and
       Three Years of Progress, " S. Observer 4(1956):161-65.

1611. _____. "William Jennings Bryan and the University of
       Florida, " F. H. Q. 39(1960):1-15.

1612. Pyburn, Nita Katharine. "Albert A. Murphee and the Col-
       lege Curriculum. " In Florida Educators, edited by the
Florida State University Research Council. Tallahassee: Florida
State University, 1959. pp. 145-60.

1613. _____. Papers and Documents Relative to Seminary
       Lands. Tallahassee: Florida State University, 1953.

1614. Rhodes, Francis Arlington. "The Legal Development of
       State Supported Higher Education in Florida. " Ph. D. dis-
sertation, University of Florida, 1949.

1615. Rogers, J. S. "Teaching of Evolution at the University of Florida," Science 59(1924):126.

1616. Rollins College: An Historical Sketch of Its First Fifty Years; 1885-1935. [Winter Park: Rollins College, n. d.]

1617. Shores, Venila Louina. "Some Historical Notes Concerning Florida State College for Women," Tallahassee Historical Society Annual 3(1937):103-20.

1618. Smith, T. L. "University of Florida as a Center for Latin American Studies," Americas 13(1961):35-38.

1619. Thrift, Charles Tinsley. Through Three Decades at Florida Southern College, Lakeland, Florida. Published Upon the Thirtieth Anniversary of Ludd Myrl Spivey as President of the College. Lakeland: Florida Southern College Press, 1955.

XIX. CULTURAL ASPECTS

A. Folklore and Immigrants

1620. Anderson, Russell H. "The Shaker Community in Florida," F. H. Q. 38(1959):29-44.

1621. Beeson, Kenneth H., Jr. "Fromajadas and Indigo: The Minorcan Colony in Florida." Master's thesis, University of Florida, 1960.

1622. Doggett, Caritta. Dr. Andrew Turnbull and the New Smyrna Colony of Florida. The Drew Press, 1919.

1623. Fernandez-Flores, Dario. "The Spanish Heritage in the United States." Madrid: Publicaciones Españolas, 1965.

1624. Georges, Robert A. "The Greeks of Tarpon Springs: An American Folk Group," S. Folklore Q. 29(1965):129-41.

1625. Grandoff, Victor C. "Folklore Notes about the Minorcans of Old St. Augustine, Florida," Revista Inter-Americana 1(1940):31-34.

1626. Hall, Wade H. The Smiling Phoenix: Southern Humor From 1865-1914. Gainesville: University of Florida Press, 1965.

1627. Halley, Helen. "A Historical Functional Approach to the Study of the Greek Community of Tarpon Springs." Ph. D. dissertation, Columbia University, 1952.

1628.   Korn, Bertram Wallace.   The Early Jews in New Orleans.
        Waltham, Mass.:   American Jewish Historical Society,
1969.

1629.   LaGodna, Martin M.   "Agriculture and Advertising: Flori-
        da State Bureau of Immigration, 1923-1960, " F. H. Q.
46(1968):195-208.

1630.   Laney, Harrison Jean.   "Slavia: A Culture Pocket in
        Florida."   Master's thesis, University of Florida, 1937.

1631.   Lehrman, Irving.   "The Jewish Community of Greater
        Miami, 1896-1955. "   In Jewish Theological Seminary of
America, American Jewish History Center.   Proceedings of the
Conference on the Writing of Regional History in the South.   ([New
York], 1956.)   pp. 116-30.

1632.   Long, Durward.   "La Resistencia: Tampa's Immigrant
        Labor Union, " Labor Hist.   5(1965):193-213.

1633.   Lovejoy, Gordon Williams.   "The Greeks of Tarpon Springs,
        Florida."   Master's thesis, University of Florida, 1938.

1634.   Morris, Alton Chester, ed.   Folksongs of Florida...Musi-
        cal Transcriptions by Leonhard Deutsch.   Gainesville: Uni-
versity of Florida Press, 1950.

1635.   Muniz, Jose Rivero.   "Los Cubanos en Tampa, " Revista
        Bimestre Cubana (Havana) 74(1958):1-144.

1636.   Panagopoulos, E. P.   New Smyrna: An Eighteenth Century
        Greek Odyssey. Gainesville: University of Florida Press, 1966.

1637.   Parsons, Elsie Clews.   "Folk-tales Collected at Miami,
        Fla. , " J. Am. Folklore Assn.   30(1917):222-27.

1638.   Proctor, Samuel.   "Pioneer Jewish Settlement in Florida,
        1765-1900. "   In Jewish Theological Seminary of America,
American Jewish History Center.   Proceedings of the Conference
on the Writing of Regional History in the South.   ([New York],
1956.)   pp. 81-115.

1639.   Ramirez, Manuel D.   "Italian Folklore From Tampa, Flori-
        da, Introduction, " S. Folklore Q.   5(1941):101-06.

1640.   Rawlings, M. K.   "Cracker Chidlings; Real Tales From
        the Florida Interior, " Scribner's Mag.   89(1931):127-34.

1641.   Reaver, J. Russell.   "Folk History From Northern Flori-
        da, " S. Folklore Q.   32(1968):7-16.

1642.   Remington, Frederick.   "Cracker Cowboys of Florida, "
        Harpers Mag.   91(1895):339-45.

1643. Reyes, E. L. "Legends of the King's Highway (Anecdotes From St. Augustine)." Reported by J. Russell Reaver. S. Folklore Q. 20(1956):225-39.

1644. Roselli, Bruno. The Italians in Colonial Florida; a Repertory of Italian Families Settled in Florida Under the Spanish (1513-1762, 1784-1831) and British (1762-1784) Regimes. Jacksonville: Drew Press, 1940.

1645. Scott, Taylor Carver. "The Mennonites of Sarasota, Florida." Master's thesis, University of Florida, 1949.

1646. Simonhoff, Harry. Jewish Participants in the Civil War. New York: Arco Publishing Company, 1963.

1647. Smiley, P. "Folklore From Virginia, South Carolina, Georgia, Alabama, and Florida," J. Am. Folklore Assn. 32(1919):357-83.

1648. Smith, G. H. "Three Miami Tales," J. Am. Folklore Assn. 52(1939):194-208.

1649. Stuart, Mary Frances. "The Uchee Valley Scots." Master's thesis, Florida State University, 1956.

1650. Sweet, F. H. "Cracker Lore and Humor," Cath. World 130(1929):78-82.

1651. Umble, John Sylvanus. "The Mennonites in Florida [1924-57]," Mennonite Life 12(1957):108-15.

B. Communication Media

1652. Bellamy, Jeanne. "Newspapers of America's Last Frontier ['Florida's Gold Coast,' 1829-1950]," Tequesta 12(1952):3-18.

1653. Boiler, William Fred, Jr. "A Study of the Reporting and Interpreting of the League of Nations by a Selected Group of Florida Newspapers." Master's thesis, University of Florida, 1958.

1654. Brigham, C. S. "East Florida Gazette, 1783-1784," Proc. Am. Ant. Soc. New series, Part 2, 23(1913):369.

1655. Davis, Horace Gibbs, Jr. "Florida Journalism During the Civil War." Master's thesis, University of Florida, 1952.

1656. _____. "Pensacola Newspapers, 1821-1900," F. H. Q. 37(1959):418-45.

1657.   DeBerard, Philip E., Jr.   "Promoting Florida: Some As-
        pects of the Use of Advertising and Publicity in the Develop-
ment of the Sunshine State."   Master's thesis, University of Florida, 1951.

1658.   Derby, Clyde L.   "Leon County Imprints Prior to 1860,"
        Tallahassee Historical Society Annual 4(1939):80-87.

1659.   Dosh, R. N.   "Marion County Newspapers," F.H.Q.
        37(1958):53-65.

1660.   Dutchak, Eugene M.   "Florida Press and the 1952 Presi-
        dential Campaign."   Master's thesis, University of Florida,
1955.

1661.   Fuller, Thomas Melville.   "A Critical Analysis of How
        Selected Florida Newspapers Reported the Cuban Revolution."
Master's thesis, University of Florida, 1965.

1662.   Gaines, J. Pendleton, Jr.   "A Century in Florida Journal-
        ism."   Master's thesis, University of Florida, 1949.

1663.   Kennerly, Arthur.   "The Democrat [Tallahassee]," F.H.Q.
        37(1958):150-55.

1664.   Kilgore, John.   "Leon County's Newspapers," Tallahassee
        Historical Society Annual 4(1939):68-79.

1665.   Knauss, James O.   "Florida Newspapers and Their Value
        to Historians," F.H.Q. 4(1924):42-43.

1666.   McMurtrie, Douglas C.   The First Printing in Florida.   At-
        lanta: Privately Printed, 1931.

1667.   Newton, V. M.   Crusade For Democracy.   Ames: Iowa
        University Press, 1961.

1668.   Nichols, L. Nelson.   "Early Florida Printing," Am. Printer
        89(1929):36-37.

1669.   Ott, Eloise Robinson.   "Early Newspapers of Ocala,"
        F.H.Q. 35(1957):303-11.

        C.   Libraries

1670.   Adams, Katharine B.   "The Growth and Development of the
        University of Florida Libraries, 1940-1958."   Master's
thesis, Catholic University of America, 1959.

1671.   Anders, M. E.   "Southeastern Library Association, 1920-
        1950," S. E. Lib. 6(1956):9-39, 68-81.

1672. Barfield, I. R. "History of the Miami Public Library."
       Master's thesis, Atlanta University, 1958.

1673. Barker, Tommie Dora. "Libraries in the Southeastern
       States, 1942-1946." In Twelfth Biennial Conference, Papers
and Proceedings. Asheville, N. C.: Southeastern Library Association, 1946. pp. 13-29.

1674. _____. "Library Progress in the South, 1936-1942,"
       Lib. Q. 12(1942):353-62.

1675. Baroco, John Vincent. "The Library Association of Pensa-
       cola, 1885-1933." Master's thesis, Florida State Univer-
sity, 1953.

1676. "The Carnegie Library at Ocala, Florida," L. J. 42(1917):
       379-81.

1677. Chalker, W. J. "Historical Development of the Florida
       State Library, 1945-1949." Master's thesis, George Pea-
body College for Teachers, 1951.

1678. Chapman, Margaret. "Florida Collections in Florida Li-
       braries," Fla. Lib. 11(1960):22-25.

1679. "Comparing the Library Surveys of 1935 and 1947," Fla.
       Pub. Lib. Newsletter 2(1949):4-8.

1680. Conduitte, Gretchen Garrison. "Changing Character of
       Southern Libraries," L. J. 81(1956):1112-18.

1681. Copeland, Emily A. "The Florida Agricultural and Mechan-
       ical University Department of Library Service, Tallahassee,
Florida," Fla. Lib. 7(1956):28-29.

1682. Dodd, Dorothy. "From Stationer's Reading Room to...?"
       Fla. Lib. 7(1956):16+

1683. Gill, S. C. "History of the Miami, Florida, Public Li-
       brary." Master's thesis, Western Reserve University,
1954.

1684. Hansen, Alice M. "Rollins College Library." In Pursuit
       of Library History, edited by John David Marshall. Talla-
hassee: Florida State University Library School, 1961.

1685. Husselbee, M. V. "History of the University of Miami Li-
       braries, 1928-1960." Master's thesis, University of North
Carolina, 1962.

1686. Kantor, David and Elizabeth Cole. Survey of Public Li-
       brary Service in Volusia County. Tallahassee: Florida
State Library, 1964.

1687. Miltimore, Cora. "Later Days of the Florida Library As-
       sociation, " Fla. Lib. Bull. 1(1927):3-9.

1688. Nistendirk, Verna R. "Ten Years of Florida Library Pro-
       gress, " ALA Bull. 56(1962):413-15.

1689. Obenaus, Kathryn M. "Private Subscription Built the Indian
       River County Library, " L. J. 87(1962):4353-54.

1690. Patane, Jane Seager. "A History of the Public Library in
       St. Petersburg, Florida. " Master's thesis, Florida State
University, 1960.

1691. Perres, M. J. "History and Development of Public Li-
       brary Service for Negroes in Pensacola, Florida, 1947-
1961. " Master's thesis, Atlanta University, 1963.

1692. Shaw, Beatrice W. "Curriculum Library of the Florida
       State Department of Education. " In Pursuit of Library His-
tory, edited by John David Marshall. Tallahassee: Florida State
University Library School, 1961.

1693. Shaw, Bradford. "University of Florida's Chinsegut Hill
       Library, " L. J. 81(1956):1118-20.

1694. Shores, Louis S. "Portrait of a Library School; Florida
       State University, " Fla. Lib. 7(1956):17+ .

1695. Thomas, Evelyn F. "The Origin and Development of the
       Society of the Four Arts Library, Palm Beach, Florida. "
Master's thesis, Florida State University, 1958.

1696. U. S. Works Progress Administration, Florida. Florida
       Libraries. Jacksonville: Works Progress Administration,
1939.

1697. Utley, George B. "Early Days of the Florida Library As-
       sociation, " Fla. Lib. Bull. 1(1927):1-2.

1698. Wallace, Anne. "The Library Movement in the South Since
       1899, " L. J. 32(1907):253-58.

       D. Music, Theatre, Architecture and Clubs

1699. Bagley, Russell E. "An Historical Study of Theatrical En-
       tertainment in Pensacola, Florida: 1882-1892. " Master's
thesis, University of Florida, 1949.

1700. Blackman, Lucy Worthington. The Florida Audubon Society,
       1900-1935. Edited from Documents, Letters, and Reminis-
censes. Florida Audubon Society, 1935.

1701. Bowser, Isadore Whitley. "The Theatre in Key West,"
       Martello 2(1965):2-6.

1702. Brooke, Bissell, ed. "An Old French Custom in the Gay
       Nineties," Hobbies 62(1957):54.

1703. Dodd, William G. "Theatrical Entertainment in Early
       Florida," F. H. Q. 25(1946):121-74.

1704. Fisher, Primrose Watson. A History of the Rotary Club
       of Jacksonville, Florida, Club No. 41. Jacksonville: Con-
       vention Press, 1962.

1705. History of the Miami Woman's Club, 1900-1955. Miami,
       1957.

1706. History of the Old Confederate Soldiers and Sailors Home,
       1890-1914. Jacksonville: Drew Press, 1914.

1707. Housewright, Wiley L. "Music of 18th Century Florida,"
       Apalachee 5(1957-62):48-62.

1708. Lay, Chester Frederick. Fifty Golden Years, 1918-1968;
       a Brief History of Lakeland Rotary. Lakeland: Lakeland
       Rotary, 1968.

1709. Meginnis, Ben A. "Munro's Opera House [Tallahassee],"
       Apalachee 5(1957-62):72-75.

1710. Minor, William Richard, ed. History of Ezra Lodge, Num-
       ber 67...1873-1948.... Jacksonville: Ezra Lodge, 1948.

1711. Mizner, Addison. Florida Architecture. New York: Hel-
       burn, Inc., 1928.

1712. Newton, Earle W., ed. Historic Architecture of Pensacola.
       Pensacola: Historic Pensacola Preservation Board, 1969.

1713. Parramore, Annie Elaine. "An Historical Study of Theatri-
       cal Presentations at the Jacksonville (Florida) Opera House:
       1883-1887." Master's thesis, University of Florida, 1954.

1714. Priestly, John Boynton. Trumpets Over the Sea: Being a
       Rambling and Egotistical Account of the London Symphony
       Orchestra's Engagement at Daytona Beach, Florida, 1967. London:
       Heinemann, 1968.

1715. Richmond, Mrs. Henry L. "Bryant and Emerson in Flori-
       da," Papers of the Jacksonville Historical Society 1(1947):
       19-27.

1716. Stolee, Marilyn S. "The Federal Music Project in Miami
       1935-1939," Tequesta 30(1970):3-12.

1717.   West, William. "An Historical Study of Professional Thea-
              ter Activities in Tallahassee, Florida, 1874-1893." Mas-
        ter's thesis, Florida State University, 1954.

1718.   Williams, Grier Moffatt. "A History of Music in Jackson-
              ville, Florida, From 1822 to 1922." Ph.D. dissertation,
        Florida State University, 1961.

XX.   MEDICINE AND HEALTH SERVICES

1719.   Barton, C. H. Florida's Yellow Fever Epidemic. New
              York: D. Appleton and Co., 1904.

1720.   Chardkoff, Richard B. "The Development of State Respon-
              sibility for the Care of the Insane in Florida." Master's
        thesis, Florida State University, 1964.

1721.   Day, Samuel M. "Medical Leadership," J. Fla. Med.
              Assn. 52(1965):468-76.

1722.   Diddle, Albert W. "Medical Events in the History of Key
              West," Tequesta 6(1946):14-37.

1723.   _____. "Medical Events in the History of Key West:
        The African Depot," J. Fla. Med. Assn., 31(1944):207-09.

1724.   Driscoll, C. D. "Early Florida Dentistry," Am. Coll.
              Dentists J. 22(1955):166-73.

1725.   Du Puis, John Gordon. History of Early Medicine, History
              of Early Public Schools, [and] History of Early Agricultural
        Relations in Dade County: Some Of The Experiences And Activities
        Of The Author. [Miami?, 1954.]

1726.   Duval County Medical Society, Jacksonville, Fla. Duval
              County Medical Society, Hundreth Birthday, 1853-1953.
        Edited by Webster Merritt. Jacksonville: Centennial Committee
        & Officers of the Society, 1954.

1727.   Fairlie, Margaret C. "The Yellow Fever Epidemic of 1888
              in Jacksonville," F. H. Q. 19(1940):95-108.

1728.   _____. "First Hospital--U. S. A.," Fla. Health Notes
              60(1968):30-54.

1729.   Florida. State Board of Health. Life and Death in Florida,
              1940-1949. Jacksonville: Florida State Board of Health,
        1950.

Medicine   147

1730.   Foraker, Alvan G., and Lucien Y. Dyrenforth. "Practice
        of Pathology in Florida, 1908-1941, " J. Fla. Med. Assn.
54(1967):799-800.

1731.   Goggins, L. M. "Florida's First Institute for Midwives, "
        Pub. Health Nursing 26(1934):133-36.

1732.   Haines, Helen S., and Robert Thoburn. 75 Years of Den-
        tistry: The Diamond Jubilee Volume Of The Florida State
Dental Society. Gainesville: University of Florida Press, 1962.

1733.   Hammond, E. Ashby. "Health and Medicine in Key West,
        1832-1845, " J. Fla. Med. Assn. 56(1969):637-43.

1734.   _____. "Notes on the Medical History of Key West,
        1822-1832, " F. H. Q. 46(1967):93-110.

1735.   Hardy, Albert Victor. "The Public Health Laboratory
        [Florida, 1903-53]. Pub. Health Reports 68(1953):968-74.

1736.   Harlan, William H. "Community Adaptation to the Presence
        of Aged Persons: St. Petersburg, Florida [1940-53], " Am.
J. Socio. 59(1955):332-39.

1737.   Harrell, Laura D. S. "Colonial Medical Practice in
        British West Florida, 1763-1781, " Bull. Hist. Med.
41(1967):539-50.

1738.   Holmes, Jack D. L. "Medical Practice in the Lower Mis-
        sissippi Valley During the Spanish Period, 1769-1803, " Ala.
J. Med. Sci. 1(1964):332-38.

1739.   Knipling, E. F. "Insect Control Investigations of the Or-
        lando, Florida Laboratory During World War II, " Smith-
sonian Institute Report (1948):331-38.

1740.   Langdon, Paul E. "Sewage Disposal at Tampa, Florida
        [since 1924], " Sewage and Industrial Wastes 23(1951):643-55.

1741.   Long, Durwood. "An Immigrant Co-Operative Medicine
        Program in the South, 1887-1963, " J. S. Hist. 31(1965):
417-34.

1742.   MaClachlan, John Miller. Planning Florida's Health Leader-
        ship: Health And The People In Florida [Mainly Since 1920].
Gainesville: University of Florida Press, 1954.

1743.   Merritt, Webster. A Century of Medicine in Jacksonville
        and Duval County [1796-ca. 1900]. Gainesville: University
of Florida Press, 1949.

1744.   _____. "A History of Medicine in Duval County, " J. Fla.
        Med. Assn. 31(1944):214-16; 31(1945):310-13, 365-72, 523-28;

32(1945):31-39, 137-44, 305-12; 32(1946):596-601; 33(1946):196-99;
33(1947):502-05; 34(1947):38-40, 280-89; 34(1948):513-16.

1745. _____. "Medical Men and Medical Events in Early St.
        Augustine, " J. Fla. Med. Assn. 52(1965):494-97.

1746. _____. "Physicians and Medicine in Early Jacksonville,"
        F. H. Q. 24(1946):266-86.

1747. _____. "Physicians and Medicine in Early Jacksonville, "
        Papers of the Jacksonville Historical Society 1(1947):93-112.

1748. _____. "West Florida, Three Centuries Under Four
        Flags, Conquest and Disease, " J. Fla. Med. Assn.
39(1953):749-65.

1749. Michael, Max, Jr. and Mark V. Barrow. " 'Old Timey'
        Remedies of Yesterday and Today, " J. Fla. Med. Assn.
54(1967):778-84.

1750. Mitchell, Martha Carolyn. "Health and the Medical Pro-
        fession in the Lower South, 1845-1860, " J. S. Hist.
10(1944):424-46.

1751. Mulrennan, John A. and Wilson T. Sowder. "Florida's
        Mosquito Control System [1918-53], " Pub. Health Reports
69(1954):613-18.

1752. Ninety Years of Service 1873-1963: The Story of St. Luke's
        Hospital, Jacksonville, Florida. Jacksonville, 1963.

1753. Palmer, Henry E. "Physicians of Early Tallahassee and
        Vicinity, " Apalachee 1(1944):29-46.

1754. Palmer, Theresa Yeager, and Hugh Archer Palmer. "Phy-
        sicians, A Family Tradition, " J. Fla. Med. Assn. 53(1966):
718-23.

1755. Paul, John R. and F. Ramirez Dorria and Dorothy M.
        Horstmann. "Analyses From a Tropical Epidemic of Polio-
myelitis Which Occurred in Florida and Cuba in 1946, " Am. J.
Trop. Med. 29(1952):543-54.

1756. Porter, Joseph Y. "The Battleship Maine as a Florida
        State Board of Health Quarantine Vessel, " F. H. Q. 3(1925):
11-14.

1757. Reams, Gerald B. "A Review of 250 Thyroid Operations
        [Jackson Memorial Hospital, Miami, Fla. , 1948-53], " Am.
J. Surgery 88(1954):594-98.

1758. Robinson, Leigh F. A Half Century in Retrospect: Un-
        winding A Story Of Broward County Doctors And Their

Medical Society. Ft. Lauderdale: Broward County Medical Association, 1962.

1759. Smith, Mary Catherine. "Hospitals and the Practice of Medicine in Spanish Pensacola, " J. Fla. Med. Assn. 56(1969):630-31.

1760. Smith, W. H. Y. "Birth and Early Days of Florida's First County Health Unit [Taylor County, 1930-33], " Pub. Health Reports 68(1953):1088-90.

1761. Snyder, Clifford C. "Don Juan Ponce de Leon and the First Operation in Florida, " J. Fla. Med. Assn. 52(1965): 488-93.

1762. Sowder, Wilson T. "The Growth of Local Health Units in Florida [1930-53], " Pub. Health Reports 68(1953):1083-88.

1763. _____. "Recruitment and Retention of Public Health Personnel in Florida, 1945-1952, " Am. J. Pub. Health 42(1952):1276-82.

1764. Stover, Ann Spears. "History of Mental Health in Florida, " J. Fla. Med. Assn. 54(1967):809-17.

1765. Straight, William M. "The Frontier Physician of Dade County, " J. Fla. Med. Assn. 52(1965):479-85.

1766. _____. "Jackson Memorial Hospital: A Half Century of Community Service, " J. Fla. Med. Assn. 54(1967):785-95.

1767. _____. "The Lady Doctor of the [Coconut] Grove, " J. Fla. Med. Assn. 56(1969):615-21.

1768. _____. "Life in the Spanish Colonial Hospital in the Late 18th Century, " J. Fla. Med. Assn. 55(1968):765-69.

1769. _____. "A Medical Flashback, " J. Fla. Med. Assn. 56(1969):929-31.

1770. _____. "Medicine in St. Augustine During the Spanish Period, " J. Fla. Med. Assn. 55(1968):731-41.

1771. _____. "The Pensacola Campaign Through a Nurse's Eye, " J. Fla. Med. Assn. 56(1969):632-36.

1772. Tolle, Robert L. "History of the Orange County Medical Society, " J. Fla. Med. Assn. 52(1965):477-78.

1773. Waring, Joseph I. "John Moultrie, Jr., M.D.: Lieutenant Governor Of East Florida--His Thesis On Yellow Fever, " J. Fla. Med. Assn. 54(1967):772-77.

1774. Wood, Rowland E. "Some Medical Highlights of Florida's
       West Coast, " J. Fla. Med. Assn. 52(1965):486-87.

XXI. THE LAW

1775. Barns, Paul D. "Florida's Final Appellate Jurisdiction
       [1838-1953], " Fla. Bar J. 28(1954):282-89.

1776. Bartley, Ernest R. "Legal Problems in Florida Municipal
       Zoning [1926-53], " U. Fla. Law R. 6(1953):355-84.

1777. Bashful, Emmett Wilfort. "The Florida Supreme Court: a
       Study in Judicial Selection [1943-54]. " Ph. D. dissertation,
University of Illinois, 1955.

1778.   . The Florida Supreme Court: A Study in Judicial
       Selection. Tallahassee: Florida State University, 1958.

1779. Bishop, Jim. The Murder Trial of Judge Peel. New York:
       Trident Press, 1962.

1780. Carson, James Milton. "Attorney's Fees in Divorce [1895-
       1949], " Miami Law Q. 4(1949):22-31.

1781.   . "Historical Background of Florida Law [1821-
       85], " Miami Law Q. 3(1949):254-68.

1782. Crosby, Harold B. and George John Miller. "Our Legal
       Chameleon, the Florida Homestead Exemption, " U. Fla.
Law R. 2(1949):12-84, 219-42, 346-90.

1783. Dauer, Manning Julian. "The Florida Constitution of 1885--
       a Critique, " U. Fla. Law R. 8(1955):1-92.

1784.   , and George John Miller. "Municipal Charters in
       Florida: Law and Drafting [1868-1953], " U. Fla. Law R.
6(1953):413-80.

1785.   , and William C. Havard. The Florida Constitu-
       tion of 1885; a Critique. Gainesville: Public Administra-
tion Clearing Service, 1955.

1786. Day, James W. "Extent to Which the English Common
       Law and Statutes are in Effect [Florida, 1829-1949], " U.
Fla. Law R. 3(1950):303-18.

1787. Dietz, George A. "Sketch of the Evolution of Florida Law
       [1822-50], " U. Fla. Law R. 3(1950):74-82.

The Law   151

1788. Doherty, Herbert J., Jr. "Code Duello in Florida [1824-
       62]," F. H. Q. 29(1951):243-52.

1789. Erickson, Walter T. "Manslaughter by Automobile in Flor-
       ida [1923-50]," U. Fla. Law R. 4(1951):360-69.

1790. Falk, Jack A. "Motion to Strike and Motion for Compul-
       sory Amendment in Florida [1861-1949]," Miami Law Q.
       4(1950):224-32.

1791. Feibelman, Herbert U. "How Well Has the Bankruptcy Act
       Succeeded--in Florida?" Fla. Law J. 23(1949):335-40.

1792. Gramling, J. Carrington, Jr. "The Development of Florida
       Labor Law [1893-1952]," Miami Law Q. 7(1953):188-204.

1793. Hoskins, F. W. "The St. Joseph Convention; the Making
       of Florida's First Constitution," F. H. Q. 16(1937):33-43, 97-
109; (1938):242-50; 17(1938):125-31.

1794. Hunt, Richard H. "Riparian Rights in Florida [1818-1955],"
       U. Fla. Law R. 8(1955):393-410.

1795. Johnson, Robert M. and William P. Owen, Jr. "Criminal
       Law: Double Jeopardy in Florida [1891-1949]," U. Fla.
Law R. 2(1949):250-57.

1796. Joslin, G. Stanley. "Florida's Charitable 'Mortmain' Act
       [1933-53]," Miami Law Q. 7(1953):488-96.

1797. Kanner, Samuel J. and John P. Corcoran, Jr. "Florida
       Employment Peace Statute--Compelling Union Recognition
[1941-49]," Miami Law Q. 4(1950):161-77.

1798. Knauss, James Owen. "The Growth of Florida's Election
       Laws," F. H. Q. 5(1926):3-17.

1799. _____. "St. Joseph, an Episode of the Economic and
       Political History of Florida," F. H. Q. 17(1938):84-102.

1800. McIntosh, Russell H. "Decrees and Judgments Awarding
       Custody of Children in Florida [1921-48]," U. Fla. Law R.
1(1948):360-76.

1801. McMurray, Carl D. The Impeachment of Circuit Judge
       Richard Kelly. Tallahassee: Institute of Governmental Re-
search, Florida State University, 1964.

1802. Messick, Hank. Syndicate in the Sun. New York: Mac-
       millan Company, 1968.

1803. Middleton, James W. "Judicial Review of Administrative
       Findings of Fact: The Doctrine of Jurisdictional Facts in

152   Florida History

Florida [1892-1949]," U. Fla. Law R. 2(1949):86-94.

1804. _____ . "Judicial Review of Findings of Fact in Florida
[1847-1950]," U. Fla. Law R. 3(1950):281-302.

1805. Parker, Daisy. "The Leon County Court, 1825-1833,"
Apalachee 3(1948-50):30-42.

1806. Parker, Eugene. "Declaratory Judgments in Florida [1943-
54]," Miami Law Q. 9(1955):179-85.

1807. Parker, Julius F. "Problems in Florida and Other Coastal
States Caused by the California Tidelands Decision [1853-
1947]," U. Fla. Law R. 1(1948):44-60.

1808. Parsons, Malcolm B. "The Selection and Tenure of Florida
Supreme Court Judges [1885-1955]," Miami Law Q. 9(1955):
271-79.

1809. _____ . "The Substantial Evidence Rule in Florida Administrative Law [1911-53]," U. Fla. Law R. 6(1953):481-
518.

1810. Porter, Emily. "The Reception of the St. Joseph Constitution," F. H. Q. 17(1938):103-24.

1811. Pratt, Kathleen Falconer. "The Development of the Florida
Prison System." Master's thesis, Florida State University,
1949.

1812. Price, Hugh Douglas and J. Allen Smith. "Municipal Tort
Liability: A Continuing Enigma [Florida, 1850-1953]," U.
Fla. Law R. 6(1954):330-54.

1813. "The Quincy Conservative Convention [March 31, 1868],"
F. H. Q. 18(1940):267-69.

1814. Richard, Melvin J. "Tidelands and Riparian Rights in
Florida [1845-1948]," Miami Law Q. 3(1949):339-64.

1815. Rogers, William H. "Florida Curative Statutes," Fla. Law
J. 22(1948):153-58.

1816. Ropes, Lawrence G., Jr. "Torts' Doctrine of Municipal
Immunity [Florida, 1849-1953]--a Myth," Miami Law Q.
8(1954):555-69.

1817. "A St. Joseph Diary of 1839," F. H. Q. 17(1938):132-51.

1818. Sebring, Harold L. "The Appellate System of Florida
[1887-1951]," Fla. Law J. 25(1951):141-7.

1819. Shofner, Jerrell H. "The Constitution of 1868, " F. H. Q.
       41(1963):356-74.

1820. Silver, Morton H. "Annulment [of marriage] in Florida
       [1851-1950], " U. Fla. Law R. 3(1950):339-50.

1821. Silverstein, Mark. "Florida Mechanics' Lien Law [1935-
       53]--Visible Commencement, " Miami Law Q. 7(1953):477-
87.

1822. Smith, Harry B. and Harvey Fishbein. "Freedom of
       Speech: Fact or Fiction [1897-1949]?" Miami Law Q.
4(1949):67-77.

1823. Smith, J. Allen. "Destructibility of Contingent Remainders
       in Florida [1931-50], " U. Fla. Law R. 3(1950):319-37.

1824. _____. "The Doctrine of Recrimination in Florida
       [1925-48], " U. Fla. Law R. 1(1948):62-69.

1825. Steinhardt, Irving and Tobias Simon. "Florida's Last
       Clear Chance Doctrine [1933-53], " Miami Law Q. 7(1953):
457-76.

1826. Stern, David S. and Henry T. Troetschel, Jr. "The Role
       of Modern Arbitration in the Progressive Development of
Florida Law [1828-1952], " Miami Law Q. 7(1953):205-10.

1827. Strichartz, Richard. "Legal Aspects of Municipal Incorpor-
       ation in Florida [1889-1949], " Miami Law Q. 4(1949):78-97.

1828. _____. "Masters and Their Fees, " Miami Law Q.
       3(1949):403-23.

1829. Sturgis, Wallace E., Jr. "Abolition of the Diploma Privi-
       lege, " U. Fla. Law R. 4(1951):370-81.

1830. Thompson, William Earl. "Tax Titles in Florida [1885-
       1952], " U. Fla. Law R. 6(1953):1-76.

1831. Udell, Barton S. "Contempt of Court in Florida [1916-54],"
       Miami Law Q. 9(1955):281-303.

1832. University of Florida Law Review. The Extraordinary
       Writs in Florida: A Symposium. Gainesville: College of
Law, University of Florida, 1951.

1833. Waldby, Hubert Odell. "The Public Officer--Public Em-
       ployee Distinction in Florida [1885-1955], " U. Fla. Law R.
(1956):47-63.

1834. Waybright, Roger J. "Attorneys vs. Administrators in
       Adoption [Florida, 1885-1952], " Fla. Law. J. 27(1953):192-
96.

1835. _____. "Why a Constitutional Amendment Relating to
        Juvenile Courts?" Fla. Law J. 22(1948):308-12.

1836. Whitfield, James B. "Florida's First Constitution," F. H. Q.
        17(1938):73-83.

1837. _____. "Notes on the Constitutional Conventions of
        Florida [1838, 1861, 1865, 1868, 1885]," Tallahassee His-
torical Society Annual 3(1937):55-81.

1838. Williams, Everett H., Jr., Robert M. Thorner, and Win-
        ston Ehrmann. "Illegitimacy in Florida [1917-53]," Eugenics
Q. 3(1956):219-27.

1839. Williamson, Edward C. "The Constitutional Convention of
        1885," F. H. Q. 41(1962):116-26.

1840. Wilson, James R. and E. Martin McGehee. "Probate
        Claims in Florida [1828-1948]," U. Fla. Law R. 1(1948):
1-26.

1841. Wright, Floyd Asher. "Zoning Under the Florida Law
        [1908-53]," Miami Law Q. 7(1953):324-57.

XXII.   POLITICS AND GOVERNMENT

1842. Abbey, Kathryn T. "Florida Versus the Principles of Pop-
        ulism, 1896-1911," J. S. Hist. 4(1938):462-75.

1843. Akerman, Robert H., ed. Theodore Roosevelt in Florida.
        Lakeland: Florida Southern College Press, 1958.

1844. Andrews, Charles O., Jr. "Regulation of Campaign Ex-
        penditures," Fla. Law J. 27(1953):15-17.

1845. Bain, Richard E. "Legislative Representation in Florida:
        Historic and Contemporary." Master's thesis, Florida
State University, 1960.

1846. Blackwell, Carl W. "An Analysis of the Functional Cost
        of Florida State Government for the Period 1948 Through
1957 and a Projection for the Period 1958 Through 1970." Master's thesis, Florida State University, 1959.

1847. Cash, William T. History of the Democratic Party in
        Florida, Including Biographical Sketches of Prominent Flor-
ida Democrats. Tallahassee: Florida Democratic Historical
Foundation, 1936.

1848.   Chalmers, David. "The Ku Klux Klan in the Sunshine
        State: The 1920's, " F. H. Q. 42(1964):209-15.

1849.   Christie, Terry L. "The Collins-Johns Election, 1954:   A
        Turning Point, " Apalachee 6(1963-67):5-19.

1850.   Conoley, Rudolph Evauder. "A History of Public Land
        Policies in Florida, 1819-1900. " Master's thesis, Duke
University, 1941.

1851.   Cory, Lloyd Walter. "The Florida Farmer's Alliance, 1887-
        1892. " Master's thesis, Florida State University, 1963.

1852.   Cowley, William A. "Public Speaking in Florida: 1900-
        1904. " Master's thesis, University of Florida, 1954.

1853.   Cubberly, Frederick. "Florida Against Georgia; a Story of
        the Boundary Dispute, " F. H. Q. 3(1924):20-28.

1854.   Davis, Frederich T. "Florida's Part in the War With Mex-
        ico, " F. H. Q. 20(1942):235-59.

1855.   Doherty, Herbert J., Jr. "Florida and the Presidential
        Election of 1928, " F. H. Q. 26(1947):174-86.

1856.   _____ . "Liberal and Conservative Voting Patterns in
        Florida [1928-48], " J. Politics 14(1952):403-17.

1857.   Doty, Franklin A. "Florida and Iowa: A Contemporary
        View, " F. H. Q. 36(1957):24-32.

1858.   Doyle, Wilson Keyser, Angus McKenzie Laird, and S. Sher-
        man Weiss. The Government and Administration of Florida.
New York: Crowell, 1954.

1859.   Dunn, Hampton. "Florida Ex-Governors Lose Voter Ap-
        peal, " Fla. Trend 12(1970):26-27.

1860.   Flory, Claude R. "Marcellus Stearns and John Wallace, "
        Apalachee 6(1963-67):65-76.

1861.   Flynt, J. Wayne. "Florida Labor and Political Radicalism,
        1919-1920, " Labor Hist. 9(1968):73-90.

1862.   _____ . "Florida's 1926 Senatorial Primary, " F. H. Q.
        42(1963):142-53.

1863.   _____ . "The 1908 Democratic Senatorial Primary in
        Florida. " Master's thesis, Florida State University, 1962.

1864.   _____ . "Pensacola Labor Problems and Political Radi-
        calism, 1908, " F. H. Q. 43(1965):315-32.

1865.   Garwood, Saunders B.   "Florida State Grange, " F. H. Q.
        47(1968):165-79.

1866.   Green, George Norris.   "Florida Politics and Socialism at
        the Crossroads of the Progressive Era, 1912. "   Master's
thesis, Florida State University, 1962.

1867.   _____ . "The Florida Press and the Democratic Presi-
        dential Primary of 1912, " F. H. Q. 44(1966):169-80.

1868.   _____ . "Republicans, Bull Moose, and Negroes in Flor-
        ida, 1912, " F. H. Q. 43(1964):153-64.

1869.   Havard, William C. and Loren P. Beth.   The Politics of
        Mis-representation: Rural-Urban Conflict in the Florida
Legislature.   Baton Rouge, La.: Louisiana State University Press,
1962.

1870.   Hester, Lewis Alexander.   "An Exploratory Study of the
        Florida Legislature's View of the Role of the Executive
Branch of Government in the Enactment of Administrative Bills. "
Master's thesis, Florida State University, 1960.

1871.   Hubbell, Samuel Michael.   "The Election of 1876 in Flori-
        da. "   Master's thesis, University of Florida, 1966.

1872.   Jennings, Warren A.   "Sidney J. Catts and the Democratic
        Primary of 1920, " F. H. Q. 39(1961):203-20.

1873.   Johnson, Kenneth R.   "The Administration of William Dun-
        nington Bloxham, 1881-1885. "   Master's thesis, Florida
State University, 1959.

1874.   _____ . "Florida Women Get the Vote, " F. H. Q. 48(1970):
        299-312.

1875.   _____ . "The Woman Suffrage Movement in Florida. "
        Ph. D. dissertation, Florida State University, 1966.

1876.   Kendrick, Baynard.   Flight From a Firing Wall.   New
        York: Simon and Schuster, 1966.

1877.   Knauss, James Owen.   "The Farmers' Alliance in Florida, "
        S. Atl. Q. 25(1926):300-15.

1878.   Link, Arthur S.   "The South and the Democratic Campaign
        of 1912. "   Ph. D. dissertation, University of North Carolina,
1945.

1879.   Lord, Dorothy.   "Sidney J. Catts and the Gubernatorial
        Election of 1916, " Apalachee 6(1963-67):45-64.

1880. McDonnel, Victoria Harden. "The Businessman's Politician:
      A Study of the Administration of John Wellborn Martin,
      1925-1929." Master's thesis, University of Florida, 1968.

1881. Mills, Jack. "The Speaking of William Jennings Bryan in
      Florida, 1915-1925." Master's thesis, University of Flori-
      da, 1949.

1882. Murphy, Pat. " 'Through Green Glasses, ' Being a Histori-
      cal Sketch of Legislatures of Florida for Thirty Years." In
      Legislative Blue Book, 1917. Tallahassee: T. J. Appleyard,
      1917.

1883. Parker, Daisy. "An Examination of the Florida Executive."
      Ph. D. dissertation, University of Virginia, 1959.

1884. _____. "The Inauguration of Albert Waller Gilchrist,
      Nineteenth Governor of the State of Florida," Apalachee
      6(1963-67):20-32.

1885. Prior, Leon O. "German Espionage in Florida During
      World War II," F. H. Q. 39(1961):374-77.

1886. Proctor, Samuel. "The National Farmer's Alliance Con-
      vention of 1890 and Its 'Ocala Demands, ' " F. H. Q.
      28(1950):161-81.

1887. Richardson, Joe M. "The Florida Excursion of President
      Chester A. Arthur," Tequesta 24(1964):41-47.

1888. Ripley, C. Peter. "Alabama's 1963 Attempt to Annex West
      Florida," Apalachee 6(1963-67):87-94.

1889. _____. "Intervention and Reaction: Florida Newspapers
      and United States Entry Into World War I," F. H. Q.
      49(1971):255-67.

1890. Roberts, Albert Hubbard. "The Senatorial Deadlock of
      1897," Apalachee 1(1944):1-12.

1891. Safransky, Robert J. "The Contested Presidential and Gu-
      bernatorial Election of 1876 in Florida." Master's thesis,
      Stetson University, 1965.

1892. Sanford, Henry Shelton. "Florida Politics in 1881." Edited
      by Edward C. Williamson. F. H. Q. 31(1953):279-81.

1893. Shappee, Nathan D. "Zangara's Attempted Assassination of
      Franklin D. Roosevelt [1933]," F. H. Q. 37(1958):101-10.

1894. Shofner, Jerrell H. "Florida Courts and the Disputed Elec-
      tion of 1876," F. H. Q. 48(1969):26-46.

1895. _____ . "Florida in the Balance: The Electoral Count
      of 1876," F. H. Q. 47(1968):122-50.

1896. _____ . "Fraud and Intimidation in the Florida Election
      of 1876," F. H. Q. 42(1964):321-30.

1897. _____ . "The Presidential Election of 1876 in Florida."
      Master's thesis, Florida State University, 1961.

1898. Smith, C. Lynwood, Jr. Strengthening the Florida Legisla-
      ture: An Eagleton Study and Report. New Brunswick:
      Rutgers University Press, 1970.

1899. Stearns, Marcellus L. "The Election of 1876 in Florida."
      Edited by Edward C. Williamson. F. H. Q. 32(1953):81-91.

1900. Sweets, John F. "The Civilian Conservation Corps in Flor-
      ida," Apalachee 6(1963-67):77-86.

1901. Taylor, A. Elizabeth. "The Woman Suffrage Movement in
      Florida," F. H. Q. 36(1957):42-60.

1902. Warren, Fuller. How to Win in Politics. Tallahassee:
      Peninsular Publishing Company, 1949.

1903. Whitfield, James Bryan. Political and Legal History of
      Florida. Atlanta: Harrison Company, 1943.

1904. Williamson, Edward C. "The Era of the Democratic County
      Leader: Florida Politics, 1877-1893." Ph. D. dissertation,
      University of Pennsylvania, 1954.

1905. _____ , ed. "Florida Politics in 1881; a Letter of Henry
      S. Sanford," F. H. Q. 31(1953):279-81.

1906. _____ . "Independentism: A Challenge to the Florida
      Democracy of 1884," F. H. Q. 27(1948):131-56.

XXIII. AGRICULTURE, COMMERCE, AND INDUSTRY

A. General

1907. Brown, C. K. "The Florida Investment of George W.
      Swepson," N. C. Hist. Rev. 5(1928):275-88.

1908. Covington, James W. "The Rockets Come to Florida,"
      Tequesta 28(1968):37-51.

1909. _____. "Trade Relations Between Southwestern Florida and Cuba--1600-1840, " F. H. Q. 38(1959):114-28.

1910. Florida State Chamber of Commerce. 50 Creative Years: A Brief History Of The Florida State Chamber Of Commerce. Jacksonville: Florida State Chamber of Commerce, 1966.

1911. "Fred N. Varn's Account Book, 1869-1875, " F. H. Q. 38(1959):71-73.

1912. Harper, Roland M. "The Population of Florida. Regional Composition and Growth as Influenced by Soil, Climate, and Mineral Discoveries, " Geog. Rev. 2(1916):361-67.

1913. Holman, Mary A. , and Ronald M. Knokel. "Manned Space Flight and Employment, " Monthly Labor Rev. 90(1968):30-36.

1914. Hudson, E. Clinton. "Tampa's Foreign Trade From 1948 Until 1958. " Master's thesis, University of Florida, 1960.

1915. Kilpatrick, Wylie. "Florida City Debt--A Case Study [1930-53], " J. Fin. 10(1955):350-62.

1916. Laessle, Albert Middleton. The Plant Communities of the Welaka Area. Gainesville: University of Florida Press, 1942.

1917. Nelson, Wallace Martin. "The Economic Development of Florida, 1870-1930. " Ph. D. dissertation, University of Florida, 1962.

1918. Nichols, Judy R. "The Middle Florida Agricultural Fair, 1879-1885, " Apalachee 7(1968-70):80-98.

1919. Paisley, Clifton L. "Van Brunt's Store, Iamonia, Florida, 1902-1911, " F. H. Q. 48(1970):353-67.

1920. Rogers, Ben F. "Florida in World War II: Tourists And Citrus, " F. H. Q. 39(1960):34-41.

1921. Sessa, Frank B. "Anti-Florida Propaganda and Counter Measures During the 1920's, " Tequesta 21(1961):41-51.

1922. Stockton, J. Roy. "Spring Training [Baseball] in Florida, " F. H. Q. 39(1961):221-30.

1923. Strickland, Alice. "Florida's Golden Age of Racing, " F. H. Q. 45(1967):253-69.

1924. Swenson, Lloyd S. , Jr. "The Fertile Crescent: The South's Role In The National Space Program, " S. W. Hist. Q. 71(1968):377-92.

160 Florida History

1925. Tischendorf, Alfred Paul. "Florida and the British Investor: 1880-1914," F.H.Q. 33(1954):120-29.

1926. Whitaker, Arthur Preston. "The Spanish Contribution to American Agriculture," Ag. Hist. 3(1929):1-14.

1927. Wolff, Reinhold P. "Recent Economic Trends in South Florida," Tequesta 1(1944):45-49.

1928. Young, Robert James. "Administering Florida's Natural Resources." Master's thesis, University of Florida, 1952.

B. Banking and Real Estate

1929. Abbey, Kathryn T. "The Union Bank of Tallahassee: An Experiment In Territorial Finance," F.H.Q. 15(1937):207-31.

1930. Adams, Adam G. "Some Pre-boom Developers of Dade County," Tequesta 17(1957):31-46.

1931. Amundson, Richard J. "The Florida Land and Colonization Company," F.H.Q. 44(1966):153-68.

1932. Barnd, Merle Oliver. "A Study of A Group of Florida State Bank Failures in 1929." Master's thesis, University of Florida, 1930.

1933. Barnett, Bion H. Reminiscences of Fifty Years in the Barnett Banks.... Jacksonville: Arnold Printing Company, 1927.

1934. Dovell, Junius E. History of Banking in Florida, 1828-1954. Orlando: Florida Bankers Association, 1955.

1935. _____. History of Banking in Florida, 1st Supplement, 1954-1963. Orlando: Florida Bankers Association, 1963.

1936. Hicks, John D. Rehearsal for Disaster: The Boom And Collapse Of 1919-1920. Gainesville: University of Florida Press, 1961.

1937. Leynes, Bernhardt Crevasse, Jr. "Developments in Land Ownership and Land Use on Large Holdings in Leon County, Florida, Since 1950." Master's thesis, Florida State University, 1959.

1938. Mendenhall, Herbert D. "The History of Land Surveying in Florida [1513-1931]," Surveying and Mapping 10(1950):278-83.

1939. Mullen, Harris H. A History of the Tampa Bay Hotel. Tampa: University of Tampa Foundation, 1966.

1940. Sessa, Frank Bowman. "The Real Estate Boom in Miami and Its Environs [1923-1926]." Ph. D. dissertation, University of Pittsburgh, 1950.

1941. Tindall, George B. "The Bubble in the Sun," Am. Heritage 16(1965):76-83, 109-11.

1942. Vanderblue, Homer B. "The Florida Land Boom," J. of Land and Public Utility Econ. 3(1927):113-31.

1943. Yoder, Lowell C. The Consumer Finance Industry in Florida [1909-1955]. Gainesville: University of Florida Press, 1957.

C. Industry

1944. Bass, Joe. "The Development of Manufacturing in Florida: 1899-1929. A Statistical Analysis." Master's thesis, University of Florida, 1932.

1945. Benzoni, Frank. "Oil and Gas Conservation Laws of Florida [1945-50]," F. Law J. 24(1950):262-6.

1946. Bernard, H. Russell. "Greek Sponge Boats in Florida," Anthro. Q. 38(1965):41-54.

1947. Blakey, Arch Frederic. "The Florida Phosphate Industry, 1888-1918." Master's thesis, Florida State University, 1964.

1948. Burkhardt, Henry J. "Starch Making: A Pioneer Florida Industry," Tequesta 12(1952):47-53.

1949. Carter, James Asbury. "Florida and Rumrunning During National Prohibition," F. H. Q. 48(1969):47-56.

1950. _____. "Florida and Rumrunning During National Prohibition." Master's thesis, Florida State University, 1965.

1951. Cobb, John N. "Sponge Fishery of Florida," Scientific Am. Supp. 57(1904):23581-83.

1952. Cunkle, Arthur. Retail, Wholesale, and Service Trades in Florida [1939-48]. Gainesville: University of Florida, Bureau of Economic and Business Research, 1952.

1953. Dodd, Dorothy. "Captain Bunce's Tampa Bay Fisheries," F. H. Q. 25(1947):246-56.

1954. "Florida Power and Light," Fortune 41(1950):84-89, 144, 147-48, 150, 152, 154.

1955. Frantzis, George T. Strangers at Ithaca; the Story of the
       Spongers at Tarpon Springs. St. Petersburg: Great Out-
doors Publishing Company, 1962.

1956. Gearhart, Ernest G., Jr. "South Florida's First Industry
       [Arrowroot Starch, Dade County]," Tequesta 12(1952):55-57.

1957. Kilpatrick, Wylie. Manufacturing in Florida [1904-52].
       Gainesville: University of Florida, Bureau of Economic
and Business Research, 1952.

1958. _____ . Manufacturing in Florida Counties and Cities
       [1939-47]. Gainesville: University of Florida, Bureau of
Economic and Business Research, 1951.

1959. _____ . Revenue and Debt of Florida Municipalities and
       Overlying Governments [1931-51]. Gainesville: University
of Florida, Bureau of Economic and Business Research, 1953.

1960. Lawren, Joseph. "The Sponge Capital of America," Travel
       91(1948):23-25, 34.

1961. Layng, Charles. "High in the Prow," Ships and the Sea
       2(1953):18-20.

1962. Proctor, Samuel. "Florida Phosphate Industry: Origins
       and Development," Can. Mining J. 75(1956):53-55.

1963. Rhodes, F. A. "Salt Making on the Apalachee Bay," Talla-
       hassee Historical Society Annual 2(1935):17-21.

1964. Shubow, David. "Sponge Fishing on the Florida East Coast,"
       Tequesta 29(1969):3-15.

1965. Tilden, Paul M. "Donax the Builder," Rocks and Minerals
       29(1954):571-73.

       D. Agriculture and Related Industries

1966. Arnade, Charles W. "Cattle Raising in Spanish Florida,
       1513-1763," Ag. Hist. 35(1961):116-24.

1967. Baker, Harry Lee. Forest Fires in Florida. Jacksonville:
       Florida Forestry Association, 1926.

1968. Broadus, Edmund Kemper. "The Reclamation of an Indus-
       try [Orange Industry After the Freezes of 1894-1895],"
Gulf State Hist. Mag. 1(1903):262-67.

1969. Brown, Mercer W. "The Parson Brown Orange," F. H. Q.
       30(1951):129-32.

1970.   Clark, Morita Mason. "The Development of the Citrus In-
        dustry in Florida Before 1895." Master's thesis, Florida
State University, 1947.

1971.   Crist, Raymond E. "The Citrus Industry in Florida [1565-
        1953]," Am. J. Econ. and Sociol. 15(1955):1-12.

1972.   Dacy, George H. Four Centuries of Florida Ranching. St.
        Louis: Privately Printed, Britt Printing Company, [1940].

1973.   Davis, T. Frederick. "Early Orange Culture in Florida
        and the Epochal Cold of 1835," F. H. Q. 15(1937):232-41.

1974.   Dodd, Dorothy. "The Manufacture of Cotton in Florida Be-
        fore and During the Civil War," F. H. Q. 13(1934):3-15.

1975.   _____. "The Manufacture of Cotton in Florida, Before
        and During the Civil War," Tallahassee Historical Society
Annual 2(1935):1-7.

1976.   Dodson, Pat. "Hamilton Disston's St. Cloud Sugar Planta-
        tion, 1887-1901," F. H. Q. 49(1971):356-69.

1977.   Dorn, Harold W. "Mango Growing Around Early Miami,"
        Tequesta 16(1956):37-53.

1978.   Dupont, C. H. "History of the Introduction and Culture of
        Cuba Tobacco in Florida," F. H. Q. 6(1928):149-55.

1979.   Florida. Department of Agriculture. Citrus Industry of
        Florida. Tallahassee: Florida Department of Agriculture,
1955.

1980.   Gober, William. "Lumbering in Florida [1743-1956]," S.
        Lumberman 193(1956):164-66.

1981.   Graham, William A. "The Pennsuco Sugar Experiment,"
        Tequesta 11(1951):27-49.

1982.   Harper, Roland McMillan. "History of Soil Investigation in
        Florida and Description of the New Soil Map." In Florida
Geological Survey, 1907-   . 17th Annual Report. Tallahassee,
1926.

1983.   _____. "Natural Resources of Southern Florida." In
        Florida Geological Survey, 1907-   . 18th Annual Report.
Tallahassee, 1927.

1984.   Holmes, Jack D. L. "Louisiana Trees and Their Uses:
        Colonial Period," La. Studies 8(1969):36-67.

1985.   _____. "Naval Stores in Colonial Louisiana and the
        Floridas," La. Studies 7(1968):295-309.

1986. _____. "Observations on the Wax-Tree in Colonial
       Louisiana and the Floridas, " Miss. Q. 20(1966):47-52.

1987. Hopkins, James T. Fifty Years of Citrus: The Florida
       Citrus Exchange, 1909-1959. Gainesville: University of
Florida Press, 1960.

1988. Jordan, Weymouth T., ed. Herbs, Hoecakes, and Husban-
       dry: The Daybook of a Planter of the Old South. Florida
State University Studies, No. 34. Tallahassee: Florida State University, 1960.

1989. La Dunca, Charles Edward. "A Preliminary Study of the
       Tobacco Industry in Gadsden County, Florida." Master's
thesis, Florida State University, 1949.

1990. Lathrop, Harry Owen. "Distribution and Development of
       the Beef Cattle Industry of Florida [since 1910], " J. Geog.
50(1951):133-44.

1991. Leon, Joseph Manuel. "The Cigar Industry and Cigar Leaf
       Tobacco in Florida During the Nineteenth Century." Mas-
ter's thesis, Florida State University, 1962.

1992. Linn, Edward R. "Florida's Forests are Different, " Am.
       Forests 54(1948):76-78, 94.

1993. McPhee, John. Oranges. New York: Farrar, Straus, and
       Giroux, 1967.

1994. Massey, Richard W., Jr. "A History of the Lumber In-
       dustry in Alabama and West Florida, 1880-1914." Ph.D.
dissertation, Vanderbilt University, 1960.

1995. Mayo, Nathan. Activities of the Florida State Department
       of Agriculture: A Review of the Departments and Divisions,
the Activities and Functions, the Growth and Enlargements That
Have Marked Its Progress for a Quarter of a Century [1925-55].
Tallahassee: Florida Department of Agriculture, 1955.

1996. Moore, Theophilus Wilson. Treatise and Hand-book of
       Orange Culture in Florida. New York: E. R. Pelton and
Company, 1881.

1997. Paisley, Clifton. "Thirty Cent Cotton at Lloyd, Florida, "
       F.H.Q. 49(1971):219-31.

1998. Rummel, Virginia C. "Crackers and Cattle Kings, " Améri-
       cas 22(1970):36-41.

1999. Siebert, Wilbur H. "The Early Sugar Industry in Florida,"
       F.H.Q. 35(1957):312-19.

2000. Smith, Julia F. "Cotton and the Factorage System in Ante-
      bellum Florida," F. H. Q. 49(1970):36-48.

2001. Tyson, Willie Kate. "History of the Utilization of the Long-
      leaf Pine (Pinus Palustris) in Florida From 1513 Until the
Twentieth Century." Master's thesis, University of Florida, 1956.

2002. Van Holmes, Jeanne. "The Big Cypress," Am. Forests
      61(1955):28-31.

      E. Labor-Management History

2003. Amundson, Richard J. "Henry S. Sanford and Labor Prob-
      lems in the Florida Orange Industry [1870]," F. H. Q.
43(1965):229-43.

2004. Appel, John Conrad. "The Unionization of Florida Cigar-
      makers and the Coming of the War With Spain [1893-98],"
Hisp. Am. Hist. Rev. 36(1956):38-49.

2005. Atkins, Emily Howard. "The 1913 Campaign for Child La-
      bor in Florida," F. H. Q. 35(1957):233-45.

2006. Burton, M. Dudley. "Florida Workmen's Compensation,
      1935 to 1950," Miami Law Q. 5(1950):74-92.

2007. Carper, N. Gordon. "The Convict-Lease System in Florida,
      1866-1923." Ph. D. dissertation, Florida State University,
1964.

2008. Flynt, Wayne. "Pensacola Labor Problems and Political
      Radicalism, 1908," F. H. Q. 43(1965):315-32.

2009. Grubbs, Donald H. "The Story of Florida's Migrant Farm
      Workers," F. H. Q. 40(1961):103-12.

2010. Long, Durward. " 'La Resistencia' Tampa's Immigrant La-
      bor Union," Labor Hist. 6(1965):193-213.

2011. _____. "The Open-Closed Shop Battle in Tampa's Cigar
      Industry, 1919-1921," F. H. Q. 47(1968):101-21.

2012. Lowe, John William. "Union Security in Florida Industries
      Under the Right-to-Work Amendment [to the Florida Consti-
tution, 1944-55]." Ph. D. dissertation, University of Florida, 1956.

XXIV.   TRANSPORTATION

        A.   Railroads

2013.   Adams, O. Burton.   "Construction of Florida's Overseas
        Railway," Apalachee 7(1968-70):5-19.

2014.   Atlantic Coast Line Railroad Company.   The Story of the
        Atlantic Coast Line, 1830-1930.   Wilmington, N. C.: Wil-
mington Stamp and Printing Company, 1930.

2015.   Bathe, Grenville.   The St. Johns Railroad, 1858-1895.   St.
        Augustine's Record Press, for the St. Augustine Historical
Society, 1958.

2016.   Blake, Sallie E.   "Old Street Railway of Tallahassee,"
        Tallahassee Historical Society Annual 2(1935):34-36.

2017.   Browne, Jefferson B.   "Across the Gulf by Rail to Key
        West," Nat. Geo. Mag. 7(1896):204-07.

2018.   "Building of the Overseas Railroad," Martello 1(1964):6-8.

2019.   Corliss, Carlton Jonathan.   "Building the Overseas Railway
        to Key West," Tequesta 13(1953):3-21.

2020.   _____ .   "Henry M. Flagler--Railroad Builder," F. H. Q.
        38(1960):195-205.

2021.   _____ .   "The Iron Horse on the Florida Keys," Tequesta
        29(1969):17-26.

2022.   Davis, T. Frederick.   "Pioneer Florida: The First Rail-
        roads," F. H. Q.   23(1945):177-83.

2023.   Dodd, Dorothy.   "Railroad Projects in Territorial Florida."
        Master's thesis, Florida State University, 1929.

2024.   _____ .   "The Tallahassee Railroad and the Town of St.
        Marks," Apalachee (1950-56):1-12.

2025.   Dovell, Junius Elmore.   "The Railroads and the Public
        Lands of Florida, 1879-1905," F. H. Q.   34(1956):236-58.

2026.   Fenlon, Paul E.   "The Florida, Atlantic, and Gulf Central
        R. R.:   The First Railroad in Jacksonville [1855-60],"
F. H. Q.   32(1953):71-80.

2027.   _____ .   "The Notorious Swepson-Littlefield Fraud; Rail-
        road Financing in Florida, 1868-1871," F. H. Q.   32(1954):
        231-61.

2028. _____ . "The Struggle for Control of the Florida Central
       Railroad (1867-1882)." Ph. D. dissertation, University of
Florida, 1955.

2029. _____ . "The Struggle for Control of the Florida Central
       Railroad, 1867-1882," F. H. Q. 34(1956):213-35.

2030. Florida East Coast Railway Company. The Story of a Pi-
       oneer, a Brief History of the Florida East Coast Railway.
St. Augustine: Record Press, 1936.

2031. Hildreth, Charles H. "Railroads Out of Pensacola, 1833-
       1883," F. H. Q. 37(1959):397-417.

2032. Johnson, Dudley S. "The Florida Railroad After the Civil
       War," F. H. Q. 47(1969):292-309.

2033. _____ . "The Railroads of Florida, 1865-1900." Ph. D.
       dissertation, Florida State University, 1965.

2034. Joubert, William A. "A History of the Seaboard Air Line
       Railway." Master's thesis, University of Florida, 1935.

2035. Layng, Charles. "Cars Across the Sea," Ships and the Sea
       2(1953):18-19.

2036. Long, Durward. "Florida's First Railroad Commission,
       1887-1891," F. H. Q. 42(1963):103-24; (1964):248-57.

2037. McCullough, Mildred. "Legislative Regulation of Florida
       Railroads From Statehood to 1897." Master's thesis, Flori-
da State University, 1940.

2038. Parks, Pat. The Railroad That Died at Sea: The Florida
       East Coast; Key West Extension. Brattleboro, Vt.: Step-
hen Green Press, 1968.

2039. Pettengill, George Warren, Jr. The Story of the Florida
       Railroads, 1834-1903. Boston: Railway & Locomotive His-
torical Society, 1952. [Railway and Locomotive Hist. Soc. Bull.
86(1952).]

2040. Railway & Locomotive Historical Society. "Additions and
       Corrections to Locomotive Rosters of the Florida Railroads
in Bulletin 86," Railway and Locomotive Hist. Soc. Bull. 88(1953):
86-99.

2041. Roberts, Merrill, J. Taxation of Railroad and Other State-
       assessed Companies in Florida [1950-51]. Tallahassee:
Florida State University, 1957.

2042. Shappee, Nathan D. "The Celestial Railroad to Juno [Jupi-
       ter and Lake Worth R. R. 1890+]," F. H. Q. 40(1962):329-49.

2043.   Shofner, Jerrell H. and William Warren Rogers.   "Con-
        federate Railroad Construction: The Live Oak to Lawton
Connector, " F. H. Q. 43(1965):217-28.

2044.   Thompson, Arthur William.   "The Railroad Background of
        the Florida Senatorial Election of 1851, " F. H. Q. 31(1953):
181-95.

2045.   Willing, David L.   "Florida's Overseas Railroad, " F. H. Q.
        35(1957):287-302.

        B.   Waterways

2046.   Barbour, Ralph Henry.   Pirates of the Shoals.   New York:
        Femar and Rinehart, 1932.

2047.   Bennett, Charles E.   "Early History of the Cross-Florida
        Barge Canal, " F. H. Q. 45(1966):132-44.

2048.   Brookfield, Charles M.   "Cape Florida Light, " Tequesta
        9(1949):5-12.

2049.   Brown, Carl Raymond.   "The Peninsular & Occidental
        Steamship Company--Fifty Years of Service [Miami-Havana,
1900-1955], " Steamboat Bill of Facts 13(1956):25-30.

2050.   Carse, Robert.   Keepers of the Lights: A History of
        American Lighthouses.   New York: Charles Scribners'
Sons, 1969.

2051.   Chamberlain, Robert S.   "Discovery of the Bahama Chan-
        nel, " Tequesta 8(1948):109-16.

2052.   Corse, Herbert M.   "Names of the St. Johns River, "
        F. H. Q. 21(1942):127-34.

2053.   DeBerard, Ella Teaque.   Steamboats in the Hyacinths.
        Daytona Beach: College Publishing Co. , 1956.

2054.   Dodd, Dorothy.   "The Steamboats Home and Pulaski, "
        Apalachee 4(1950-56):66-75.

2055.   _____, ed.   " 'Volunteers' Report Destruction of Light-
        houses, " Tequesta 14(1954):67-70.

2056.   DuBois, Bessie Wilson.   "Jupiter Lighthouse, " Tequesta
        20(1960):5-17.

2057.   Green, A. A.   "Cape Florida Light, " D. A. R. Mag.
        87(1953):1049-50.

2058.   Hunn, Max and Bob French. "The Transmutation of Bay Mabel," Ships and the Sea 3(1955):20-21.

2059.   Jacksonville Seafarer. "34-foot Channel is Open," Jacksonville Seafarer 1(1953):4-5.

2060.   Manier, John T. "Tall Stacks and Paddlewheels: Colorful History of Merrill-Stevens Dry Dock and Repair Company," Jacksonville Seafarer 1(1953):10-13.

2061.   Mayo, Lawrence Shaw. The St. Mary's River, a Boundary. Boston: Privately Printed by T. R. Marvin & Son, Printers, 1914.

2062.   Mitchell, C. Bradford. "Paddle-Wheel Inboard," Am. Neptune 7(1947):115-66;224-39.

2063.   Mueller, Edward A. "East Coast Florida Steamboating, 1831-1861," F. H. Q. 40(1962):241-60.

2064.   _____. "Florida's Clipper Ship," Tequesta 27(1967):3-6.

2065.   _____. "Kissimmee Steamboating," Tequesta 26(1966): 53-87.

2066.   _____. "Suwannee River Steamboating," F. H. Q. 45(1967): 271-88.

2067.   Owens, Harry P. "Port of Apalachicola," F. H. Q. 48(1969): 1-25.

2068.   _____. "Sail and Steam Vessels Serving the Apalachicola-Chattahoochee Valley [1828-1861]," Ala. Rev. 21(1968):195-210.

2069.   Peterson, Mendel L. The Last Cruise of H. M. S. "Loo." Washington, D. C.: Smithsonian Institution, 1955.

2070.   Rawls, Oscar G. "Ninety-six Years of Engineering Development on the St. Johns River [1835-1949]," Papers of the Jacksonville Historical Society 2(1949):45-61.

2071.   Redfearn, D. H. "The Steamboat Home--Presumption as to Order of Death in Common Calamity," Fla. Law J. 9(1935): 405-24.

2072.   Rogers, Benjamin F. "The Florida Ship Canal," F. H. Q. 36(1957):14-23.

2073.   Ryan, Lanue B. "The Cross-Florida Barge Canal: Fact or Folly," Apalachee 7(1968-70):130-42.

2074. Sewell, J. Richard. "Cross-Florida Barge Canal, 1927-1968, " F. H. Q. 46(1968):369-83.

2075. Somerville, J. W. "The Steamer Queen of St. Johns, " Am. Neptune 9(1949):298-99.

2076. Vernon, Robert O. Trans-Florida Barge Canal. Tallahassee: Florida Geological Survey, 1959.

2077. Voss, Gilbert L. "The Orange Grove House of Refuge No. 3, " Tequesta 28(1968):3-17.

2078. Will, Lawrence E. "Digging the Cape Sable Canal, " Tequesta 19(1959):29-63.

          C. Road and Air

2079. Boyd, Mark F., ed. "The First American Road in Florida, Papers Relating to the Survey and Construction of the Pensacola-St. Augustine Highway, " F. H. Q. 14(1935):73-106; (1936):139-92.

2080. Cash, W. T. "Roads of Early Days in Florida, " Fla. Highways 9(1931):20-21.

2081. Derrick, David Surridge. "The Sunshine Skyway: Its Influence on Some Land-use and Economic Developments in St. Petersburg, Florida. " Master's thesis, Florida State University, 1960.

2082. Dovell, Junius Elmore. The State Road Department of Florida. Gainesville: Public Administration Clearing Service of the University of Florida, 1955.

2083. Goza, William M. "The Fort King Road--1963 [built 1825], " F. H. Q. 43(1964):52-70.

2084. Hebel, Ianthe B. "The King's Road, " J. Halifax Hist. Soc. 2(1957):30-31.

2085. Hunt, Richard H. "Aviation and Airports in Florida, " Fla. Law J. 22(1948):72-79.

2086. Kendrick, Baynard. Florida Trails to Turnpikes, 1914-1964. Gainesville: University of Florida Press, 1964.

2087. Lazarus, William C. Wings in the Sun: The Annals of Aviation in Florida [1895-1950]. Orlando: Tyn Cobb's Florida Press, 1951.

2088. Smith, H. D., Jr. "The Florida Highway Patrol, " Apalachee 7(1968-70):47-60.

2089.   Walker, James Lorenzo. "Dedication of Tamiami Trial
        Marker, " Tequesta 19(1959):23-28.

        D.   Shipwreck and Salvage

2090.   Brookfield, Charles M.   "Cannon on Florida Reefs Solve
        Mystery of Sunken Ship Wreck of H. M. S. Winchester, "
        Nat. Geo. Mag. 80(1941):807-27.

2091.   Cheetham, Joseph M.   "Wreck on the Reef, " Tequesta
        18(1958):3-5.

2092.   Davis, T. Frederick.   "Pioneer Florida: Indian Key and
        Wrecking in 1833, " F. H. Q. 22(1943):57-61.

2093.   Diddle, Albert W.   "Adjudication of Shipwrecking Claims at
        Key West in 1831, " Tequesta 6(1946):44-49.

2094.   Dodd, Dorothy.   "Jacob Housman [1799-1841] of Indian Key,"
        Tequesta 8(1948):3-19.

2095.   _____ .   "The Wrecking Business on the Florida Reef,
        1822-1860, " F. H. Q. 22(1944):171-99.

2096.   Dubois, Bessie Wilson.   "The Wreck of the Victor [in Jupi-
        ter Inlet 1872], " Tequesta 23(1963):15-22.

2097.   Gilpin, Vincent.   "Brandish W. Johnson, Master Wrecker;
        1846-1914, " Tequesta 1(1941):21-32.

2098.   Hammond, E. A. , ed.   "Wreckers and Wrecking on the
        Florida Reef, " F. H. Q. 41(1963):239-73.

2099.   "In Defense of the Wreckers; the New York Times of July
        7, 1954 Compares Their Services to the Art of the Physi-
        cian, " Martello 1(1964):9-10.

2100.   "Key West and Salvage in 1850, " F. H. Q. 8(1929):47-63.

2101.   Marx, Robert F.   Shipwrecks in Florida Waters.   Eau
        Gallie: Scott Publishing Company, 1969.

2102.   Peterson, Mendel L.   History Under the Sea: Underwater
        Exploration of Shipwrecks.   Washington, D. C.: Smithsonian
        Institution, 1954.

2103.   Saunders, William H.   "The Wreck of Houseboat No. 4,
        October 1906, " Tequesta 19(1959):15-21.

2104.   Scott, Kenneth.   " 'The City of Wreckers, ' Two Key West
        Letters of 1838, " F. H. Q. 25(1946):191-201.

2105. Shepard, Birse. Lore of the Wreckers. Boston: Beacon
       Press, 1961.

2106. "Wrecks, Wrecking, Wreckers, and Wreckees on Florida
       Reef, " Hunt's Merchants Mag. 6(1842): 349-54.

XXV.   THE INDIAN IN FLORIDA [See also Sections 9G and 10-B,
       C, and D]

2107. Alden, John Richard. "The Albany Congress and the Crea-
       tion of the Indian Superintendencies, " Miss. Val. Hist. Rev.
27(1940): 193-210.

2108. _____. John Stuart and the Southern Colonial Frontier.
       Ann Arbor: University of Michigan Press, 1944.

2109. Andrews, Charles M. "The Florida Indians in the Seven-
       teenth Century, " Tequesta 1(1943): 36-48.

2110. Boyd, Mark F. "Horatio S. Dexter and Events Leading to
       the Treaty of Moultrie Creek With the Seminole Indians, "
Fla. Anthro. 11(1958): 65-94.

2111. Blassingame, Wyatt. Seminoles of Florida. Tallahassee:
       Florida Department of Agriculture, 1959.

2112. Brannon, Peter A. "The Pensacola Indian Trade, " F. H. Q.
       31(1952): 1-15.

2113. Brown, Tom O. "Locating Seminole Indian War Forts
       [Fort Clinch at Frostproof], " F. H. Q. 40(1967): 310-13.

2114. Bullen, Ripley P. "Southern Limit of Timucua Territory, "
       F. H. Q. 47(1969): 414-19.

2115. Capron, Louis. "Florida's Emerging Seminoles, " Nat. Geo.
       Mag. 136(1969): 716-34.

2116. _____. "The Medicine Bundles of the Florida Seminole
       and the Green Corn Dance, " Bull. Bureau Am. Ethnology
151(1953): 155-210.

2117. Casey, R. R. "Tree Kings of the Everglades, " S. W. Lore
       8(1942): 20-24.

2118. Chaney, Margaret A. "A Tribal History of the Seminole In-
       dians. " Master's thesis, University of Oklahoma, 1928.

2119. Coe, Charles H. Red Patriots: The Story of the Semi-
       noles. Cincinnati: The Editor Publishing Company, 1898.

2120. Corkran, David H. The Creek Frontier, 1540-1783. Nor-
       man: University of Oklahoma Press, 1967.

2121. Corse, Carita Doggett. Shrine of the Water Gods. Gaines-
       ville: Paper Printing Company, 1935.

2122. Cotterill, R. S. The Southern Indians; the Story of the
       Civilized Tribes Before Removal. Norman: University of
Oklahoma Press, 1954.

2123. Covington, James W. "The Apalachee Indians Move West,"
       Fla. Anthro. 17(1964):221-25.

2124. _____, ed. "The Florida Seminoles in 1847," Tequesta
       24(1964):49-57.

2125. _____. "Migration of the Seminoles Into Florida, 1700-
       1820," F. H. Q. 46(1968):340-57.

2126. _____. "A Seminole Census: 1847," Fla. Anthro.
       21(1968):120-22.

2127. _____. "White Control of Seminole Leadership," Fla.
       Anthro. 18(1965):137-46.

2128. Craig, Alan, and David McJunkin. "Stranahan's: Last of
       the Seminole Trading Posts," Fla. Anthro. 24(1971):45-50.

2129. Cubberly, F. "Malee, Pocahontas of Florida," Nat. Rep.
       21(1933):21-22.

2130. Davis, Hilda J. "The History of Seminole Clothing and Its
       Multicolored Designs [1838-1954]," Am. Anthro. 57(1955):
974-80.

2131. Davis, T. Frederick. "Milly Francis and Duncan McKrim-
       mon; an Authentic Florida Pocahontas," F. H. Q. 21(1943):
254-65.

2132. Densmore, Frances. Seminole Music. Washington, D. C.:
       U. S. Government Printing Office, 1956.

2133. _____. "Three Parallels Between the Seminole Indians
       and the Ancient Greeks [Florida, 1931-33]," Masterkey
25(1951):76-78.

2134. Doering, Frederick J. "Legends From Canada, Indiana,
       and Florida," S. Folklore Q. 2(1938):213-20.

174   Florida History

2135.   Drew. Frank, "Florida Place-names of Indian Origin,"
        F. H. Q. 6(1928):197-205.

2136.   . "Notes on the Origin of the Seminole Indians of
        Florida," F. H. Q. 6(1927):21-24.

2137.   . "Some Florida Place Names of Indian Origin,"
        F. H. Q. 4(1926):181-82.

2138.   East, Omega G. "Apache Indians in Fort Marion, 1886-
        1887," El Escribano (1969):11-27; (1969):3-23; (1969):4-23;
(1969):20-38.

2139.   , and Albert C. Manucy. "Arizona Apaches as
        'Guests' in Florida [1886-87]," F. H. Q. 30(1952):294-300.

2140.   Ehrmann, W. W. "The Timucua Indians of Sixteenth Cen-
        tury Florida," F. H. Q. 18(1940):168-91.

2141.   Elderdice, D. "Pocahontas of Florida," Mentor 16(1928):
        56-57.

2142.   Ellis, Leonora B. "The Seminoles of Florida," Gunton's
        Mag. 25(1903):495-505.

2143.   Emerson, William Canfield. The Seminoles, Dwellers of
        the Everglades: The Land, History, and Culture of the
Florida Indians [1750-1953]. New York: Exposition Press, 1954.

2144.   Foreman, Grant. The Five Civilized Tribes. Norman:
        University of Oklahoma Press, 1934.

2145.   Freeman, Ethel Cutler. "Two Types of Cultural Response
        to External Pressures Among the Florida Seminoles," An-
thro. Q. 38(1965):55-61.

2146.   Gallaher, Art, Jr. "A Survey of the Seminole Freedmen."
        Master's thesis, University of Oklahoma, 1951.

2147.   Gifford, John C. "Five Plants Essential to the Indians and
        Early Settlers of Florida," Tequesta 1(1944):36-44.

2148.   Goggin, John M. "A Florida Indian Trading Post, Circa
        1763-1784," S. Indian Stud. 1(1949):35-38.

2149.   . Indian and Spanish Selected Writings. Coral
        Gables: University of Miami Press, 1964.

2150.   . "The Indians and History of the Matecumbe Re-
        gion [1513-1840]," Tequesta 10(1950):13-24.

2151.   . "The Seminole Negroes of Andros Island, Ba-
        hamas," F. H. Q. 24(1946):201-06.

2152. _____. "Silver Work of the Florida Seminole," El Palacio 43(1940):25-32.

2153. _____. "The Tekesta Indians of Southern Florida," F. H. Q. 18(1940):274-84.

2154. Gonciar, B. "Indian Princess of Florida: Ulehlah, Daughter of Ucita, Chief of the Hirrihigua Tribe," Hobbies 52(1948):124.

2155. Goodyear, Albert C. "Pinellas Point: A Possible Site of Continuous Indian Habitation," Fla. Anthro. 21(1968):74-82.

2156. Greenlee, Robert F. "Cerimonial Practices of the Modern Seminoles," Tequesta 1(1942):25-33.

2157. _____. "Folktales of the Florida Seminole," J. Am. Folklore Assn. 58(1945):138-44.

2158. _____. "Medicine and Curing Practices of the Modern Florida Seminoles," Am. Anthro. 46(1944):317-28.

2159. Greenman, E. F. "Hopewellian Traits in Florida," Am. Antiquities 3(1938):327-32.

2160. Griffin, John W., ed. The Florida Indian and His Neighbors. Winter Park: Rollins College Press, 1949.

2161. _____. "Some Comments on the Seminole in 1818," Fla. Anthro. 10(1957):41-49.

2162. Haas, Mary R. "The Position of Apalachee in the Muskogean Family," Inter. J. Am. Linguistics 15(1949):121-27.

2163. Harrison, Benjamin. "Home Life of the Florida Indians," F. H. Q. 3(1924):17-28.

2164. _____. "Indian Races of Florida," F. H. Q. 3(1924):29-37.

2165. Harshberger, Emmet Leroy. "A Brief History of the Seminole Indians." Master's thesis, Ohio State University, 1929.

2166. Holmes, Jack D. L. "The Southern Boundary Commission, the Chattahooche River, and the Florida Seminoles, 1799," F. H. Q. 44(1966):312-41.

2167. _____. "Spanish Treaties With West Florida Indians, 1784-1802," F. H. Q. 48(1969):140-54.

2168. Kennedy, Stetson. "Nanigo in Florida," S. Folklore Q. 4(1940):153-56.

2169.   Kersey, Harra A., Jr.   "Educating the Seminole Indians of
        Florida 1879-1970, " F.H.Q. 49(1970):16-35.

2170.   Kiker, Ernest.   "Education Among the Seminole Indians. "
        Master's thesis, Oklahoma A & M, 1932.

2171.   Krogman, Wilton Marian.   "The Radical Composition of the
        Seminole Indians of Florida and Oklahoma, " J. Neg. Hist.
19(1934):412-30.

2172.   Laxson, D. D.   "A Historic Seminole Burial in a Hialeah
        Midden [Dade County, 'mid-19th-century'], " Fla. Anthro.
7(1954):111-18.

2173.   Lightfoot, Eloise Arlene.   "The Seminoles of Florida. "
        Master's thesis, Stetson University, 1931.

2174.   MacCauley, C.   "The Seminole Indians of Florida, " An.
        Rep. Bur. Am. Ethnology 5(1884):469-531.

2175.   McKenney, Thomas Lorraine.   Memoirs, Official and Per-
        sonal, With Sketches of Travels Among Northern and South-
ern Indians.   New York: Paine and Burgess, 1846.

2176.   McNicoll, Robert E.   "The Caloosa Village Tequesta: A
        Miami of the Sixteenth Century, " Tequesta 1(1941):11-20.

2177.   McReynolds, Edwin C.   The Seminoles.   Norman: Univer-
        sity of Oklahoma Press, 1957.

2178.   Marmon, K. A.   The Seminole Indians of Florida.   River-
        side, Calif.: Sherman Institute, 1956.

2179.   Miller, Josephine Eugenia.   "The Culture of the Florida
        Seminoles. " Master's thesis, University of Southern Cali-
fornia, 1931.

2180.   Miller, Lou Whitfield.   "Mallee, " Tallahassee Historical
        Society Annual 3(1937):22-26.

2181.   Neill, Wilfred T.   "The Calumet Ceremony of the Seminole
        Indians [1765-1838], " Fla. Anthro. 8(1955):83-88.

2182.   . "Dugouts of the Mikasuki Seminole, " Fla. Anthro.
6(1953):77-84.

2183.   . Florida's Seminole Indians [since 1750].   Silver
        Springs: Ross Allen's Reptile Institute, 1952.

2184.   . "The Identity of Florida's 'Spanish Indians, ' "
        Fla. Anthro. 8(1955):43-57.

2185. _____. "Preparation of Rubber by the Florida Seminole," Fla. Anthro. 9(1956):25-8.

2186. _____. "Sailing Vessels of the Florida Seminole [19th century]," Fla. Anthro. 9(1956):79-86.

2187. Peithmann, Irvin M. The Unconquered Seminole Indians: Pictorial History of the Seminole Indians [since ca. 1775]. St. Petersburg: Great Outdoors Association, [1956].

2188. Porter, Kenneth Wiggins. "The Cowkeeper Dynasty of the Seminole Nation [1740?-1884?]," F.H.Q. 30(1952):341-49.

2189. _____. "Davy Crockett and John Horse," Am. Lit. 15(1943):10-15.

2190. _____. "Farewell to John Horse," Phylon 8(1947):265-73.

2191. _____. "The Founder of the 'Seminole Nation': Secoffee or Cowkeeper [1717-85]?" F.H.Q. 27(1949):362-84.

2192. _____. "Notes on the Seminole Negroes in the Bahamas," F.H.Q. 24(1945):56-60.

2193. _____. "Origins of the St. John's River Seminole: Were They Mikasuki?" Fla. Anthol. 4(1951):39-45.

2194. _____. "Relations Between Negroes and Indians Within the Present Limits of the United States," J. Neg. Hist. 17(1932):287-368.

2195. _____. "The Seminole in Mexico, 1850-1861," Hisp. Am. Hist. Rev. 31(1951):1-36.

2196. _____. "The Seminole Negro-Indian Scouts, 1870-1881," S.W. Hist. Q. 55(1952):358-77.

2197. _____. "Thlonoto-Sassa: A Note on an Obscure Seminole Village of the Early 1820's," Fla. Anthro. 13(1960):115-19.

2198. _____. "Wildcats Death and Burial," Chron. Okla. 21(1943):41-43.

2199. Pratt, Richard Henry. Battlefield and Classroom: Four Decades With the American Indian, 1867-1904. Edited by Robert M. Utley. New Haven: Yale University Press, 1964.

2200. Pratt, Theodore. Seminole: A Drama of the Florida Indian. Gainesville: University of Florida Press, 1953.

2201.   Rainey, F. G. "An Indian Burial Site at Crystal River,
        Florida," F. H. Q. 13(1935):185-92.

2202.   Read, William Alexander. Florida Place-names of Indian
        Origin and Seminole Personal Names. Baton Rouge, La.:
Louisiana State University Press, 1934.

2203.   Schell, Rolfe F. 1, 000 Years on Mound Key. The Story
        of the Caloosa Indians on West Coast Florida, Centering
Around Ft. Myers Beach and Its Surrounding Bay Waters.... Ft.
Myers Beach, 1962.

2204.   Simmons, William Hayne. Notices of East Florida, With
        an Account of the Seminole Nation of Indians.... Charles-
ton: Printed for the Author by A. E. Miller, 1822.

2205.   Skinner, Alanson. "Notes on the Florida Seminole," Am.
        Anthro. 15(1913):63-78.

2206.   Small, J. K. "Seminole Bread--The Conti," J. N. Y. Bo-
        tanical Garden 22(1921):121-37.

2207.   Smith, Hale G. "The European and the Indian: European-
        Indian Contacts in Georgia and Florida," Fla. Anthro.
9(1956):whole no.

2208.   Spellman, Charles W. "The Agriculture of Early North
        Florida Indians," Fla. Anthro. 1(1948):37-48.

2209.   Spoehr, Alexander. Camp, Clan, and Kin Among the Cow
        Creek Seminole of Florida. Chicago: Field Museum Press,
1941.

2210.   Sturtevant, William C. "Chakaika and the 'Spanish Indians':
        Documentary Sources Compared With Seminole Tradition,"
Tequesta 13(1953):35-73.

2211.   _____. "The Medicine Bundles and Busks of the Florida
        Seminole," Fla. Anthro. 7(1954):31-70.

2212.   _____. "A Newly-Discovered 1838 Drawing of a Semi-
        nole Dance," Fla. Anthro. 15(1962):73-82.

2213.   _____, ed. "R. H. Pratts Report on the Seminole in
        1879," Fla. Anthro. 9(1956):1-24.

2214.   _____. "A Seminole Personal Document," Tequesta
        16(1956):55-75.

2215.   Swanton, John R. Early History of the Creek Indians and
        Their Neighbors. Smithsonian Institution, Bureau of Ameri-
can Ethnology, Bulletin No. 73. Washington, D. C.: Government
Printing Office, 1922.

2216. U. S. Bureau of Indian Affairs. The Seminole Indians of Florida: A Summary of Seminole Indian History, Indian Bureau Activities, and Social, Religious, Educational, and Economic Conditions. [n. p., 1956.]

2217. Van Beck, John C., and Linda M. Van Beck. "The Marco Midden, Marco Island, Florida, " Fla. Anthro. 18(1965):1-20.

2218. Wager, Ralph E. "An Indian Stockade and Fort in Northwest Florida, " F. H. Q. 40(1962):417-21.

2219. Wallace, Fred W. "The Story of Captain John C. Casey, " F. H. Q. 41(1962):127-44.

2220. Wardle, H. Newell. "The Pile Dwellers of Key Marco, " Archaeol. 4(1951):181-86.

2221. Webb, Helen Amelia. "The Seminoles in Modern Times." Master's thesis, Florida State University, 1940.

2222. Welsh, Herbert. Apache Prisoners in Fort Marion, St. Augustine, Florida. Philadelphia: Office of the Indian Rights Association, 1887.

2223. Willey, Gordon R. "Culture Sequence in the Manatee Region of West Florida, " Am. Antiquities 13(1948):209-18.

2224. _____. Excavations in Southeast Florida. University Publications in Anthropology, No. 42. New Haven: Yale University Press, 1949.

2225. _____. "The Florida Indian and His Neighbors: A Summary." In The Florida Indian and His Neighbors, edited by John W. Griffen. Winter Park: Rollins College, 1949. pp. 139-67.

2226. Wilson, Minnie Moore. The Birds of the Everglades and Their Neighbors the Seminole Indians. Tampa: Tampa Tribune Publishing Company, 1931.

2227. _____. "Glimpses of Seminole Life, " Fla. Mag. 2(1901):227-30.

2228. _____. "The Seminole Indians of Florida, " F. H. Q. 7(1928):75-87.

2229. _____. The Seminoles of Florida. Philadelphia: American Printing House, 1896.

2230. _____. "Seminoles of Florida. Relationship to the Aztecs and Eastern Tribes, " Fla. Mag. 4(1902):5-11.

2231. _____. "Tales From an Old Bandana Mammy. Dat Seminole Treaty Dinner," Fla. Mag. 6(1903):29-33.

2232. Work Projects Administration, Florida Writer's Project. The Seminole Indians in Florida. Tallahassee: The Florida State Department of Agriculture, 1940.

XXVI. THE NEGRO IN FLORIDA [See also Section 10-D]

2233. Akerman, Robert Howard. "The Triumph of Modernization in Florida Thought and Politics: A Study Of The Race Issue From 1954 to 1960." Ph. D. dissertation, American University, 1967.

2234. Anderson, Robert L. "The End of an Idyll," F. H. Q. 42(1963):35-47.

2235. Barr, Ruth B., and Modeste Hargis. "The Voluntary Exile of Free Negroes of Pensacola," F. H. Q. 17(1938):3-14.

2236. Bates, Thelma. "The Legal Status of the Negro in Florida," F. H. Q. 6(1928):159-81.

2237. _____. "A Preliminary Study of the Legal Status of the Negro in Florida." Master's thesis, Florida State University, 1927.

2238. Bowman, Robert Lewis. "Negro Politics in Four Southern Counties." Ph. D. dissertation, University of North Carolina, 1964.

2239. Carleton, William Graves and Hugh Douglas Price. "America's Newest Voter: A Florida Case Study," Antioch R. 14(1954):441-57.

2240. "Dispatches of Spanish Officials Bearing on the Free Negro Settlement of Gracia Real de Santa Teresa de Mose, Florida [1688-1759]," J. Neg. Hist. 9(1924):144-95.

2241. Dodd, Dorothy. "The Schooner Emperor: An Incident Of The Illegal Slave Trade In Florida," F. H. Q. 13(1935):117-28.

2242. Doherty, Herbert J., Jr., ed. "A Free Negro Purchases His Daughter: Two Letters From The Richard Keith Call Collection," F. H. Q. 29(1950):38-43.

2243. Dresser, Amos. The Narrative of Amos Dresser, With Stone's Letters From Natchez. New York: American Anti-

Slavery Society, 1836.

2244.   Farris, Charles D. "The Reenfranchisement of Negroes in
        Florida [1889-1947]," J. Neg. Hist. 39(1954):259-83.

2245.   Garvin, Russell. "The Free Negro in Florida Before the
        Civil War," F. H. Q. 46(1967):1-17.

2246.   Gilliam, Farley M. "The 'Black Codes' of Florida," Apa-
        lachee 6(1963-67):111-20.

2247.   Hines, Margie Trapp. "Negro Suffrage and the Florida
        Election Laws, 1860-1950." Master's thesis, University
of North Carolina, 1953.

2248.   Jackson, Jesse Jefferson. "The Negro and the Law in
        Florida, 1821-1921: Legal Patterns Of Segregation And
Control In Florida, 1821-1921." Master's thesis, Florida State
University, 1960.

2249.   Johnston, J. H. "Documentary Evidence of the Relations
        of Negroes and Indians," J. Neg. Hist. 14(1929):21-43.

2250.   Kiple, Kenneth F. "The Case Against a Nineteenth Cen-
        tury Cuba--Florida Slave Trade," F. H. Q. 49(1971):346-55.

2251.   Lisenby, Julie Ann. "The Free Negro in Antebellum Flori-
        da." Master's thesis, Florida State University, 1967.

2252.   Mannix, Daniel P. and Malcolm Cowley. Black Cargoes:
        A History Of The Atlantic Slave Trade, 1518-1865. New
York: Viking Press, 1965.

2253.   Meier, August and Elliott Rudwick. "Negro Boycotts of
        Segregated Streetcars in Florida, 1901-1905," S. Atl. Q.
69(1970):525-33.

2254.   Murdoch, Richard K. "The Return of Runaway Slaves,
        1790-1794," F. H. Q. 38(1959):96-113.

2255.   Palmer, Henry E. "The Proctors---a True Story of Anti-
        Bellum Days and Since," Tallahassee Historical Society An-
nual 1(1934):14-16.

2256.   Parker, Rosalind. "The Proctors--Antonio, George, and
        John," Apalachee 2(1946):19-29.

2257.   Porter, Kenneth Wiggins. "Negroes and the East Florida
        Annexation Plot, 1811-1813," J. Neg. Hist. 30(1945):9-29.

2258.   _____. "Negroes on the Southern Frontier, 1670-1763,"
        J. Neg. Hist. 33(1948):53-78.

2259.   Price, Hugh Douglas. "The Negro and Florida Politics,
         1944-1954," J. Politics 17(1955):198-220.

2260.   . The Negro and Southern Politics; a Chapter of Flor-
         ida History. New York: New York University Press, 1957.

2261.   . "The Role of the Negro in Florida Politics:
         1944-1952." Master's thesis, University of Florida, 1953.

2262.   Prior, Leon O. "Lewis Payne, Pawn of John Wilkes
         Booth," F. H. Q. 43(1964):1-20.

2263.   Roady, Elston Edward. "The Expansion of Negro Suffrage
         in Florida (1940-57)," J. Neg. Ed. 26(1957):297-306.

2264.   Siebert, Wilbur H. "Slavery and White Servitude in East
         Florida, 1726-1776," F. H. Q. 10(1931):3-23.

2265.   . "Slavery in East Florida, 1776-1785," F. H. Q.
         10(1932):139-61.

2266.   Smith, Rhea. "Racial Strains in Florida," F. H. Q.
         11(1932):17-32.

2267.   Southall, Eugene Portlette. "Negroes in Florida Prior to
         the Civil War," J. Neg. Hist. 19(1934):77-86.

2268.   Stafford, Frances J. "Illegal Importations: Enforcement
         Of The Slave Trade Laws Along The Florida Coast, 1810-
         1828," F. H. Q. 46(1967):124-33.

2269.   Stakely, Charles A. "Introduction of the Negro Into the
         United States: Florida, Not Virginia, The First State To
         Receive Him," Mag. Am. Hist. (1891):349-63.

2270.   Williams, Edwin L., Jr. "Negro Slavery in Florida (1565-
         1863)," F. H. Q. 28(1949):93-110, 182-204.

2271.   Williamson, Edward C. "Black Belt Political Crisis: The
         Savage-James Lynching, 1882," F. H. Q. 45(1967):402-09.

2272.   Wilson, Theodore B. The Black Codes of the South. Ala-
         bama: University of Alabama Press, 1965.

Biography   183

XXVII.   BIOGRAPHY

       A.   Collected Biographies

2273.   Blackman, Lucy Worthington.   The Women of Florida.   2
        vols.   Jacksonville: Southern Historical Publishing Asso-
ciates,   1940.

2274.   Boldt, Albert Walter.   "The Honorary Leadership Frater-
        nity in American Society: a Survey Analysis of Florida
Blue Key Members and Nonmembers [since 1823]."   Ph.D. dissertation, University of Florida, 1956.

2275.   Jerome, Father.   Early Celts in America.   St. Leo: Ab-
        bey Press, 1962.

2276.   Florida Poets and Poets Visiting Florida...an Anthology of
        Poems Published in the Miami Daily News....   Dallas:
Manfred, VanNort and Company, 1931.

2277.   Hume, Harold H.   "Botanical Explorers of the Southeastern
        United States,"   F.H.Q.   21(1943):289-302.

2278.   Makers of America, an Historical and Biographical Work
        by an Able Corps of Writers.   2 vols.   Published under the
patronage of the Florida Historical Society, Jacksonville, Florida.
Atlanta: A. B. Caldwell, 1909.

2279.   Monroe, Mary Barr.   "Pioneer Women of Dade County,"
        Tequesta 1(1943):49-56.

2280.   Wagner, Henry J.   "Early Pioneers of South Florida [1840-
        80],"   Tequesta 9(1949):61-72.

       B.   Individual Biographies [alphabetical by subject]

2281.   Yonge, Julia J.   "Walker Anderson, 1801-1857,"   F.H.Q.
        11(1933):173-83.

2282.   Ford, Alice.   John James Audubon.   Norman: University
        of Oklahoma Press, 1964.

2283.   Pyburn, Nita Katharine.   "Owen M. Avery and School Leg-
        islation."   In Florida Educators, edited by the Florida
State University Research Council.   Tallahassee: Florida State
University, 1959.   pp. 10-21.

2284.   Pyburn, Nita Katharine.   "Thomas Baltzell and Universal
        Education."   In Florida Educators, edited by the Florida
State University Research Council.   Tallahassee: Florida State

University, 1959. pp. 1-9.

2285. _____ . "John Beard and the Changing Curriculum." In
        Florida Educators, edited by the Florida State University
Research Council. Tallahassee: Florida State University, 1959.
pp. 250-80.

2286. Goulding, R. L. "Charles Beecher." In Florida Educators,
        edited by the Florida State University Research Council.
Tallahassee: Florida State University, 1959. pp. 45-59.

2287. Bell, Emily Lagow. My Pioneer Days in Florida, 1876-
        1898. Miami: McMurray Printing Company, 1928.

2288. Grenelle, Eleanore Hortense. "The Bellamys of Territorial
        Florida." Master's thesis, University of Florida, 1953.

2289. Holt, Rackham. Mary McLeod Bethune: A Biography.
        New York: Doubleday and Company, 1964.

2290. Ledin, R. Bruce. "John Loomis Blodgett (1809-1853): A
        Pioneer Botanist of Southern Florida," Tequesta 13(1953):
23-33.

2291. Feibelman, Herbert U. "William Alexander Blount [1851-
        1921], 'Florida's Greatest Lawyer,' Native of Alabama,"
Ala. Law. 17(1956):156-60.

2292. Carson, Ruby Leach. "William Dunnington Bloxham, Flori-
        da's Two-Term Governor." Master's thesis, University of
Florida, 1945.

2293. _____ . "William Dunnington Bloxham: the Years to the
        Governorship," F. H. Q. 27(1949):207-36.

2294. Boggess, Francis Calvin Morgan. A Veteran of Four Wars.
        The Autobiography of F. C. M. Boggess. A Record of Pi-
oneer Life and Adventure, and Heretofore Unwritten History of the
Florida Seminole Indian Wars. Arcadia: Printed at the Champion
Job Rooms, 1900.

2295. Thrift, Charles T. "Isaac Boring, Pioneer Florida Circuit
        Rider," Rel. in the Making 3(1943):185-204.

2296. Brookfield, Charles Mann. "The Guy Bradley Story," Audu-
        bon Mag. 57(1955):170-74.

2297. Jones, Joseph J., Jr. "The Political Career of John
        Branch [Governor of Florida Territory, 1840]," Apalachee
5(1957-62):76-84.

2298. Long, Barbara Lou Rich. "John Branch, Florida's Last
        Territorial Governor," Apalachee 7(1968-70):120-29.

2299. Hanna, James Scott. The Brandon Family of Southwest
       Florida. Leander, Texas: Washington Press, Inc., 1968.

2300. Blanchard, Richard E. We Remember John: A Biography
       of John W. Branscomb, First Bishop Elected From Florida
Methodism. Lakeland: Florida Conference of the Methodist Church,
1964.

2301. Buford, Rivers H. "Napoleon B. Broward," Apalachee
       2(1946):1-4.

2302. Proctor, Samuel. Napoleon Bonaparte Broward [1857-1910]:
       Florida's Fighting Democrat. Gainesville: University of
Florida Press, 1950.

2303. _____. "Napoleon B. Broward: The Years to the Gover-
       norship," F. H. Q. 26(1947):117-34.

2304. Roberts, Derrell C. "Joseph E. Brown and Florida's New
       South Economy," F. H. Q. 46(1967):53-57.

2305. Lewis, Mary D. "Thomas Brown," Apalachee 1(1944):90-
       95.

2306. Ranson, Robert. A Memoir of Captain Mills Olcott Burn-
       ham, a Florida Pioneer; Written for Members of His Fam-
ily and Friends and All Interested in the State's Early History.
Tallahassee: Printed by T. J. Appleyard, Inc., 1926.

2307. Brevard, Caroline Mays. "Richard Keith Call," F. H. Q.
       1(1908):3-12; 1 No. 3 (1908):8-20.

2308. Doherty, Herbert J., Jr. "Richard Keith Call: Southern
       Unionist." Ph. D. dissertation, University of North Caro-
lina, 1953.

2309. _____. Richard Keith Call: Southern Unionist. Gaines-
       ville: University of Florida Press, 1961.

2310. Halsell, Willie D., ed. "Early Letters From R. K. Call
       [1819]," F. H. Q. 39(1961):266-69.

2311. Parker, Daisy. "R. K. Call: Whig Leader," Tallahassee
       Historical Society Annual 4(1939):12-19.

2312. Waldo, Horatio. "Richard Keith Call--Thomas Brown,"
       F. H. Q. 6(1928):156-58.

2313. Roberts, Albert Hubbard. "Wilkinson Call, Soldier and
       Senator," F. H. Q. 12(1934):95-113, 179-97.

2314.   Campbell, Doak Sheridan.   Doak S. Campbell, Southern Ed-
        ucator: Selected Addresses.   Tallahassee: Florida State
University, 1957.

2315.   Austin, Elizabeth S., ed.   Frank M. Chapman in Florida;
        Historical Journals and Letters.   Gainesville: University
of Florida Press, 1967.

2316.   Williamson, Edward C.   "William D. Chipley, West Flori-
        da's Mr. Railroad, " F. H. Q.   25(1947):333-35.

2317.   Fleming, C. Seton.   "George J. F. Clarke, " F. H. Q.
        4(1925):31-42.

2318.   Hill, Louise Biles.   "George J. F. Clarke, 1774-1836, "
        F. H. Q.   21(1943):197-253.

2319.   Patrick, Rembert W.   Aristocrat in Uniform: General
        Duncan L. Clinch.   Gainesville: University of Florida
Press for the Florida Historical Society, 1963.

2320.   Holmes, Jack D. L.   "Jose Del Rio Cosa, " Tequesta
        26(1966):39-52.

2321.   Gilkes, Lillian.   Cora Crane: A Biography of Mrs. Step-
        hen Crane.   Bloomington: Indiana University Press, 1960.

2322.   Russell, May Hill.   "William Curry [Key West Millionaire],"
        Martello 3(1966):16-18.

2323.   Scharff, Robert, and Walter S. Taylor.   Over Land and
        Sea.   New York: David McKay Company, 1968.

2324.   Darrow, Anna.   "Old Doc Anna, " J. Fla. Med. Assn.
        55(1968):749-56.

2325.   "Thomas Frederick Davis, " F. H. Q.   25(1947):279-80.

2326.   Erickson, Ruth.   Frederick DeBary, the Man and His Man-
        sion.   Sanford: Celery City Printing Company, 1964.

2327.   Morrison, A. J.   "John G. DeBrahm, " S. Atl. Q.
        21(1922):252-58.

2328.   Adams, Adam G.   "Viscaya, " Tequesta 15(1955):29-39.
        [James Deering]

2329.   Hanna, A. J.   The Music Master of Solano Grove [Freder-
        ick Delius].   New York: American Society of the French
Legion of Honor, 1943.

2330. Jahoda, Gloria. The Road to Samarkand: Frederick Delius
       and His Music. New York: Charles Scribner's Sons, 1969.

2331. Kriese, Paul. "Florida in the Life and Works of Frederick
       Delius, " Papers of the Jacksonville Historical Society
       1(1947):77-92.

2332. Groene, Bertram H. "Justice Samuel Douglas as Governor
       Marvin Remembered Him, " F. H. Q. 49(1971):268-77.

2333. Douglas, Thomas. Autobiography of Thomas Douglas, Late
       Judge of the Supreme Court of Florida. New York: Calkins
and Stiles, 1856.

2334. Shofner, Jerrell H. "A Note on Governor George F. Drew,"
       F. H. Q. 48(1970):412-14.

2335. Williamson, Edward C. "George F. Drew, Florida's Re-
       demption Governor, " F. H. Q. 38(1960):206-15.

2336. Strickland, Alice. "The Dummett Family Saga, " J. Halifax
       Hist. Soc. 2(1957):3-14.

2337. Cash, W. T. "William Pope Duval, " Tallahassee Historical
       Society Annual 1(1934):10-13.

2338. Knauss, James Owen. "William Pope DuVal, Pioneer and
       State Builder, " F. H. Q. 11(1933):95-139.

2339. Eppes, Mrs. Nicholas Ware. "Francis Eppes (1801-1881),
       Pioneer of Florida, " F. H. Q. 5(1926):94-102.

2340. Fackler, Samuel A. Ups and Downs of a Country Editor,
       Mostly Downs. Tallahassee: Collins Job Print, 1908.

2341. Fleming, F. P. "Major George Rainsford Fairbanks, "
       F. H. Q. 1(1908):5-7.

2342. Burdett, Susan. "The Military Career of Brigadier General
       Joseph Finegan of Florida...." Master's thesis, Columbia
University, 1947.

2343. LeFevre, Edwin. "Flagler and Florida, " Everybody's Mag.
       22(1910):168-86.

2344. Martin, John Wellborn. Henry Morrison Flagler, 1830-
       1913: Florida's East Coast is His Monument! New York:
Newcomen Society in North America, 1956.

2345. Martin, Sidney Walter. "Flagler Before Florida, " Tequesta
       5(1945):3-15.

2346.   . "Flagler's Associates in East Florida Developments, " F. H. Q. 26(1948):256-63.

2347.   . Florida's Flagler. Athens, Ga.: The University of Georgia Press, 1949.

2348.   . "Henry M. Flagler: Florida Benefactor, " Ga.
Rev. 3(1949):322-28.

2349.   . "Henry Morrison Flagler, " F. H. Q. 25(1947):257-
76.

2350. Rachlis, Eugene and John E. Marqusee. The Land Lords.
[H. M. Flagler] New York: Random House, 1963.

2351. Shappee, Nathan D. "Flagler's Undertakings in Miami in
1897, " Tequesta 19(1959):3-13.

2352. Fleishel, M. L. "The First Forty-two Years, " S. Lumber-
man 193(1956):173-76.

2353. Flynt, James Wayne. "Duncan Upshaw Fletcher: Florida's
Reluctant Progressive." Ph. D. dissertation, Florida State
University, 1965.

2354. Wells, William James. "Duncan Upshaw Fletcher, Florida's
Grand Old Man." Master's thesis, Stetson University, 1942.

2355. Black, Marian Watkins. "Eleazer K. Foster; State Superintendent of Public Instruction January 31, 1881-February
21, 1884. " In Florida Educators, edited by the Florida State University Research Council. Tallahassee: Florida State University,
1959.

2356. Silver, James W. Edmund Pendleton Gaines, Frontier
General. Baton Rouge: Louisiana State University Press,
1949.

2357. Fain, Marjorie. "Some Extracts From the History of the
Gamble Family in Florida, " Tallahassee Historical Society
Annual 1(1934):28-31.

2358. Lambright, Edwin D. The Life and Exploits of Gasparilla,
Last of the Buccaneers, With the History of Ye Mystic
Krewe of Gasparilla. Tampa: Hillsboro Printing Company, 1936.

2359. Watt, Margaret Gibbs. The Gibbs Family of Long Ago and
Near at Hand, 1337-1967. Privately Printed, 1968.

2360. Troetschel, Henry, Jr. "John Clayton Gifford [1870-1949]:
an Appreciation, " Tequesta 10(1950):35-47.

2361.   Staid, Sister Mary E. "Albert Waller Gilchrist, Florida's
        Middle of the Road Governor." Ph. D. dissertation, Uni-
versity of Florida, 1950.

2362.   Howe, George D. "The Father of Modern Refrigeration
        [John Gorrie]," F. H. Q. 1(1909):19-23.

2363.   Jelkes, Edward. "John Gorrie, M. D.," J. Fla. Med.
        Assn. 54(1967):796-98.

2364.   _____. "Doctor John Gorrie; Inventor of the First Arti-
        ficial Ice Machine," Jacksonville Historical Society Annual
(1933-34):76-80.

2365.   Mier, Ruth E. "More About Dr. John Gorrie and Refriger-
        ation," F. H. Q. 26(1947):167-73.

2366.   Dodd, Dorothy. "The Miller of Okahumpka [James Gough],"
        F. H. Q. 22(1944):140-42.

2367.   Beecher, Charles. "K. L. Goulding." In Florida Educa-
        tors. Florida State University Studies, no. 30. Tallahas-
see: Florida State University, 1959.

2368.   Keene, Jessee L. "Gavino Gutierres and His Contributions
        to Tampa," F. H. Q. 36(1957):33-41.

2369.   Black, Marian Watkins. "William Penn Haisley; Superin-
        tendent of Public Instruction of the State of Florida, 1877-
1881." In Florida Educators, edited by the Florida State University Research Council. Tallahassee: Florida State University,
1959.

2370.   American Swedish Historical Foundation. "Saga of a Flori-
        da Swede [Axel Hallstrom]," Chronicle 2(1955):20-22.

2371.   Trumbull, Marian R. "Hiram F. Hammon, Pioneer Home-
        steader of Palm Beach," F. H. Q. 19(1940):140-44.

2372.   Archer, Jules. Indian Friend, Indian Foe: The Story of
        William S. Harney. New York: Macmillan, 1969.

2373.   Black, Marian Watkins. "William Watkin Hicks; Superin-
        tendent of Public Instruction of the State of Florida, March
1, 1875-December 31, 1876." In Florida Educators, edited by the
Florida State University Research Council. Tallahassee: Florida
State University, 1959.

2374.   Venable, Elizabeth Marshall. William Adam Hocker (1844-
        1918), Justice of the Supreme Court of Florida: a Biogra-
phy With Some Account of His Ancestry and Family Connections.
Jacksonville: The Miller Press, 1941.

2375. Ball, Bruce W. "Samuel Hodgman, Haines City, Florida
       Pioneer, " Tequesta 30(1970): 55-63.

2376. Kuehl, Warren F. Hamilton Holt: Journalist-Internationa-
       list-Educator. Gainesville: University of Florida, 1960.

2377. Hortt, M. A. Gold Coast Pioneer. New York: Exposition
       Press, 1953.

2378. Pratt, Theodore. "Zora Neale Hurston, " F. H. Q. 40(1961):
       35-40.

2379. Tanner, Earl C. "The Early Career of Edwin T. Jenckes;
       a Florida Pioneer of the 1830's, " F. H. Q. 30(1952): 261-75.

2380. Johnson, James Weldon. Along This Way: The Autobiog-
       raphy of James Weldon Johnson. New York: Viking Press,
1968.

2381. Tarry, Ellen. Young Jim. [James Weldon Johnson] New
       York: Dodd, Mead and Company, 1968.

2382. James, Joseph B. "Edmund Kirby-Smith's Boyhood in
       Florida, " F. H. Q. 14(1936): 244-54.

2383. Parks, Joseph Howard. General Edmund Kirby-Smith.
       Baton Rouge, La.: Louisiana State University Press, 1954.

2384. Ferguson, Thomas M. and others. Claude R. Kirk, Jr.:
       A Man and His Words. Tallahassee: Executive Press,
1968.

2385. Fuller, Walter P. "Who Was the Frenchman of French-
       man's Creek? [Alfred Lechevalier], " Tequesta 29(1969): 45-
59.

2386. Eastman, Joel Webb. "Claude L'Engle, Florida Muckraker,"
       F. H. Q. 45(1967): 243-52.

2387. Huhner, Leon. "Moses Elias Levy: An Early Florida Pi-
       oneer and the Father of Florida's First Senator, " F. H. Q.
19(1941): 319-45.

2388. Ley, John Cole. Fifty-two Years in Florida. Nashville,
       Tenn., Dallas, Tex.: Publishing House of the Methodist
Episcopal Church, South, Barbee and Smith, Agents, 1899.

2389. "Joseph Byrne Lockey, " F. H. Q. 26(1947): 99-100.

2390.   Pfeifer, Rose M.   "The Life and Works of Joseph B. Loc-
         key."   Master's thesis, University of Florida, 1960.

2391.   Ingram, James M.   "Dr. Howell Tyson Lykes: Founder of
         an Empire," J. Fla. Med. Assn. 55(1968):742-48.

2392.   Kaufman, Le Roy.   "Captain George M. Lynch, Florida
         Educator...."   Master's thesis, University of Florida, 1950.

2393.   Galphin, Rosa.   "John C. McGehee," F. H. Q. 4(1926):186-91.

2394.   Morse, M. E.   "Alexander McGillivray, Who Put Not His
         Trust in Princes."   Master's thesis, Florida State Univer-
sity, 1936.

2395.   Rhodes, Francis A.   "Samuel B. McLain."   In Florida Ed-
         ucators.   Florida State University Studies, No. 30. Talla-
hassee: Florida State University, 1959.

2396.   Muir, Andrew Forest.   "David Betton Macomb, Frontiers-
         man," F. H. Q. 32(1954):189-201.

2397.   Clubbs, Occie.   "Stephen Russell Mallory, The Elder."
         Master's thesis, University of Florida, 1936.

2398.   _____. "Stephen Russell Mallory: United States Sena-
         tor From Florida and Confederate Secretary of the Navy,"
F. H. Q. 25(1947):221-45, 295-318; 26(1947):56-76.

2399.   Durkin, Joseph T.   Stephen R. Mallory: Confederate Navy
         Chief.   Chapel Hill: University of North Carolina Press,
1954.

2400.   Patrick, Rembert W.   Jefferson Davis and His Cabinet
         [Stephen T. Mallory] Baton Rouge, La.:   Louisiana State
University Press, 1944.

2401.   Stephen R. Mallory, Secretary of the Navy, Confederate
         States of America.   Pensacola: Pensacola Home and Sav-
ings Association, 1968.

2402.   Altland, Patti.   "Governor William C. Marvin [Governor
         1865]," Martello 2(1965):23-27.

2403.   Kearney, Kevin E.   "Autobiography of William Marvin,"
         F. H. Q. 36(1958):179-222.

2404.   Massolo, Arthur D., tran.   The Wonderful Life of Angelo
         Massari: An Autobiography.   New York: Exposition Press,
1965.

2405. Cooper, John C. "In Memorium; David Elwell Maxwell,"
       F. H. Q. 1(1909):3-5.

2406. May, Ellis Connell. Gaters, Skeeters, and Malary: Recol-
       lections of a Pioneer Florida Judge. New York: Vantage
Press, 1953.

2407. _____. From Dawn to Sunset: Recollections of a Pio-
       neer Florida Judge. 2 vol. Inverness, 1955.

2408. Smiley, Nora K. "Montgomery Cunningham Meigs," Mar-
       tello 3(1966):8-13.

2409. Freeland, Helen C. "George Edgar Merrick," Tequesta
       1(1942):1-7.

2410. Gammon, William Lamar. "Governor John Milton of Flori-
       da, Confederate States of America." Master's thesis, Uni-
versity of Florida, 1948.

2411. Parker, Daisy. "Governor John Milton," Tallahassee His-
       torical Society Annual 3(1937):14-21.

2412. _____. "John Milton, Governor of Florida; a Loyal Con-
       federate," F. H. Q. 20(1942):346-61.

2413. Townsend, Eleanor Winthrop. "John Moultrie, Junior, M.
       D., 1729-1798: Royal Lieutenant-Governor of East Flori-
da," Annals Med. Hist. 3d ser., 2(1940):98-109.

2414. Hanna, A. J. A Prince in Their Midst: The Adventurous
       Life of Achille Murat on the American Frontier. Norman:
University of Oklahoma Press, 1946.

2415. Long, Ellen Call. "Princessee Achille Murat: A Bio-
       graphical Sketch," F. H. Q. 2(1909):27-38.

2416. Armstrong, Orland Ray. Life and Work of Dr. A. A.
       Murphree. A Labor of Love, Endeavoring to Perpetuate
the Memory of a Truly Great Man Who Was President of the University of Florida From 1909-1927. St. Augustine: Published by
the author for the Murphree Memorial Fund, 1928.

2417. Murphy, Frank. The Frank Murphy Story. Edited by
       Thomas Helm. New York: Dodd, Mead, and Company,
1968.

2418. Dovell, J. E. "John Newhouse, Upper Everglades Pioneer
       and Historian," Tequesta 27(1967):23-28.

2419. Strickland, Alice. "James Ormond, Merchant and Soldier,"
       F. H. Q. 41(1963):209-22.

2420. Pasco, Samuel (the younger). "Samuel Pasco (1834-1917),"
       F. H. Q. 7(1928):135-39.

2421. Doherty, Herbert J., Jr. "Rembert Wallace Patrick,"
       F. H. Q. 46(1968):305-13.

2422. Eckert, Edward K. "Rembert Wallace Patrick: A Bibliog-
       raphy," F. H. Q. 46(1968):314-21.

2423. Prior, Leon O. "Lewis Payne, Pawn of John Wilkes Booth,"
       F. H. Q. 43(1964):1-20.

2424. Jelks, Edward. "Dr. Henry Perrine," J. Fla. Med. Assn.
       20(1934):459-63.

2425. Klose, Nelson. "Dr. Henry Perrine [1797-1840]: Tropical
       Plant Enthusiast," F. H. Q. 27(1948):189-201.

2426. Robinson, T. Ralph. "Henry Perrine, Pioneer Horticul-
       turist of Florida," Tequesta 1(1942):16-24.

2427. _____. "Perrine and Florida Tree Cotton," Tequesta
       7(1947):67-68.

2428. Feibelman, Herbert U. "Edward Aylsworth Perry, Briga-
       dier-General, C. S. A., and Former Governor of Florida,"
       Fla. Law J. 23(1949):250-57.

2429. Parker, Daisy. "The Inauguration of Edward Aylesworth
       Perry (1884) as the 14th Governor of Florida," Apalachee
       5(1957-62):85-95.

2430. Prince, Sigsbee C., Jr. "Edward Alysworth Perry, Flori-
       da's Thirteenth Governor." Master's thesis, University of
       Florida, 1949.

2431. _____. "Edward Alysworth Perry [1831-89]: Yankee
       General of the Florida Brigade," F. H. Q. 29(1951):197-205.

2432. Straight, William M. "Odet Phillippe: Friend of Napoleon,
       Naval Surgeon and Pinellas Pioneer," J. Fla. Med. Assn.
       53(1966):704-08.

2433. Pierce, Charles W. Pioneer Life in Southeast Florida.
       Coral Gables: University of Miami Press, 1970.

2434. Blacker, John C. "Henry Bradley Plant," Papers of the
       Jacksonville Historical Society 2(1949):62-74.

2435.   Johnson, Dudley S.   "Henry Bradley Plant and Florida,"
        F. H. Q.   45(1966):118-31.

2436.   _____ .   "Plant's Lieutenants, " F. H. Q.   48(1970):381-91.

2437.   Martin, Sidney Walter.   "Henry Bradley Plant. " In Georg-
        ians in Profile, edited by Horace Montgomery.   Athens:
The University of Georgia Press, 1959.

2438.   Smyth, G. Hutchinson.   Life of Henry Bradley Plant,
        Founder and President of the Plant System of Railroads
and Steamships, and Also the Southern Express Company.   New
York: Putnam, 1898.

2439.   Altland, Patti.   "Dr. J. Y. Porter [1847-1927], " Martello
        2(1965):10-13.

2440.   Sowder, Wilson T.   "Joseph Yates Porter, M. D. :   The
        Merchant's Son Who Became Florida's First State Health
Officer, " J. Fla. Med. Assn.   54(1967):801-08.

2441.   Rand, Jacob Batchelder.   "History of the Rand Family, "
        D. A. R. Mag.   87(1953):799-800.

2442.   Meginniss, Benjamin A.   "George Pettus Raney, 1845-1911,"
        Apalachee 1(1944):81-89.

2443.   Bellman, Samuel Irving.   "Marjorie Kinnan Rawlings: A
        Solitary Sojourner in the Florida Backwoods, " Kan. Q.
(1970):78-87.

2444.   Bigelow, Gordon E.   Frontier Eden: The Literary Career
        of Marjorie Kinnan Rawlings.   Gainesville: University of
Florida Press, 1966.

2445.   Reed, Adelaide H.   "Florida Pioneer [Adelaide H. Reed], "
        F. H. Q.   37(1958):111-49.

2446.   Current, Richard N.   Three Carpetbag Governors.   [Harri-
        son Reed] Baton Rouge, La. :   Louisiana State University
Press, 1967.

2447.   North, Henry Ringling and Alden Hatch.   The Circus Kings--
        Our Ringling Family Story.   Garden City, N. Y. :   Double-
day and Company, 1960.

2448.   Plowden, Gene.   Those Amazing Ringlings and Their Circus.
        Caldwell, Idaho: Caxton Printers, 1967.

2449.   Phillips, P. Lee.   Notes on the Life and Works of Bernard
        Romans.   Florida State Historical Society Publication, No.

Biography 195

2. De Land: Florida State Historical Society, 1924.

2450.   Carothers, Milton W. "Albert J. Russel, 1829-1896; Fa-
        ther of Graded Schools in Florida." In Florida Educators,
edited by the Florida State University Research Council. Tallahassee: Florida State University, 1959. pp. 107-18.

2451.   Amundson, Richard James. "The American Life of Henry
        Shelton Sanford." Ph.D. dissertation, Florida State Uni-
versity, 1963.

2452.   _____. "[Henry S.] Sanford and [Giuseppi] Garibaldi,"
        Civil War Hist. (1968):40-45.

2453.   Tarbox, Increase N. Memoirs of James N. Schneider and
        Edward M. Schneider. Boston: Sabbath School Society,
1867.

2454.   Parker, O. S. "William N. Sheats, Florida Educator."
        Master's thesis, University of Florida, Gainesville, 1949.

2455.   Pyburn, Nita Katharine. "William N. Sheats and the Flori-
        da High Schools." In Florida Educators, edited by the
Florida State University Research Council. Tallahassee: Florida
State University, 1959. pp. 129-41.

2456.   Cox, Merlin G. "David Sholtz: New Deal Governor (1932+)
        of Florida," F.H.Q. 43(1964):142-52.

2457.   Spurrier, Steve. It's Always Too Soon to Quit: The Steve
        Spurrier Story. Edited by Mel Larson. Grand Rapids,
Mich.: Zondervan House, 1968.

2458.   Flory, Claude R. "Marcellus L. Stearns, Florida's Last
        Reconstruction Governor," F.H.Q. 44(1966):181-92.

2459.   Stoddard, Herbert L., Sr. Memoirs of a Naturalist. Nor-
        man, Okla.: University of Oklahoma Press, 1969.

2460.   Douglas, Marjory Stoneman. "Frank Bryant Stoneman,"
        Tequesta 1(1944):3-12.

2461.   Wilson, Forrest. Crusader in Crinoline--the Life of Har-
        riet Beecher Stowe. Philadelphia: Lippincott Company,
1941.

2462.   Burghard, August. Mrs. Frank Stranahan, Pioneer. Fort
        Lauderdale: Fort Lauderdale Historical Society, 1968.

2463.   Will, Lawrence E. "King of the Crackers [Jacob Summer-
        lin]," Tequesta 26(1966):31-38.

2464. Sharp, Helen R. "The Activities of Samuel A. Swann in
       the Development of Florida, 1855-1909." Master's thesis,
Florida State University, 1940.

2465. _____. "Samuel A. Swann and the Development of Flori-
       da, 1855-1900, " F. H. Q. 20(1941):169-96.

2466. Tenney, John Francis. Slavery, Secession and Success;
       the Memoirs of a Florida Pioneer. San Antonio, Tex.:
Southern Literary Institute, 1934.

2467. Johnson, Evans C. "Oscar W. Underwood: The Develop-
       ment of a National Statesman, 1894-1915. " Ph. D. disser-
tation, University of North Carolina, 1953.

2468. Gannon, Michael V. Rebel Bishop: The Life and Era of
       Augustin Verot. Milwaukee, Wis.: Bruce Publishing Com-
pany, 1964.

2469. Cotterill, R. S. "David Shelby Walker, " Tallahasse His-
       torical Society Annual 1(1934):56-60.

2470. Pyburn, Nita Katharine. "David S. Walker and a State
       System of Education. " In Florida Educators, edited by the
Florida State University Research Council. State University Studies,
No. 30. Tallahassee: Florida State University, 1959.

2471. _____. "David Shelby Walker (1815-1891): Educational
       Statesman of Florida, " F. H. Q. 34(1955):159-71.

2472. Bullen, Ripley P. "S. T. Walker, an Early Florida Ar-
       chaeologist, " Fla. Anthro. 4(1953):46-49.

2473. Ingram, James M. "John Perry Wall: A Man For All
       Seasons, " J. Fla. Med. Assn. 53(1966):709-17.

2474. Ware, John D. , comp. Genealogy of the Descendants of
       Joseph Ware of Fenwick Colony, England, 1675, and His
Successors in Florida. Tampa: Privately Printed, 1969.

2475. Dovell, J. E. "Thomas Elmer Will [1861-1937]: Twentieth
       Century Pioneer, " Tequesta 8(1948):21-55.

2476. Buckman, Henry H. III, ed. "Letters of Captain Charles
       Willey, " Papers of the Jacksonville Historical Society
2(1949):16-22.

2477. Fleming, F. P. "George West Wilson, " F. H. Q. 1(1908):
       40-42.

2478.   Gifford, G. E., Jr. "John George F. Wurdemann (1810-
        49): A Forgotten Southern Physician-Naturalist, " J. Hist.
        Med. 24(1969):44-46.

2479.   Clubbs, Occie. "Philip Keyes Yonge, 1850-1934, " F. H. Q.
        13(1935):167-72.

2480.   Patrick, Rembert W. "Julien Chandler Yonge, " F. H. Q.
        41(1962):103-115.

2481.   Huhner, Leon. "David L. Yulee, Florida's First Senator, "
        Pub. Am. Jewish Hist. Soc. 25(1917):1-29.

2482.   Lord, Mills M., Jr. "David Levy Yulee, Statesman and
        Railroad Builder." Master's thesis, University of Florida,
        1940.

2483.   Thompson, Arthur W. "David Yulee: A Study of Nineteenth
        Century American Thought and Enterprise." Ph. D. disser-
        tation, Columbia University, 1954.

2484.   Yulee, C. W. "Senator Yulee, " F. H. Q. 2(1909):26-43; 2
        No. 2 (1909):3-22.

2485.   Fairbanks, George R. "Moses Elias Levy Yulee, " F. H. Q.
        18(1940):165-67.

XXVIII.   LOCAL HISTORY

        A.   Cities and Towns [alphabetic by subject]

2486.   Pink, Helen Ross. "Amelia Island: A Resource Unit for
        Teachers in Secondary Schools...." Master's thesis, Uni-
        versity of Florida, 1949.

2487.   Owens, Harry P. "Apalachicola: The Beginning, " F. H. Q.
        47(1969):276-91.

2488.   _____. "Port of Apalachicola, " F. H. Q. 48(1969):1-25.

2489.   Avon Park Diamond Jubilee, Inc. 75th Anniversary of
        Avon Park. Avon Park: Avon Park Diamond Jubilee, Inc.,
        1964.

2490.   Bartow Chamber of Commerce. Bartow, Florida, the
        County Seat of Polk County, a Condensed History. Bartow:
        Chamber of Commerce, 1965.

2491. Will, Lawrence E. Swamp to Sugar Bowl: Pioneer Days
       in Belle Glade. St. Petersburg: Great Outdoors Publishing
Company, 1968.

2492. Pratt, Theodore. The Story of Boca Raton [1925-53].
       [Boca Raton: Roy S. Patten, 1953.]

2493. Jones, James H., ed. History of Brooksville City Govern-
       ment. Brooksville: Central Florida Publishers, 1965.

2494. Caidin, Martin. Spaceport, U.S.A.; the Story of Cape
       Canaveral. New York: Dutton, 1959.

2495. Tebeau, Charlton W. The Story of the Chokoloskee Bay
       Country; With The Reminiscences of Pioneer C. S. 'Ted'
Smallwood. Coral Gables: University of Miami Press, 1955.

2496. Will, Lawrence E. A Dredgeman of Cape Sable. St.
       Petersburg: Great Outdoors Publishing Company, 1967.

2497. Beach, Rex Ellingwood. The Miracle of Coral Gables.
       New York: Printed by Currier & Harford Ltd., 1926.

2498. Jordan, Lillian. "A Historical Sketch of my Home Town,
       Dania," F.H.Q. 10(1931):109-12.

2499. Booth, Fred. "Early Days in Daytona Beach, Florida; How
       a City Was Founded," J. Halifax Hist. Soc. 1(1951):10.

2500. Deland, Helen Parce. Story of Deland and Lake Helen,
       Florida. [Norwich, Conn.: L. H. Walden, 1928.]

2501. A Souvenir of the City of Deland Florida. Issued for the
       Purpose of Presenting to the Notice of Our Northern Friends,
the Advantages and Beauties of Our City and Its Surroundings....
De Land: The News Publishing Company, 1902.

2502. Douglas, W. Lovett. History of Dunedin. St. Petersburg:
       Great Outdoors Publishing Company, 1965.

2503. Dinkins, J. Lester. Dunnellon-Boomtown of the 1890's:
       The Story of Rainbow Springs and Dunnellon. St. Peters-
burg: Great Outdoors Publishing Company, 1969.

2504. Damkohler, Elwin E. Estero, Florida, 1882; Memoirs of
       the First Settler. Fort Myers Beach: Island Press, 1967.

2505. Lamoreaux, Leroy. Early Days on Estero Island; an Old
       Timer Reminiscenses. Fort Myers Beach: Estero Island
Publishers, 1967.

2506.   Knight, Raymond D.   "Fernandina, " Jacksonville Historical
        Society Annual (1933-34):55-61.

2507.   Ashby, Hammond E., ed.   "Sketches of the Florida Keys,
        1829-1833, " Tequesta 29(1969):73-94.

2508.   Beare, Nikki.   Pirates, Pineapples and People: A History,
        Tales, and Legends of the Upper Florida Keys.   Miami
Beach: Atlantic Publishing Company, 1961.

2509.   Griswold, Oliver.   The Florida Keys and the Coral Reef.
        Miami: The Graywood Press, 1965.

2510.   Sanger, Marjory Bartlett.   World of the Great White Heron:
        A Saga of the Florida Keys.   New York: Devin-Adair Com-
pany, 1967.

2511.   Burghard, August.   "Fort Lauderdale; a Superb Florida
        Home Town of Tropical Splendor, " Fla. Pub. Works
21(1944):3-7.

2512.   Collver, Leon L. W.   The Pocket History of Fort Lauder-
        dale.   Fort Lauderdale: Tropical Press, [1940].

2513.   Moninger, Arthur V.   Guide to Fort Lauderdale and Vicinity,
        1951.   Fort Lauderdale, 1951.

2514.   Weilding, Philip J. and August Burghard.   Checkered Sun-
        shine: The Story of Fort Lauderdale, 1793-1955.   Gaines-
ville: University of Florida Press, 1966.

2515.   Brown, Barrett.   A Short History of Fort Myers Beach,
        Estero and San Carlos Islands, Florida.   Fort Myers
Beach: Estero Island Publishers, 1965.

2516.   Fritz, Florence Irene.   Bamboo and Sailing Ships: The
        Story of Thomas A. Edison and Fort Myers, Florida [1885-
1931].   [Fort Myers, 1949.]

2517.   Gonzalez, Thomas A., comp.   The Caloosahatchee, Miscel-
        laneous Writings Concerning the History of the Caloosahat-
chee River and the City of Fort Myers, Florida.   Estero: Kore-
shan Unity Press, 1932.

2518.   Grismer, Karl Hiram.   The Story of Fort Myers: The
        History of the Land of the Caloosahatchee and Southwest
Florida [1513-1949].   St. Petersburg: St. Petersburg Printing
Company, 1949.

2519.   Petersen, Johann.   I Am a Fugitive From Injustice, From
        a Cesspool of Intolerance, Greed, and Corruption.   [Fort
Myers and Lee County.]   [San Jose, Costa Rica?], 1952.

2520.   Schell, Rolfe. 1, 000 Years on Mound Key. Fort Myers
        Beach: Island Press, 1962. [Rev. ed., 1969.]

2521.   Vickers-Smith, Lillian D. The History of Fruitland Park,
        Florida.... [Fruitland Park]: Fruitland Park Chamber of
Commerce [1924].

2522.   Cook, Edgar Dallas. "An Economic Base Study of the
        Metropolitan Area of Gainesville, Florida." Master's the-
sis, University of Florida, 1964.

2523.   Davis, Jess G. History of Gainesville, Florida With Bio-
        graphical Sketches of Families. Gainesville, 1966.

2524.   Hamilton, William Ray. "Changing of the Guard: Gaines-
        ville, 1963." Master's thesis, University of Florida, 1963.

2525.   Hildreth, Charles Halsey. "A History of Gainesville, Flor-
        ida." Ph. D. dissertation, University of Florida, 1954.

2526.   Hussain, Farhat. "Gainesville, Florida: A Geographic
        Study of a City in Transition." Master's thesis, University
of Florida, 1959.

2527.   McVoy, Edgar Cornelius. "A Sociological Study of Gaines-
        ville, Florida." Master's thesis, University of Florida,
1937.

2528.   Miller, Edward Loring. "Negro Life in Gainesville; a So-
        ciological Study." Master's thesis, University of Florida,
1938.

2529.   Schneider, Michael Paul. "Decisions in Gainesville."
        Master's thesis, University of Florida, 1963.

2530.   Stallworth, Herbert Farish. "Gainesville, Florida; a Study
        in Municipal Administration." Master's thesis, University
of Florida, 1949.

2531.   Hebel, Ianthe Bond. "The Samuel Williams Family; Early
        Residents on the Halifax," J. Halifax Hist. Soc. 2(1957):
25-29.

2532.   Stanton, Edith P. Ruins of the Early Plantations of the
        Halifax Area, Volusia County, Florida. Daytona Beach:
Burgman and Son for the Volusia County Historical Commission,
1955.

2533.   Biddle, Margaret Seton Fleming. Hibernia, "the Unreturn-
        ing Tide." New York: Privately Printed, 1947.

2534. Ten Eick, Virginia Elliot. History of Hollywood (1920-1950). Hollywood: The City of Hollywood, 1966.

2535. Carswell, Elba Wilson. Holmes Valley: A West Florida Cradle of Christianity. Bonifay: Central Press, 1969.

2536. Hellier, Walter R. Indian River: Florida's Treasure Coast. Coconut Grove: Hurricane Press, 1965.

2537. Frantzis, George. Strangers at Ithaca. St. Petersburg: Great Outdoors Publishing Company, n. d.

2538. Craig, James C. "[31 Articles on Jacksonville Reprinted From the (Jacksonville) Florida Times-Union]," Papers of the Jacksonville Historical Society 3(1954):1-177.

2539. Daniel, Richard P. "The Spirit of Jacksonville in the Fire of 1901," Papers of the Jacksonville Historical Society 1(1947):16-18.

2540. Davis, Thomas Frederick. History of Early Jacksonville, Florida; Being an Authentic Record of Events From the Earliest Times to and Including the Civil War. Jacksonville: H. and W. B. Drew Company, 1911.

2541. _____. History of Jacksonville, Florida and Vicinity 1513 to 1924. St. Augustine: Published for the Florida Historical Society by the Record Company, 1925.

2542. Florida Times-Union. ..."Jacksonville in 1914" edition. May 6, 1914.... Jacksonville: The Florida Publishing Company, [1914].

2543. _____. 100th Anniversary [Issue] 1864-1964. Jacksonville: Times-Union, 1964.

2544. Harrison, Benjamin. Acres of Ashes; the Story of the Great Fire That Swept Over the City of Jacksonville, Florida, on the Afternoon of Friday, May 3, 1901.... Jacksonville: J. A. Holloman, 1901.

2545. Keene, Otis L. "Jacksonville, Fifty-three Years Ago; Recollections of a Veteran," F. H. Q. 1(1909):9-15.

2546. Mann, F. A. "Burning of Jacksonville," Fla. Mag. 2(1901):295-305.

2547. May, Philip S. "The Old City Cemetery [Jacksonville, 1852-1949]," Papers of the Jacksonville Historical Society 2(1949):1-15.

2548.   Rawls, Carolina. The Jacksonville Story: A Pictorial Re-
        cord of a Florida City [1562-1950]. Jacksonville: Jackson-
ville's Fifty Years of Progress Association, 1950.

2549.   Snodgrass, Dena. "Collected Papers," Papers of the Jack-
        sonville Historical Society 5(1969):entire issue.

2550.   Wagstaff, Walter S. ...Jacksonville in Flames; Florida's
        Metropolis in Sackcloth and Ashes. Jacksonville: Wagstaff,
1901.

2551.   Du Bois, Bessie Wilson. "Jupiter Inlet," Tequesta
        28(1968):19-35.

2552.   Withington, Chester Merrill. Jupiter Island, a Grant From
        the Spanish Government to Eusebio M. Gomez on July 16,
1815.... [N. p.]: Hobe Sound Company, 1935.

2553.   Woodman, Jim. The Book of Key Biscayne. Miami:
        Miami Post Publishing Company, 1961.

2554.   _____. Key Biscayne: Romance of Cape Florida. Mi-
        ami: Hurricane House Press, 1961.

2555.   Hathway, James A. Key Largo Island Home. Coral Gables:
        Key Largo Foundation, 1968.

2556.   Bingham, Florence S. "Key Vaca," Tequesta 17(1957):47-
        67; 18(1958):23-75.

2557.   Allen, Joe. "Those Pirates [Key West]," Martello 3(1966):
        19-20.

2558.   Blackwell, Harriet Gray. "Thirty-nine Bridges to Cross,"
        [Key West] Frontiers 16(1952):71-73.

2559.   Browne, Jefferson B. Key West; the Old and the New.
        St. Augustine: Record Company, 1912.

2560.   Cutler, Bowman. "Architecture of [Key West] Towers,"
        Martello 1(1964):19-20.

2561.   Diddle, Dr. A. W. "Vital Statistics Compiled in Key West
        During 1835," J. Fla. Med. Assn. 30(1944):380-82.

2562.   Garnett, Burt P., ed. The Martello Towers and the Story
        of Key West. Key West: Key West Press, [1953].

2563.   Goulding, R. L. "William Hackley's Diary, 1830-1857:
        Key West and the Apalachee Area," Apalachee 6(1963-67):
33-44.

2564.   Jameson, Colin G. "Footprints on Our Welcome Mat; the
        First 80 Years, " Martello 2(1965):14-22.

2565.   _____ . "What's in a Street Name [Key West], " Martello
        3(1966):26-30.

2566.   _____ . "Who Said 'Hurricane' [Sept. 1948 in Key West],"
        Martello 2(1965):33-46.

2567.   Long, Durward. "Key West and the New Deal, 1934-1936, "
        F. H. Q. 46(1968):209-18.

2568.   _____ . "Workers on Relief, 1934-1938, in Key West, "
        Tequesta 28(1968):53-61.

2569.   Malone, Mary Wood. "Barren Ground [Early Key West--
        Gardening], " Martello 3(1966):20-25.

2570.   Maloney, Walter C. Sketch of the History of Key West,
        Florida. Edited with an introduction by Thelma Peters.
Gainesville: University of Florida Press, 1968.

2571.   Peters, Thelma, ed. "William Adee Whitehead's Remi-
        niscences of Key West, " Tequesta 25(1965):3-42.

2572.   Roth, Clayton D., Jr. "150 Years of Defense Activity at
        Key West, 1820-1970, " Tequesta 30(1970):33-51.

2573.   Smiley, Nora K. "Old Island Restoration Foundation [Key
        West], " Martello 2(1965):28-32.

2574.   _____ . "Salt-making in Key West, " Martello 2(1965):7-9.

2575.   Tebeau, Charlton W. "Two Opinions of Key West in 1834, "
        Tequesta 20(1960):45-49.

2576.   Thielen, Benedict. "Key West [1700-1948], " Sat. Even.
        Post 221(1949):20-21, 84-89.

2577.   White, Louise V. Louise White Shows You Key West; a
        Guide to an Enchanting City. St. Petersburg: Great Out-
doors Publishing Company, [1965].

2578.   _____ and Nora K. Smiley. History of Key West; Today
        and Yesterday. St. Petersburg: Great Outdoors Publishing
Company, [1959].

2579.   Whitehead, William Adee. "William Adee Whitehead's De-
        scription of Key West." Edited by Rembert Wallace Patrick.
Tequesta 12(1952):61-73.

2580.   Whitson, Mrs. Lorenzo Dow. "Away Down South;" Key
        West, Tampa, Orlando, Winter Park, St. Augustine, and

Florida in General.... Jacksonville: Times-Union Publishing
House, 1886.

2581.   Writers' Program. Florida. A Guide to Key West. Com-
        piled by Workers of the Writers' Program of the Work
Projects Administration in the State of Florida. 2d ed. New York:
Hastings House, [1949].

2582.   The Lake Worth Historian. [A Souvenir Journal. Pub-
        lished by the Ladies of Palm Beach, for the Benefit of the
Royal Poinciana Chapel, 1896.]

2583.   Marsh, Ola Gladys Hylton. History of the United States
        Postal Service on Longboat Key. Longboat Key: Delcraft
Printing Company, 1962.

2584.   McDuffee, Lillie B. The Lures of Manatee; a True Story
        of South Florida's Glamourous Past. [Nashville: Press of
Marshall and Bruce Company, 1933.]

2585.   Robie, Virginia Huntington. Sketches of Manatee. Braden-
        town, 1921.

2586.   Graff, Mary B. Mandarin on the St. Johns. Gainesville:
        University of Florida Press, 1953.

2587.   Hooker, Kenneth Ward. "A Stowe Memorial [Mandarin,
        Fla.]," F. H. Q. 18(1940):198-203.

2588.   Seiber, Truman David. "Historical and Economic Geogra-
        phy of Masarytown, Florida." Master's thesis, University
of Florida, 1957.

2589.   Thomas, Frank J. Early Days in Melbourne Beach, 1888-
        1928. Cocoa Beach: Jet Press, 1968.

2590.   Howard, Kennie L. Yesterday in Florida [Melrose, Fla.],
        New York: Carlton Press, 1970.

2591.   Ballinger, Kenneth. Miami Millions. Miami: Florida
        Franklin Press, 1936.

2592.   Bingham, Millicent Todd. "Miami: A Study in Urban Ge-
        ography," Tequesta 8(1948):73-107.

2593.   Blackman, E. V. Miami and Dade County, Florida; Its
        Settlement, Progress and Achievement, ... With a Collection
of Individual Sketches of Representative Citizens and Genealogical
Records of Some of the Old Families. Washington, D. C.: V.
Rainbolt, 1921.

2594. Buchanan, Patricia. "Miami's Bootleg Room," Tequesta 30(1970):13-31.

2595. Carney, James J. "Population Growth in Miami and Dade County, Florida," Tequesta 6(1946):50-55.

2596. Carson, Ruby Leach. "Miami: 1896-1900," Tequesta 16(1956):3-13.

2597. Cohen, Isidor. Historical Sketches and Sidelights of Miami, Florida. Miami: Privately Printed, 1925.

2598. Dorn, J. K. "Recollections of Early Miami [1870-98]," Tequesta 9(1949):43-59.

2599. Frazure, Hoyt. Memories of Old Miami.... Miami, 196?

2600. Kofoed, John Christian. Moon Over Miami. New York: Random House, [1955].

2601. Maxwell, Cora S. Miami of Yesterday. Miami, 1956.

2602. "Miami in 1843," F.H.Q. 3(1925):34-35. (From The News, St. Augustine, Florida, Dec. 30, 1843.)

2603. Muir, Helen Lennehan. Miami, U. S. A. [since 1875]. New York: Holt, [1953].

2604. Public Administration Service. The Government of Metropolitan Miami [and Dade County, 1896-1953]. [Chicago, 1954.]

2605. Sessa, Frank B. "Miami in 1926," Tequesta 16(1956):15-36.

2606. Wilson, F. Page. "Miami: From Frontier to Metropolis: An Appraisal," Tequesta 14(1954):25-49.

2607. Wolff, Reinhold Paul. Miami: Economic Pattern of a Resort Area. Coral Gables: University of Miami, 1945.

2608. Carson, Ruby Leach. "Forty Years of Miami Beach," Tequesta 15(1955):3-27.

2609. _____. "Miami Beach Reaches the Half Century Mark," Tequesta 24(1964):3-19.

2610. Linneman, William R. and Harriet Fether. "Miami Beach Hotel Names," Am. Speech 39(1964):196-200.

2611. Mehling, Harold. The Most of Everything; the Story of Miami Beach. St. Petersburg: Great Outdoors Publishing Company, 1964.

2612. Nash, Charles Edgar. The Magic of Miami Beach. A De-
       tailed Account of the Traditions, History and Phenomenal
Growth of a Wonder City Built With the Touch of Aladdin Upon the
Sands of the Semitropical Lower East Coast of Florida. Philadel-
phia: David McKay Comapny, [1938].

2613. Redford, Polly. Billion Dollar Sandbar, a Biography of
       Miami Beach. New York: E. P. Dutton and Company,

2614. Ewell, Francis A. "The Story of Middleburg, " Jacksonville
       Historical Society Annual (1933-34):46-54.

2615. Longstreet, R. J. The Story of Mount Dora, Florida.
       Published by the Mount Dora Historical Society. De Land:
E. O. Painter Printing Company, 1960.

2616. Frasca, John. The Mulberry Tree. Englewood Cliffs, N.
       J.: Prentice-Hall Inc., 1968.

2617. Cash, W. T. "New Port as a Business Center, " Apalachee
       1(1944):13-28.

2618. Detwiler, John Y. "Antiquities At and Near New Smyrna,
       Florida, " F. H. Q. 1(1908):20-23.

2619. Dumble, A. E. New Smyrna, Florida. De Land: E. O.
       Painter Printing Company, 1904.

2620. Sweett, Zelia Wilson and J. C. Marsden. New Smyrna,
       Florida, Its History and Antiquities. De Land: E. O.
Painter Printing Company, 1925.

2621. Jones, Eloise Knight, Comp. Ocala Cavalcade Through One
       Hundred Years. Ocala: S. F. McCready, [1946].

2622. Ott, Eloise Robinson. "Ocala Prior to 1868, " F. H. Q.
       6(1927):85-110.

2623. Niemeyer, Glenn A. "Oldsmar for Health, Wealth, Happi-
       ness, " F. H. Q. 46(1967):18-28.

2624. Fries, Kena. Orlando in the Long, Long Ago and Now.
       Orlando, [1938].

2625. Gore, E. H. From Florida Sand to "The City Beautiful."
       A Historical Record of Orlando, Florida. 2d ed. [N. p.,
       1951.]

2626. Hinkley, Ada Green. The Colonization of Ormond, Florida.
       De Land: E. O. Painter Printing Company, 1931.

2627. Ormond, James. Reminiscences of James Ormond Con-
       cerning the Early Days of Halifax Country. Ormond: Or-
mond Village Improvement Association, 1941.

2628. Strickland, Alice. The Valiant Pioneers, a History of Or-
       mond Beach, Volusia County, Florida. Miami: University
of Miami Press, 1963.

2629. Capron, Louis. "First in Palm Beach [c. 1867]," Tequesta
       25(1965):43-65.

2630. De Holguin, Beatrice. Tales of Palm Beach. New York:
       Vantage Press, 1968.

2631. Duryea, Nina Larre. Among the Palms [Palm Beach].
       New York, 1903.

2632. Ney, John. Palm Beach: The Place, the People, Its
       Pleasures and Palaces. Boston: Little, Brown and Com-
pany, 1966.

2633. Palm Beach Villas. Palm Beach: R. O. Davies Publishing
       Company, 1929.

2634. Pratt, Theodore. What Was Palm Beach. St. Petersburg:
       Great Outdoors Publishing Company, 1968.

2635. Travers, J. Wadsworth. History of Beautiful Palm Beach.
       Palm Beach: The Palm Beach Press, 1928.

2636. Abel, Ruth E. One Hundred Years in Palmetto. Palmetto:
       Palmetto Centennial Association, 1967.

2637. Copeland, Harry Clay. "The Development of Panama City
       and Its Newspapers." Master's thesis, Florida State Uni-
versity, 1956.

2638. Porter, Louise M. Pasqua Florida; the Feast of Flowers.
       Philadelphia: Dorance, [1954].

2639. Bliss, Charles Henry. Pensacola of To-day.... Pensa-
       cola: C. H. Bliss, [1897].

2640. Butler, Hartman L. "Historical Pensacola Bay," Coast
       Artillery J. 75(1932):125-27.

2641. Cherry, Ada Lou. "The United States Navy Yard at Pensa-
       cola, Florida, 1823-1862." Master's thesis, Florida State
University, 1953.

2642. Chipley, William D., comp. Pensacola. Louisville:
       Courier-Journal Press, [1877].

2643.   Clubbs, Occie. "Pensacola in Retrospect: 1870-1890, "
         F. H. Q. 37(1959):377-96.

2644.   Cole, John William. Pictorial History of Pensacola, City
         of Five Flags. Pensacola: Fiesta of the Five Flags Asso-
ciation, 1952.

2645.   Cumberland, Charles C. "Pensacola in 1770, " Journal of
         the Rutgers University Library 13(1949):7-13.

2646.   Davis, T. Frederick. "Pioneer Florida: The Pad-Gaud at
         Pensacola, 1830, " F. H. Q. 23(1945):220-26.

2647.   Dodd, Dorothy. "The New City of Pensacola, a Real Es-
         tate Development of 1835-1837, " F. H. Q. 9(1931):224-41.

2648.   Doherty, Herbert J. , Jr. "Ante-Bellum Pensacola: 1821-
         1860, " F. H. Q. 37(1959):337-56.

2649.   Gonzalez, S. J. "Pensacola; Its Early History, " F. H. Q.
         2(1909):9-25.

2650.   Leigh, Mrs. Townes Randolph. "The City of Pensacola,
         Florida, " Confederate Veteran 36(1928):252-53.

2651.   McLellan, Don. Fifty Years in Pensacola. Personal
         Reminiscences and Anecdotes. [Pensacola: Mayes Printing
Company, 1944.]

2652.   Manucy, Albert. "The Founding of Pensacola--Reasons and
         Reality, " F. H. Q. 37(1959):223-41.

2653.   Mordes, Sidney. "Pensacola--A Florida Seaport. " Mas-
         ter's thesis, Florida State University, 1959.

2654.   Newton, Earle W. , ed. Historic Architecture of Pensacola.
         Pensacola: Historical Restoration and Preservation Com-
mission, 1969.

2655.   "Some Officials of the City Government of Pensacola, "
         F. H. Q. 3(1925):31-33.

2656.   Wentworth, T. T. , Jr. "Pensacola Memorabilia, " F. H. Q.
         39(1960):46-51.

2657.   Bethel, John A. Bethel's History of Point Pinella, 1924....
         With a Foreward by Florence Bethel Loader. St. Peters-
burg: Great Outdoors Publishing Company, 1962.

2658.   Gatewood, George W. Oxcart Days to Airplane Era in
         Southwest Florida [Punta Gorda]. Punta Gorda: Punta
Gorda Herald, 1939.

2659. Peeples, Vernon E. "Trabue, Alias Punta Gorda, " F. H. Q.
      46(1967):141-148.

2660. Dean, Susie Kelly. On Saint Andrews Bay, 1911-1917; A
      Sequel to the Tampa of My Childhood. [Tampa, 1969.]

2661. Surber, Elsie Lillian. "A Study of the History and Folk-
      lore of the St. Andrews Bay Region." Master's thesis,
University of Florida, 1950.

2662. West, George M. St. Andrews, Florida; Historical Notes
      Upon St. Andrews and St. Andrews Bay.... St. Andrews:
The Panama City Publishing Company, 1922.

2663. Allaben, E. G. "St. Augustine in 1841 was Different, "
      Hobbies 53(1948):105.

2664. Arnade, Charles W. "The Architecture of Spanish St.
      Augustine, " The Americas 18(1961):149-86.

2665. _____. "The Avero Story: An Early St. Augustine Fam-
      ily with Many Daughters and Many Houses, " F. H. Q.
4(1961):1-34.

2666. Averette, Annie. Facts About St. Augustine, Florida. St.
      Augustine: The Record Company, 1915.

2667. Beeson, Eleanor. "The St. Augustine Historical Restora-
      tion, " F. H. Q. 16(1937):110-18.

2668. Brooks, A. M. The Unwritten History of St. Augustine,
      Copied From the Spanish Archives in Seville Spain. Trans-
lated by Annie Averette. St. Augustine: The Record Company,
1909.

2669. Calkin, Carleton I. "The Government House in St. Augus-
      tine, " Amer. Bar Assoc. Jour. 57(1971):148-50.

2670. Carter, R. "Scenes in St. Augustine, " Appelton's Journal,
      6(1871):16-20.

2671. Caravallo y Miyeres, Cesar. La Ciudad de San Augustin
      (La Florida). Habana: Editorial Lex, 1954.

2672. Chatelain, Verne E. "The St. Augustine Historical Pro-
      gram." Carnegie Institution of Washington. Yearbook
36(1936-37):372-77; 37(1937-38):389-91.

2673. Conly, Robert L. "St. Augustine, Nation's Oldest City,
      Turns 400, " Nat. Geo. Mag. 129(1966):196-229.

2674.   Connolly, Matthew J.   "Four Contemporary Narratives of
        the Founding of St. Augustine, " Cath. Hist. Rev. 51(1965):
305-34.

2675.   Davis, T. Frederick.   "Pioneer Florida: Sidelights on
        Early American St. Augustine, " F. H. Q. 23(1944):116-21.

2676.   DeCoste, Fredrik.   True Tales of Old St. Augustine.   St.
        Petersburg: Great Outdoors Publishing Co. , 1966.

2677.   Dewhurst, William W.   The History of Saint Augustine,
        Florida With an Introductory Account of the Early Spanish
and French Attempts at Exploration and Settlement in the Territory
of Florida Together with Sketches of Events and Objects of Interest
Connected With the Oldest Town in the United States to Which is
Added a Short Description of the Climate and Advantages of Saint
Augustine as a Health Resort.   New York: G. P. Putnam's Sons,
The Knickerbocker Press, 1886.

2678.   Dunkle, John R.   "Population Change as an Element in the
        Historical Geography of St. Augustine, " F. H. Q. 37(1958):
1-32.

2679.   _____. "St. Augustine, Florida: A Study In Historical
Geography. "   Ph. D. dissertation, Clark University, 1957.

2680.   Dunn, W. E.   "Pirates and Miracles in Old St. Augustine, "
        Cath. World 127(1928):596-600.

2681.   Eby, Cecil D. , Jr. , ed. "Memoir of a West Pointer [Alfred
        Beckely] in Saint Augustine: 1824-1826.   Annotated by
Doris C. Wiles and Eugenia B. Arana.   F. H. Q. 42(1964):307-20.

2682.   Fairbanks, George Ransford.   The History and Antiquities
        of the City of St. Augustine, Florida.   New York: Charles
B. Norton, 1858.

2683.   Federal Writers' Project.   St. Augustine.   St. Augustine:
        St. Augustine Record Company, 1937.

2684.   Folsom, Montgomery.   Old St. Augustine.   Atlanta, Georgia:
        The Franklin Printing and Publishing Company... , 1905.

2685.   Fraser, Walter B.   The First Landing Place of Juan Ponce
        de Leon on the North American Continent in the Year 1513.
St. Augustine, 1956.

2686.   Glenn, Joshua Nichols.   "A Diary of Joshua Nichols Glenn:
        St. Augustine in 1823, " F. H. Q. 24(1945):121-61.

2687.   Jerome, Father.   Saint Augustine in 1835.   St. Leo: The
        Abbey Press, [?].

2688. Kline, Walter D. "St. Augustine, America's Oldest City."
       Yearbook, Public Museum of Milwaukee 10(1932):167-86.

2689. Longworth, Maria Theresa. Saint Augustine, Florida. New
       York: G. P. Putnam and Son, 1869.

2690. Manucy, Albert C. The Houses of St. Augustine, 1565-
       1821. St. Augustine: St. Augustine Historical Society,
1962.

2691. Moore, John Hammond, ed. "A South Carolina Lawyer
       Visits St. Augustine--1837," F. H. Q. 43(1965):361-78.

2692. Musick, John Roy. Saint Augustine; a Story of the Hugue-
       nots in America.... New York: Funk and Wagnalls, 1892.

2693. Reeves, F. Blair. "The Architecture of Historic St. Augus-
       tine: A Photographic Essay," F. H. Q. 44(1965):94-96.

2694. Reynolds, Charles Bingham. Old Saint Augustine: A Story
       Of Three Centuries. St. Augustine: E. H. Reynolds, 1885.

2695. _____. "The Oldest House in the United States," St.
       Augustine, Fla. An Examination Of The St. Augustine His-
torical Society's Claim That Its House On St. Francis Street Was
Built In The Year 1565 By The Franciscan Monks. New York:
The Foster & Reynolds Company, 1921.

2696. _____. The St. Augustine Historical Society's Oldest
       House Hoax. [n. p., 1930.]

2697. _____. The Standard Guide to St. Augustine. St. Augus-
       tine: E. H. Reynolds, 1889.

2698. Richmond, Mrs. Henry L. "Ralph Waldo Emerson in Flor-
       ida," F. H. Q. 18(1939):75-93.

2699. Sewall, R. K. Sketches of St. Augustine with a View of its
       History.... New York: Published for the Author by G. P.
Putnam, 1848.

2700. Sharf, Frederic A. "St. Augustine: A City of Artists,
       1883-1895," Antiques 90(1966):220-23.

2701. St. Augustine Cathedral. History of Nuestra Senora de la
       Leche y Buen Parto and Saint Augustine, The Oldest Parish
in the United States. St. Augustine: Cathedral Parish of St.
Augustine, 1937.

2702. St. Augustine Evening Record. Saint Augustine. St. Augus-
       tine: [Evening Record], 1911.

2703.   St. Augustine Historical Society and Institute of Science.
         St. Augustine is the Oldest Permanent European Settlement
on the North American Continent North of Mexico.   St. Augustine:
Historical Society and Institute of Science, 1941.

2704.   .   St. Augustine's Historical Heritage as Seen To-
         day.   St. Augustine: Historical Society and Institute of
Science, 1952.

2705.   Smith, Hale G., ed.   "Evolution of the Oldest House,"
         Notes in Anthro. 7(1962):whole no.

2706.   and Robert H. Steinbach.   "Rocque 226," Notes in
         Anthro. 9(1963):whole no.

2707.   Van Camper, John Tyler.   St. Augustine: Capital of La
         Florida.   St. Augustine: For the Author, 1959.   Reprinted.
La Florida, Florida's Colonial Capital.   St. Augustine: St. Augustine Historical Society, 1965.

2708.   Vollbrecht, John L.   The Dramatic Story of Spain's Great
         17th Century Fortress in Saint Augustine [1565-1948].   St.
Augustine: Record Press, 1948.

2709.   Webb, DeWitt.   "Old St. Augustine.   Her Harbor Come
         Back To Its Own," F.H.Q. 1(1908):3-8.

2710.   White, Leigh.   "St. Augustine [1565-1949]," Sat. Even. Post
         221(1950):24-5, 100-02, 106.

2711.   Wickham, Joan.   Saint Augustine, Florida, 1565-1965.   Wor-
         cester, Mass.:   Achille J. St. Onge, 1967.

2712.   Corse, Carita Doggett.   "St. John's Town," Jacksonville
         Historical Society Annual (1933-34):44-45.

2713.   Knauss, James Owen.   "St. Joseph, An Episode Of The
         Economic And Political History Of Florida, Part 1." F.H.Q.
18(1938):84-102.

2714.   .   "St. Joseph, An Episode Of The Economic And
         Political History of Florida," F.H.Q. 5(1927):177-95;
6(1927):3-20.

2715.   "St. Joseph, Florida," F.H.Q. 2(1909):23-26.

2716.   "Investigation of St. Marks Harbor With Brief Commercial
         History of That Town and Newport [Government Documents
Excerpts 1871+]," Tallahassee Historical Society Annual 2(1935):
47-52.

2717.   Grismer, Karl H.   History of St. Petersburg, Historical
         And Biographical.   St. Petersburg: Tourist News Publish-

ing Company, 1924.

2718. _____. The Story of St. Petersburg: The History of Lower Pinellas Peninsula And The Sunshine City [ca. 1831-1948]. St. Petersburg: P. K. Smith, 1948.

2719. Jackson, Page S. An Informal History of St. Petersburg. St. Petersburg: Great Outdoors Publishing Company, 1962.

2720. Schaal, Peter. Sanford As I Knew It. Orlando: Peter Schaal, 1970.

2721. Brush, Jane D. "Tales of Old Florida," F.H.Q. 40(1962): 300-10, 408-17; (1962):85-94, 199-207, 309-23, 407-23.

2722. Grismer, Karl H. The Story of Sarasota.... Sarasota: M. E. Russell, 1946.

2723. Ulmann, Alec. The Sebring Story. Philadelphia: Chilton Book Co., 1969.

2724. Christian, Eugene. The Story of Silver Springs, The Fabled Fountain Of Youth. [Privately Printed, 1925.]

2725. Corse, Carita. Shrine of the Water Gods: Historical Account Of Silver Springs, Florida. Gainesville: Pepper Printing Company, 1935.

2726. Martin, Richard A. Eternal Spring: Man's 10,000 Years Of History At Florida's Silver Springs. St. Petersburg: Great Outdoors Publishing Co., 1966.

2727. Bradford County Telegraph. 100 Years of Starke, 1857-1957, Centennial Issue. Starke, Florida, 1957.

2728. Adams, Robert M. "The Romance of Snead Island [Lower Gulf Coast]," F.H.Q. 41(1962):94-101.

2729. Abbey, Kathryn T. "Lafayette and the Lafayette Land Grants," Tallahassee Historical Society Annual 1(1934):1-9.

2730. _____. "The Story of the LaFayette Lands in Florida," F.H.Q. 10(1932):115-33.

2731. Blake, Sallie E. Tallahassee of Yesterday. Tallahassee: T. J. Appleyard, 1924.

2732. Cash, W. T. (ed.) "Tallahassee and St. Marks in 1841: A Letter of John S. Tappan," F.H.Q. 24(1945):108-12.

2733. Cockrell, Alston W. "Reminiscences of Tallahassee," Tallahassee Historical Society Annual 2(1935):37-44.

2734.   Davis, Mary Lamar.   "Tallahassee Through Territorial
        Days, " Apalachee 1(1944):47-61.

2735.   Dodd, Dorothy.   "The Corporation of Tallahassee, 1826-
        1860, " Apalachee (1950-56):80-96.

2736.   _____ . "Old Tallahassee, " Apalachee 5(1957-62):63-71.

2737.   Dodd, William G.   "Ring Tournaments in Tallahassee, "
        Apalachee (1950-56):55-70.

2738.   Downes, Allan J.   "Change and Stability in Social Life:
        Tallahassee, Florida, 1870-1890. "   Master's thesis, Flori-
da State University, 1955.

2739.   Dozier, Annie Randolph.   "Early Settlers of Tallahassee,
        1824-1850, " Tallahassee Historical Society Annual 1(1934):
33-38.

2740.   "Dreadful Conflagration in Tallahassee, " F. H. Q. 4(1925):
        44-48.

2741.   Elliot, Carrie E.   "McDougall's Pasture, " Apalachee
        2(1946):3-34.

2742.   "The Great Storm [Tallahassee, Aug. 23, 24, 1851], " F. H.
        Q. 18(1940):270-73.

2743.   Green, Edwin L.   "Florida Historical Documents, " Gulf
        State Hist. Mag. 1(1902):199-202.

2744.   Groene, Bertram H.   "Ante-Bellum Tallahassee: It Was A
        Gay Time Then. "   Ph. D. dissertation, Florida State Uni-
versity, 1967.

2745.   _____ , ed.   "Lizzie Brown's Tallahassee, " F. H. Q.
        48(1969):155-75.

2746.   Hadd, Donald.   "The Columns [Two Buildings in Tallahas-
        see] 1830-1860, " Apalachee 5(1957-62):26-40.

2747.   Harrigan, Anthony and Mary Lamar Davis.   "Two Planta-
        tion Houses in Florida, " Antiques 64(1953):46-7.

2748.   Hayden, Clara R.   A Century of Tallahassee Girls, As
        Viewed From the Leaves Of Their Diaries. . . .   Atlanta:
Fook and Davies Company, N. D.

2749.   Hendry, F. A.   "Tallahassee Before the War, " F. H. Q.
        1(1909):16-23.

2750.   Henry, Evelyn Whitfield.   "The May Party, " Apalachee
        2(1946):35-45.

2751. _____ . "Old Houses of Tallahassee," Tallahassee Historical Society Annual 1(1934):39-55.

2752. Kilgore, John. "Florida's Capitol [buildings]," Tallahassee
Historical Society Annual 3(1937):8-13.

2753. Ley, Fred P., Jr. "The Tallahassee Fire of 1843," Apalachee 4(1950-56):11-19.

2754. Long, Reinette Gamble. An Historical Pageant of Tallahassee, Acted by The People of Tallahassee...1924. Tallahassee: T. J. Appleyard, 1924.

2755. McCord, Gayte. "List of Postmasters Who Have Served in
Tallahassee, Leon County, Florida," Tallahassee Historical
Society Annual 1(1934):32.

2756. Myers, John R. "Social Life and Recreation in Tallahassee
During Reconstruction, 1865-1877," Apalachee 7(1968-70):
20-37.

2757. "Note Sur Deux Itineraires De Charleston a Tallahasseé
(Floride)," Société de Geographic de Paris 18(1842):241-59.

2758. "The Selection of Tallahassee as The Capital," F. H. Q.
1(1908):26-44.

2759. Shores, Venila Louina. "The Laying Out of Tallahassee
[1820's-30's]," Apalachee 5(1957-62):41-47.

2760. "The Tallahassee Fire of 1843," F. H. Q. 7(1928):164-67.

2761. "Tallahassee in 1824-25," F. H. Q. 3(1925):38-40.

2762. Boggs, Ralph Steele. "Spanish Folklore From Tampa,
Florida," S. Folklore Q. 1(1917):1-13.

2763. Bullen, Ripley Pierce. "Archeology of the Tampa Bay
Area," F. H. Q. 34(1955):51-63.

2764. Covington, James W., ed. "The Establishment of Fort
Brooke; The Beginnings Of Tampa From The Letters of
Col. George M. Brooke," F. H. Q. 31(1953):273-78.

2765. _____ . "The Tampa Bay Hotel," Tequesta 26(1966):3-20.

2766. Davis, T. Frederich. "Pioneer Florida (IV): The Beginning Of Tampa," F. H. Q. 23(1944):39-44.

2767. Grismer, Karl Hiram. Tampa: A History Of The City Of
Tampa And The Tampa Bay Region Of Florida [1545-1950].
St. Petersburg: St. Petersburg Print Co., 1950.

2768.   Jackson, Lena E.   "Sidney Lanier in Florida, " F. H. Q.
        15(1936):118-24.

2769.   Long, Durward.   "The Historical Beginnings of Ybor City
        and Modern Tampa, " F. H. Q.   45(1966):31-44.

2770.   _____ . "Making of Modern Tampa: A City Of The New
        South, 1885-1911, " F. H. Q.   49(1971):333-45.

2771.   Massari, Angelo. La Comunita Italiana di Tampa. New
        York: Europe America Press, 1968.

2772.   Muniz, Jose Rivero.   "Tampa at the Close of the Nine-
        teenth Century, " translated by Charles J. Kolinski.   F. H. Q.
        41(1963):332-42.

2773.   Neill, Wilfred T.   "An Indian and Spanish Site on Tampa
        Bay, Florida, " Fla. Anthro. 21(1968):106-16.

2774.   Parrish, Charles James.   "Minority Politics in a Southern
        City: Tampa, Florida, 1950-1960. " Master's thesis, Uni-
        versity of Florida, 1960.

2775.   Pizzo, Anthony P. Tampa Town, 1824-1886: Cracker Vil-
        lage With A Latin Accent. Miami: Hurricane House Pub-
        lishers, 1968.

2776.   "The Port of Tampa, " Nautical Gazette 142(1948):36-39.

2777.   Schell, Rolfe F. De Soto Didn't Land at Tampa. Fort
        Myers Beach: Island Press, 1966.

2778.   Westmeyer, D. Paul.   "Tampa, Florida, A Geographical
        Interpretation of Its Development. " Master's thesis, Uni-
        versity of Florida, 1953.

2779.   Estey, Winifred W. Tangerine Memoirs. Tangerine:
        Sponsored and Printed by the Tangerine Improvement So-
        ciety, 1957.

2780.   Pent, R. F. The History of Tarpon Springs. St. Peters-
        burg: Great Outdoors Publishing Company, 1964.

2781.   Newman, Anna Pearl Leonard, ed. Stories of Early Life
        Along Beautiful Indian River. Stuart: Stuart Daily News,
        1953.

2782.   Richards, J. Noble. Florida's Hibiscus City: Vero Beach.
        Melbourne: Brevard Graphics, Inc. , 1968.

2783. Rich, Lou. "Wakulla Spring: Its Setting and Literary Visitors," F.H.Q. 42(1964):351-62.

2784. Bellwood, Ralph. Tales of West Pasco. Hudson: Albert J. Mabovec, Printer, 1962.

2785. Lewis, Sandra. "History of White City, Florida [1893-1953]," F.H.Q. 33(1954):48-50.

2786. Phillips, Gay. "The History of Wildwood [Fla., 1882-1954]," F.H.Q. 34(1955):93-95.

2787. MacDowell, Claire Leavitt. Chronological History of Winter Park. Winter Park, 1950.

2788. Knotts, Tom. See Yankeetown: History and Reminiscences. Yankeetown: Withlacooche Press, 1970.

2789. Yglesias, Jose. A Wake in Ybor City. New York: Holt, Rhinehart & Winston, 1963.

B. Counties

2790. Alachua County; Its Resources and Advantages. Gainesville, A Healthful, Progressive City. Gainesville: Daily Sun Book Print, 1898.

2791. Ashby, John W. Alachua, The Garden County of Florida. New York: South Publishing Co., 1898.

2792. Buchholz, F. W. History of Alachua County, Florida, Narrative and Biographical. St. Augustine: The Record Co., 1929.

2793. Davis, Jess G. History of Alachua County, 1824-1969. Gainesville, 1970.

2794. Merk, John Lamar. "The Government of Alachua County, Florida." Master's thesis, University of Florida, 1957.

2795. Smith, W. A. "Letters of a Florida Settler in 1877." Edward C. Williamson, ed. F.H.Q. 32(1954):202-17.

2796. Brief Description of Brevard County, Florida or the Indian River Country. Titusville: Florida Star, 1889.

2797. Tebeau, Charlton W. Florida's Last Frontier: The History of Collier County. Coral Gables: University of Miami Press, 1957.

2798.   DeCrois, F. W.   Historical, Industrial and Commercial
        Data of Miami and Fort Lauderdale, Dade County, Florida.
The Most Progressive and Conspicuous Section Of The East Coast.
Facts And Fancies Relating To Miami And Fort Lauderdale And
Other Growing Settlements.   St. Augustine: The Record Company,
1909.

2799.   Hollingsworth, Tracy.   History of Dade County, Florida.
        Miami: Miami Post, 1936.

2800.   Hudson, F. M.   "Beginnings in Dade County," Tequesta
        1(1943):1-35.

2801.   Martin, Richard A.   Consolidation: Jacksonville-Duval
        County; The Dynamics Of Urban Political Reform.   Jack-
sonville: Crawford Publishing Co., 1968.

2802.   Edwards, Lucy Ames.   "Stories in Stone: A Study Of Du-
        val County Grave Markers [Jacksonville And Vicinity, 1835-
1917], "   F. H. Q.   35(1956):116-29.

2803.   Gold, Pleasant Daniel.   History of Duval County, Florida...
        also Biographies Of Men And Women Who Have Done Their
Part In Making Duval County, Past And Present.   St. Augustine:
The Record Company, 1928.

2804.   Armstrong, H. Clay.   History of Escambia County, Florida.
        Narrative and Biographical.   St. Augustine: The Record
Company, 1930.

2805.   Stanley, J. Randall.   History of Gadsden County.   Quincy:
        Gadsden County Historical Commission, 1948.

2806.   Pikula, John.   "Historical Landmarks Of My County," F. H.
        Q.   15(1937):255-57.

2807.   Jones, James H., ed.   Guide to Governmental Services in
        Hernando County.   Brooksville: Central Florida Publishers,
1965.

2808.   Whitehurst, Mary K., ed.   Brooksville and Hernando County,
        Florida.   Brooksville: The Brooksville Sun, 1936.

2809.   Bailey, David Elmer.   "A Study of Hillsborough County's
        History, Legend, And Folklore, With Implications For The
Curriculum. "   Master's thesis, University of Florida, 1949.

2810.   Burns, Annie Walker.   Historical Records of Hillsborough
        County, Tampa, Florida, Compiled From The United States
Census, 1830 to 1870.   Washington, D. C.:   The Author, 1952.

2811.   Robinson, Ernest Lauren. History of Hillsborough County,
        Florida; Narrative and Biographical. St. Augustine: The
Record Company, 1928.

2812.   Rhyne, Janie Smith. Our Yesterdays. Marianna: Jackson
        County Florida Press, 1968.

2813.   Stanley, J. Randall. The History of Jackson County. Mari-
        anna: Jackson County Historical Society, 1950.

2814.   History of Jefferson County, Florida. Historians: Mary
        Oakley McRory and Edith Clarke Barrows. Monticello:
Published Under the Auspices of the Kiwanis Club, 1958.

2815.   Pasco, Samuel. "Jefferson County, Florida, 1827-1910,"
        F. H. Q. 7(1928):139-54, 234-57.

2816.   Kennedy, William Thomas, ed. History of Lake County,
        Florida.... St. Augustine: The Record Company, 1929.

2817.   Cash, W. T. "Literary History of Leon County," Talla-
        hassee Historical Society Annual 2(1935):21-33.

2818.   Paisley, Clifton. From Cotton to Quail: An Agricultural
        Chronicle Of Leon County, Florida, 1860-1967. Gaines-
ville: University of Florida Press, 1968.

2819.   Seymour, Arthur R. "Social Aspects of Leon County Wills
        and Inventories, 1826-1845," Apalachee 4(1950-56):43-54.

2820.   "Leon County [First] World War Veterans [A List]," Talla-
        hassee Historical Society Annual 3(1937):35-52.

2821.   Kimber, Donald Kay. "Population Changes in the Economic
        Development of Levy County, Florida," Master's thesis,
Florida State University Geography Department, 1960.

2822.   Ott, Eloise and Louis H. Chazal. Ocali Country, Kingdom
        of the Sun; A History of Marion County, Florida. Oklawaha:
Marion Publishers, 1966.

2823.   Blackman, William Fremont. History of Orange County,
        Florida, Narrative and Biographical. De Land: The E. O.
Painter Printing Company, 1927.

2824.   Howard, G. E. Early Settlers of Orange County, Florida....
        Orlando: C. E. Howard, 1915.

2825. Moore-Wilson, Minnie. History of Osceola County, Flori-
       da, Frontier Life. Orlando: Inland Press, 1935.

2826. Forshay, David A. and Elizabeth E. Micken, eds. Lure of
       the Sun: A Story Of Palm Beach County. Lake Worth:
First Federal Savings and Loan Association of Lake Worth, 1967.

2827. Moody, J. F. "A Letter From the Land of Flowers, Fruit,
       and Plenty, " F. H. Q. 30(1952):350-51.

2828. Staub, W. L. The Story of Pinellas County, Florida. St.
       Augustine: Record Press, 1929.

2829. Hetherington, M. F. History of Polk County, Florida;
       Narrative And Biographical. Saint Augustine: The Record
Company, 1928.

2830. Williams, Ada Coats. A Brief History of Saint Lucie
       County. Fort Pierce: T. M. Field, 1963.

2831. The Story of Swannee County. Prepared by the Suwannee
       County Extension Staff. [Live Oak, 1964?].

2832. Fitzgerald, Thomas E. Historical Highlights of Volusia
       County. Daytona Beach: Observer Press, 1939.

2833. _____. Volusia County, Past and Present. Daytona
       Beach: Observer Press, 1937.

2834. Gold, Pleasant Daniel. History of Volusia County, Florida.
       De Land: E. O. Painter Printing Company, 1927.

2835. Hebel, Ianthe B., ed. Centennial History of Volusia County,
       Florida, 1854-1954. Daytona Beach: College Publishing
Company, 1955.

2836. _____. Presenting Forty Years of Progress, 1901-1941,
       Volusia County. Daytona Beach: Fitzgerald Publications,
1941.

2837. McKinnon, John L. History of Walton County. Gainesville:
       Kallman Publishing Company, 1968.

C. Regional Studies

2838. Bickel, Karl August and Walker Evans. The Mangrove
       Coast, The Story Of The West Coast Of Florida. New York:
Coward-McCann, 1942.

2839.   Cash, W. T.   "The Lower East Coast, 1870-1890," Te-
        questa 8(1949):57-71.

2840.   Covington, James W.   The Story of Southwestern Florida.
        New York: Lewis Publishing Company, 1957.

2841.   Fritz, Florence I.   Unknown Florida.   Coral Gables: Uni-
        versity of Miami Press, 1963.

2842.   Gifford, John C.   "Some Reflections on the South Florida
        of Long Ago," Tequesta 6(1946):38-43.

2843.   Greenbie, Sydney.   "Florida's West Coast," Holiday
        3(1948):18-37, 118-26.

2844.   Harper, Roland McMillan.   Geography and Vegetation of
        Northern Florida. [Tallahassee?: 1914] From the 16th
Annual Report of the Florida State Geological Survey...1914.

2845.   _____. Geography of Central Florida.   From the 13th
        Annual Report of the Florida State Geological Survey.   Tal-
lahassee, 1917.

2846.   Hellier, Walter R.   Indian River: Florida's Treasure
        Coast.   Coconut Grove: Hurricane House Publishers, 1965.

2847.   Hutchinson, Leonard P.   History of the Playground Area of
        Northwest Florida.   St. Petersburg: Great Outdoors Pub-
lishing Company, 1964.

2848.   Lyons, Ernest.   My Florida.   New York: A. S. Barnes &
        Company, 1969.

2849.   Merrick, George E.   "Pre-Flagler Influences on the Lower
        Florida East Coast," Tequesta 1(1941):1-10.

2850.   Moore, Clarence B.   Certain Sand Mounds of the St. John's
        River, Florida.   Philadelphia: Levytype Company, 1894.

2851.   Pratt, Theodore.   Florida's Spanish River Area.   Highland
        Beach: Boca-Hi, Inc., 1969.

2852.   Strickland, Alice.   "Ponce De Leon Inlet [Northeast Fla.],"
        F. H. Q. 43(1965):244-61.

2853.   Thorner, Robert M.   Population Growth in Three South
        Florida Counties [Broward, Dade, and Palm Beach, 1940-
55].   Jacksonville: Bureau of Vital Statistics, Florida State Board
of Health, 1956.

D. Forts [alphabetical by subject]

2854. Griffin, John W. "The Addison Blockhouse," F.H.Q.
30(1952):276-93.

2855. Boyd, Mark F. "The Apalachicola or Chattahoochee Arse-
nal of the United States," Apalachee 4(1950-56):29-43.

2856. Bennett, Charles E. "Fort Caroline, Cradle of American
Freedom," F.H.Q. 35(1956):3-16.

2857. Davis, T. Frederick. "Fort Caroline," F.H.Q. 12(1933):
77-83.

2858. Manucy, Albert. "The Fort Caroline Museum," Papers of
the Tallahassee Historical Society 4(1960):45-52.

2859. National Park Service. "Fort Caroline," Papers of the
Tallahassee Historical Society 4(1960):39-44.

2860. DeCoste, Fredrik. "The Fort That Went to Sea!" Am.
Forests 70(1964):15.

2861. Harrington, J. C., Albert C. Manucy, and John M. Goggin.
"Archeological Excavations in the Courtyard of Castillo de
San Marcos, St. Augustine, Florida," F.H.Q. 34(1955):101-41.

2862. Manucy, Albert C., ed. The History of Castillo de San
Marcos and Fort Matanzas From Contemporary Narratives
and Letters. Washington: Government Printing Office for Department of the Interior, National Park Service, 1945.

2863. Laumer, Frank J. "The Fort Dade Site," Fla. Anthro.
16(1963):33-42.

2864. _____. "This Was Fort Dade," F.H.Q. 45(1966):1-11.

2865. Shapee, Nathan D. "Fort Dallas and the Naval Depot of
Key Biscayne, 1836-1926," Tequesta 21(1961):13-40.

2866. Jones, William M. "A Report on the Site of Camp Finegan
[Duval County]," F.H.Q. 39(1961):366-73.

2867. Manucy, Albert C. "The Fort at Frederica," Notes in
Anthro. 5(1962):150.

2868. Poe, Stephen R. "Archaeological Excavation at Fort Gadsden,
Florida [1814-21]," Notes in Anthro. 8(1963):35.

2869.   Corse, Carita.   The Key to the Golden Islands.   Chapel
        Hill: University of North Carolina Press, 1931.

2870.   Cubberly, Frederick.   "Fort George (St. Michael), Pensa-
        cola, " F. H. Q.   6(1928):220-34.

2871.   "Fort Jefferson; Dry Tortugas, Florida," Martello 1(1964):
        11-14.

2872.   Kinney, Sheldon H.   "Dry Tortugas," U. S. N. Inst. Proc.
        76(1950):424-29.

2873.   Manucy, Albert C. "The Gibraltar of the Gulf of Mexico, "
        F. H. Q.   21(1943):303-31.

2874.   Cubberly, Frederick.   "Fort King, " F. H. Q.   5(1927):139-52.

2875.   Ott, Eloise R.   "Fort King: A Brief History," F. H. Q.
        46(1967):29-38.

2876.   Hanna, Alfred Jackson.   Fort Maitland: Its Origin And
        History.   Maitland: The Fort Maitland Committee, 1936.

2877.   St. Augustine Institute of Science and Historical Society.
        Fort Marion and City Gates, St. Augustine, Florida; Offi-
        cial History Authorized By The St. Augustine Institute Of Science
        And Historical Society.   St. Augustine: The A. C. Press, 1915.

2878.   Cox, Oliver C. (Rev.)   Ruins of the Old Spanish Fort at
        New Smyrna, Florida.   New Smyrna: New Smyrna Chamber
        of Commerce, 1935.

2879.   Fillingim, T. D.   "Old Fort San Carlos: Fort Barrancas,
        Pensacola, Florida," Wentworth's Mag.   1(1941):9.

2880.   Goodbody, Amy.   "Fort San Luis, " Tallahassee Historical
        Society Annual 1(1934):25-27.

2881.   Shores, Venila Lovina.   "The Ruins of Fort San Luis Near
        Tallahassee, " F. H. Q.   6(1927):111-16.

2882.   Olds, Dorris La Vanture.   "History and Archaeology of
        Fort Saint Marks in Apalachee."   Master's thesis, Florida
        State University, 1962.

2883.   _____ .   "Some Highlights in the History of Fort St.
        Marks, " Fla. Anthro. 15(1962):33-40.

2884. Shenkel, J. Richard and William Westbury. "The Marine
       Hospital at Fort St. Marks, " Notes in Anthro. 12(1965):21.

2885. Holmes, Jack D. L. "Notes on the Spanish Fort San Este-
       ban de Tombeche, " Ala. Rev. 18(1965):281-90.

2886. Wenhold, Lucy L. "The First Fort of San Marcos de Apa-
       lache, " F. H. Q. 34(1956):301-14.

       E. The Everglades and Other Natural Areas

2887. Ackerman, Bill. The Florida Keys. Tallahassee: Florida
       Department of Agriculture, 1967.

2888. Altland, Patti. "Big Pine Key, " Martello 3(1966):2-7.

2889. Baker, J. H. "Saving Southwest Florida: Everglades Na-
       tional Park, " Audubon Magazine 42(1941):209.

2890. Beard, Daniel B. , Earl M. Semingsen, and C. R. Vinten.
       "Florida's Royal Palm Forest, " Nat. Parks Mag. 22(1948):
32-34.

2891. _____. "Let 'er burn?" Everglades Nat. Hist. 2(1955):
       2-8.

2892. Brookfield, Charles Mann and Oliver Tudor Griswold. They
       All Called it Tropical: True Tales Of The Romantic Ever-
glades National Park, Cape Sable, And The Florida Keys [1513-
1947]. Miami: Data Press, 1949.

2893. Butcher, Devereux. "Going, going--Florida's Royal Palm--
       Big Cypress Forest, " Nat. Parks Mag. 22(1948):3-7.

2894. Carson, Robe B. "The Florida Tropics, " Econ. Geog.
       27(1951):321-39.

2895. Carswell, E. W. Among These Hills: A History of Falling
       Waters State Park. Bonifay: Central Press, 1968.

2896. Church, Alonzo. "A Dash Through the Everglades, " Te-
       questa 9(1949):13-41.

2897. Darrow, Dorothy. "Reminiscences of the Lake Okeechobee
       Area, 1912-1922, " Tequesta 27(1967):7-22.

2898. Dickinson, W. E. "In Quest of an Adult Crocodile, " Ever-
       glades Nat. Hist. 1(1953):151-56.

2899. Dix, E. A. and J. N. MacGonigle. "Everglades of Flori-
       da, " Century 49(1905):512-27.

2900.   Douglas, Marjory Stoneman. The Everglades: River of
        Grass. New York: Rinehart and Co., 1947.

2901.   Dovell, Junias E. "A History of the Everglades of Florida."
        Ph. D. dissertation, University of North Carolina, 1947.

2902.   _____. "The Everglades Before Reclamation, " F. H. Q.
        26(1947):1-43.

2903.   _____. "The Everglades: A Florida Frontier, " Ag.
        Hist. 22(1948):187-97.

2904.   Fairchild, David. "Some Plant Reminiscences of Southern
        Florida, " Tequesta 1(1942):8-15.

2905.   Gifford, John. The Everglades and Other Essays Relating
        to Southern Florida. Kansas City: The Everglades Land
Sales Co., 1911.

2906.   Griswold, Oliver Tudor. "Have We Saved the Everglades?"
        Living Wilderness 13(1953):1-10.

2907.   Hanna, Alfred Jackson and Kathryn Abbey Hanna. Lake
        Okeechobee, Wellspring of the Everglades. . . . Indianapolis:
Bobbs-Merrill Company, 1948.

2908.   Harney, Will Wallace. "The Drainage of the Everglades, "
        Harper's New Mo. Mag. 68(1884):598-605.

2909.   Humes, Ralph H. "A Short History of Liguus Collecting
        With a List of Collectors 1744-1958, " Tequesta 25(1965):
67-82.

2910.   Marchman, Walt P., ed. "The Ingrahan Everglades Ex-
        ploring Expedition, 1892, " Tequesta 7(1947):3-43.

2911.   McMullen, Edwin Wallace. "The Origin of the Term Ever-
        glades, " Am. Speech 28(1953):26-34.

2912.   Morrison, R. D. "America's Last Frontier: Florida Ever-
        glades, Perhaps The Site Of Our Next National Park, " Na-
ture Mag. 34(1941):570-72+ .

2913.   New Orleans Times-Democrat. "Across South Central Flor-
        ida in 1882: The Account Of The First New Orleans Times-
Democrat Exploring Expedition, " Tequesta 11(1951):63-92.

2914.   "Notes on the Passage Across the Everglades from the
        News--St. Augustine: January 8, 1841, " Tequesta 20(1960):
57-65.

2915.   Pierce, Charles William. "The Cruise of the Bonton
        [1885], " Tequesta 22(1962):3-63.

226   Florida History

2916. Robertson, William B. R., Jr. Everglades, The Park
Story. Miami: University of Miami Press, 1958.

2917. Rudloe, Jack. The Sea Brings Forth. New York: Alfred
A. Knopf, 1968.

2918. Salamanca, Lucy. "With Audubon in the Florida Keys,"
Nat. Hist. 60(1951):24-31.

2919. Scott, Harold A. "Central and Southern Florida Flood Control [ca. 1906-1948]," Mil. Engineer 40(1948):502-05.

2920. Stephan, L. L. "Geographic Role of the Everglades in the
Early History of Florida," Scientific Mo. 55(1942):515-26.

2921. Tebeau, Charlton W. Man in the Everglades: 2,000 Years
Of Human History In The Everglades National Park. Coral
Gables: University of Miami Press, 1968.

2922. Truslow, Frederick Kent and Frederick G. Vosburgh.
"Threatened Glories of Everglades National Park," Nat.
Geo. Mag. 132(1967):508-53.

2923. Vinten, C. R. "Those Were the Good Old Days," Everglades Nat. Hist. 3(1955):85-88.

2924. Vosburgh, John R. "Memorial Planned for Warden Who
Died to Save Glades Birds," Audubon Mag. 55(1953):150-51.

2925. Wallace, Tom. "Florida Development," Planning and Civic
Comment 17(1952):1-5.

2926. Will, Lawrence E. Cracker History of Okeechobee. St.
Petersburg: Great Outdoors Publishing Company, 1964.

2927. _____. Okeechobee Boats and Skippers. St. Petersburg:
Great Outdoors Publishing Co., 1965.

2928. _____. Okeechobee Catfishing. St. Petersburg: Great
Outdoors Publishing Co., 1965.

2929. _____. Okeechobee Hurricane. St. Petersburg: Great
Outdoors Publishing Co., 1961.

2930. Williams, Archie P. "Across South Central Florida in
1882: The Account Of The First New Orleans Times-Democrat Exploring Expedition," Tequesta 10(1950):49-88.

2931. Wintringham, Mary K., ed. "North To South Through the
Glades in 1883; The Account Of The Second Expedition Into
The Florida Everglades By The New Orleans Times-Democrat,"
Tequesta 23(1963):33-59.

2932. Wright, Albert Hazen. Our Georgia-Florida Frontier; The
Okefinokee Swamp, Its History And Cartography. Ithaca:
Cornell University Press, 1945.

AUTHOR INDEX

(Numbers refer to entry numbers)

Barfield, W. D.; 792
Barker, T. D.; 1673, 1674
Barlow, R. H.; 143
Barnd, M. O.; 1932
Barnett, B. H.; 1933
Barns, P. D.; 1775
Barnwell, J. W.; 317
Baroco, J. V.; 1675
Barr, C. J.; 872
Barr, R. B.; 2235
Barrientos, B.; 253
Barrow, M. V.; 1593, 1749
Barrs, B.; 567
Bartholf, J. F.; 1252
Bartly, E. R.; 1776
Barton, C. H.; 1719
Bartram, J.; 1227, 1228
Bashful, E. W.; 1777, 1778
Bass, J.; 1944
Bassett, J. S.; 725
Bates, T.; 2236, 2237
Bathe, G.; 2015
Bauskett, J. S.; 166
Baxter, J. M.; 144
Beach, R. E.; 2497
Beard, D. B.; 2890, 2891
Beare, N.; 2508
Bearss, E. C.; 1124-7
Beater, J.; 167, 168
Beazley, J. S.; 145
Bécker, J.; 763
Beecher, C.; 2367
Beecher, E. W. B.; 1253
Beer, W.; 52
Beeson, E.; 2667
Beeson, K. H., Jr.; 486, 1621
Belknap, R.; 1210
Bell, E. L.; 2287
Bell, H. C.; 53
Bellamy, J.; 793, 1652
Bellamy, R.; 254
Bellman, S. I.; 2443
Bellwood, R.; 2784
Bemis, S. F.; 764
Bemrose, J.; 873-4
Bennett, C. E.; 226, 318-22,
    2047, 2856
Bentley, G. R.; 1162, 1254
Benzoni, F.; 1945
Bergquist, C. C.; 1
Bernard, H. R.; 1946
Bertolette, D. F. K.; 323
Besson, P.; 324

Beth, L. P.; 1869
Bethel, J. A.; 2657
Bevis, W. P.; 794
Bickel, K. A.; 1044, 2838
Biddle, M. S. F.; 2533
Bigelow, G. E.; 2444
Biggar, H. P.; 325
Bill, L.; 1256
Bingham, F. S.; 2556
Bingham, M. T.; 1045, 2592
Bisceglia, L. R.; 765
Bishop, J.; 1779
Bittle, G. C.; 795, 875, 876,
    1084
Black, M. W.; 1556, 2355,
    2369, 2373
Blackman, E. V.; 2593
Blackman, L. W.; 1700, 2273
Blackman, W. F.; 2823
Blackwell, C. W.; 1846
Blackwell, H. G.; 2558
Blake, S. E.; 2016, 2731
Blakey, A. F.; 1947
Blanchard, R. E.; 2300
Blanding, D.; 1378
Blassingame, W.; 2111
Blatchley, W. S.; 1379
Bliss, C. H.; 2639
Bloomfield, M.; 1258
Bogg, W. R.; 1085
Boggess, F. C. M.; 1252, 2294
Boggs, R. S.; 2762
Bohnenberger, C.; 457
Boiler, W. F., Jr.; 1653
Boldt, A. W.; 2274
Bolton, H. E.; 169, 227
Booth, F.; 2499
Born, J. D.; 513
Bourne, E. G.; 326
Bouza Brey, F.; 412
Bowe, R. J.; 170
Bowman, R. L.; 2238
Bowser, I. W.; 1701
Boyd, M. F., 146, 291, 362-4,
    423, 458, 568, 672-3, 877-8,
    969, 1128-30, 1434-6, 2079,
    2110, 2855
Boykin, E. C.; 1147
Boynton, C. B.; 1148
Bradley, L. J.; 73
Brannon, P. A.; 2112
Brawley, B.; 987
Brebner, J. B.; 228

Breeze, L. E.; 1131, 1517
Brevard, C. M.; 171, 172, 2307
Brewster, L. F.; 514
Brichard, M. R.; 1257
Bridges, J. H.; 1594
Brigham, C. S.; 1654
Brinton, D. G.; 173, 1259
Bristol, L. M.; 1595
Broadus, E. K.; 1968
Brooke, B.; 1702
Brookfield, C. M.; 2048, 2090, 2296, 2892
Brooks, A. M.; 1260, 2668
Brooks, P. C.; 766, 767
Brooks, T. J.; 174
Brooks, W. E.; 1518
Brown, B.; 2515
Brown, C. K.; 1907
Brown, C. R.; 2049
Brown, G. S.; 642
Brown, J. A.; 674
Brown, M. W.; 1969
Brown, T. O.; 2113
Brown, V. L.; 459
Browne, J. B.; 2017, 2559
Browning, E. G.; 1541
Bruce, H. A.; 726
Brunner, K. A.; 2
Brush, J. D.; 2721
Bryant, W. C.; 1261
Buchanan, P.; 2594
Buchanan, R. C.; 879
Buchholz, F. W.; 2792
Buckman, H. H.; 103
Buckman, H. H., III; 2476
Buford, R. H.; 2301
Buhler, C. F.; 229
Buker, G. E.; 230, 880
Bullen, R. P.; 292, 569, 2114, 2472, 2763
Bulske, M. E.; 1380
Burdett, S. E.; 1132, 2342
Burghard, A.; 2462, 2511
Burkhardt, H. J.; 1948
Burns, A. W.; 2810
Burns, F. P.; 643
Burns, T. J.; 1437
Burton, M. D.; 2006
Bush, G. G.; 1557
Bushnell, C. G.; 365
Bushong, A. D.; 147
Butcher, D.; 2893
Butler, H. L.; 2640

Cabeza de Vaca, A. N.; 231, 232, 233, 1229
Cahill, M.; 1163
Caidin, M.; 2494
Calderon, G. D. V.; 1438
Caldwell, C. K.; 1086
Calkin, C. I.; 2669
Callahan, N.; 570
Calvert, J. M.; 3
Camin, A.; 255
Camp, V., Jr.; 1149
Campbell, A. C.; 104
Campbell, D. S.; 1596, 2314
Campbell, J. T.; 796
Campbell, R.; 1262
Campbell, R. L.; 175
Canova, A. P.; 881, 1263
Capron, L.; 366, 2115, 2116, 2629
Caravallo y Miyeres, C.; 2671
Cardwell, G. A.; 882
Carleton, W. G.; 2239
Carney, J. J.; 2595
Carothers, M. W.; 2450
Carper, N. G.; 2007
Carr, K. L.; 148
Carroll, M. T. A.; 1439
Carse, R.; 2050
Carson, J. M.; 1780, 1781
Carson, R. B.; 2894
Carson, R. L.; 176, 1211, 2292, 2293, 2608, 2609, 2596
Carswell, E. W.; 1519, 2535, 2895
Carter, C. E.; 460, 487, 516-7, 798-802
Carter, J. A.; 1949, 1950
Carter, W. H.; 1497
Carter, R.; 2670
Casey, R. R.; 2117
Cash, W. T.; 177, 1133, 1520, 1847, 2080, 2337, 2617, 2732, 2817, 2839
Castelnau, F., Comte de; 1264
Catesby, M.; 1230
Catterall, R. C. H.; 768
Caughley, J. W.; 461, 488
Chalker, W. J.; 1677
Chalmers, D.; 1848
Chamberlain, R. S.; 2051
Chamberlain, Captain V.; 1087
Chambers, H. E.; 149
Chandler, W.; 883

Chaney, M. A.; 2118
Chapin, G. M.; 178
Chapman, M.; 1678
Chardkoff, R. B.; 1720
Charlevoix, P. F. X.; 327
Chatelain, V. E.; 424, 425, 1441, 2672
Chazal, L. H.; 2822
Cheetham, J. M.; 2091
Cherry, A. L.; 2641
Chester, D.; 462
Childs, T.; 884
Chipley, W. D.; 2642
Choate, C. A.; 293, 1349
Christian, E.; 2724
Christie, T. L.; 1849
Church, A.; 2896
Clark, Anna; 727
Clark, J. H.; 1088
Clark, M. M.; 1970
Clark, P.; 1000
Clarke, G. I. F.; 703, 803
Clarke, R. L.; 1046, 1134
Claureaul, H. P.; 1443
Clausen, C. J.; 367, 885
Clendenen, C. C.; 1164
Cloyd, W. C.; 1266
Clubbs, O.; 2397, 2398, 2479, 2643
Coale, E. J.; 1267
Cobb, A.; 1597
Cobb, J. N.; 1951
Cockran, T. E.; 1558
Cockrell, A. W.; 2733
Coe, C. H.; 971, 972, 2119
Coffman, F. L. V.; 150
Cohen, I.; 2597
Cohen, M. M.; 888
Coker, W. S.; 54
Cole, E.; 1686
Cole, J. W.; 2644
Cole, R. H.; 1135
Cole, T. L.; 4
Colee, H.; 328
Collver, L. L. W.; 2512
Conduitte, G. G.; 1680
Conly, R. L.; 2673
Connolly, M. J.; 234, 2674
Connor, J. T.; 256, 368, 426
Conoley, R. E.; 1850
Conrad, M. D.; 1165
Cook, D. L.; 1559
Cook, E. D.; 2522

Cooper, J.; 704
Cooper, J. C.; 2405
Copeland, E. A.; 1681
Copeland, H. C.; 2637
Copeland, L. S.; 179
Copeland, R. W., Jr.; 1560
Copp, B. A.; 717
Copp, E. J.; 1089
Corbitt, D. C.; 489, 592, 593, 594, 595, 644, 675
Corcoran, J. P., Jr.; 1797
Corkran, D. H.; 2120
Corliss, C. J.; 2019-21
Corse, C. D.; 105, 490, 676, 2121, 2712, 2725, 2869
Corse, H. M.; 2052
Cortada, J. W.; 1047
Cory, C. B.; 1268, 1269
Cory, L. W.; 1851
Cotterill, R. S.; 677, 2122, 2469
Covington, J.; 180, 257, 436, 463, 491, 596, 804-7, 889-95, 988, 1598, 1908-9, 2123-7, 2765, 2840
Cowley, M.; 2252
Cowley, W. A.; 1852
Cox, I. J.; 369-70, 645-8
Cox, J.; 1166
Cox, L.; 1166
Cox, M. G.; 1167, 1381, 2456
Cox, O. C.; 2878
Coxe, D.; 1231
Craig, A. K.; 151, 2128
Craig, J. C.; 2538
Crandall, R. K.; 697
Cresson, W. P.; 728
Crist, R. E.; 1971
Croom, W. D.; 1090
Crosby, H. B.; 1782
Crosby, O. M.; 1270
Cross, J. H.; 571
Crow, C. L.; 1599, 1600
Cubberly, F.; 769, 896, 1853, 2129, 2870, 2874
Cumberland, C. C.; 2645
Cumming, W. P.; 152, 153
Cunkle, A.; 1952
Curley, M. J.; 1444
Current, R. N.; 2446
Curry, J. L. M.; 770
Cushman, J. D., Jr.; 808, 1150, 2498-9, 1500-1

Dumble, A. E. ; 2619
Dumont, M. W. ; 1419
Dunkle, J. R. ; 160, 2678, 2679
Dunn, H. ; 187, 823, 1859
Dunn, W. E. ; 438, 439, 2680
Dupont, C. H. ; 1978
Dupre Brown, G. ; 373
DuPuis, J. G. ; 1725
Duren, C. M. ; 1093
Durkin, J. T. ; 2399
Duryea, N. L. ; 2631
Dusenburg, G. ; 1385
Dutchak, E. M. ; 1660
Dyrenforth, L. Y. ; 1730

Easley, P. S. ; 1386
Eason, H. H. ; 1562
East, O. G. ; 1054, 2138, 2139
Eastman, J. W. ; 2386
Eaton, J. H. ; 733
Eby, C. D., Jr. ; 899, 2681
Eckert, E. K. ; 1169, 2422
Eddy, H. M. ; 109, 110
Edwards, J. L. ; 1275
Edwards, L. A. ; 2802
Egan, C. L. ; 650
Egan, P. ; 1094
Ehrmann, W. ; 1838
Ehrmann, W. W. ; 2140
Elderdice, D. ; 2141
Ellicott, A. ; 598
Elliot, C. E. ; 2741
Ellis, L. B. ; 2142
Emerson, W. C. ; 2143
Emig, E. J. ; 57
Engelhardt, Z. ; 1447
Eppes, Mrs. N. W. ; 2339
Erickson, R. ; 2326
Erickson, W. T. ; 1789
Estey, W. W. ; 2779
Evans, J. B. ; 1448
Evans, W. ; 2838
Ewell, F. A. ; 2614
Ewing, C. A. M. ; 1170
Ezell, B. F. ; 1582

Fackler, S. A. ; 2340
Fain, M. ; 2357
Fairbanks, G. R. ; 188, 189, 190, 374, 1503, 2485, 2682
Fairchild, D. ; 2904
Fairlie, M. C. ; 191, 1727, 1728

Falero, F., Jr. ; 1153
Falk, J. A. ; 1790
Farmar, R. ; 519
Farney, C. M. ; 192
Farris, C. D. ; 824, 2244
Favrot, H. L. ; 651, 652
Faye, S. ; 427, 440, 653
Feibelman, H. U. ; 1791, 2291, 2428
Fenlon, P. E. ; 2026-9
Ferguson, T. M. ; 2384
Fernandez-Florez, D. ; 375, 376, 1623
Ferrel, S. S. ; 1055
Fether, H. ; 2610
Fillingim, T. D. ; 2879
Fisackerly, H. G. ; 211
Fishbein, H. ; 1822
Fisher, P. W. ; 1704
Fisher, R. A. ; 735
Fitzgerald, T. E. ; 2832, 2833
Flannery, E. F. ; 900
Fleishel, M. L. ; 2352
Fleming, C. S. ; 2317
Fleming, F. P. ; 1095, 2341, 2477
Fletcher, D. U. ; 111
Flory, C. R. ; 1860, 2458
Flynn, S. J. ; 194
Flynt, J. W. ; 1861, 1862, 1863, 1864, 2008, 2353
Folmer, H. ; 331
Folsom, M. ; 2684
Foraker, A. G. ; 1730
Forbes, J ; 679
Forbes, J. G. ; 1288
Ford, A. ; 2282
Ford, L. C. ; 441
Foreman, G. ; 902, 2144
Forry, S. ; 903
Forshay, D. A. ; 2826
Foss, J. H. ; 1289
Foster, G. ; 1521
Fowler, A. ; 1504
Fox, C. D. ; 1403
France, A. ; 1404
France, R. H. ; 1405
Francoise de La Porte, C. de C. ; 827
Frantzis, G. ; 1955, 2537
Frasca, J. ; 2616
Fraser, W. B. ; 2685
Frazure, H. ; 2599

234

Freeland, H. C.; 2409
Freeman, E. C.; 2145
French, B. F.; 238, 2058
French, S.; 1290
Fries, K.; 2624
Fritot, J. R.; 572
Fritz, F. I.; 195, 2516, 2841
Fry, A.; 1584
Fuller, A. W. F.; 239
Fuller, B. D.; 466
Fuller, H. B.; 772
Fuller, T. M.; 1661
Fuller, W. P.; 2385
Futch, O. L.; 1057, 1058

Gadsden, Captain J.; 114, 738, 904
Gaines, J. P., Jr.; 1662
Gallaher, A., Jr.; 2146
Galphin, R.; 2393
Galvez, B. de; 520, 599
Gammon, W. L.; 2410
Gannon, M. V.; 60, 1449-52, 2468
Garcia, G.; 240
Gardiner, R. S.; 1292
Garnett, B. P.; 2562
Garvin, R.; 2245
Garwood, H. C.; 1603
Garwood, S. B.; 1865
Gatewood, G. W.; 1406, 1523, 2658
Gatewood, W. B., Jr.; 1212
Gauld, C. A.; 521
Gauld, G.; 1236
Gearhart, E. B.; 1505
Gearhart, E. G., Jr.; 1956
Geiger, M. J., Father; 1453, 1454, 1455
Georges, R. A.; 1624
Gibson, J. L.; 297
Giddings, J. R.; 719, 905
Gifford, G. E., Jr.; 2478
Gifford, J. C.; 906, 2147, 2842, 2905
Gilkes, L.; 2321
Gill, S. C.; 1683
Gillaspie, W. R.; 377, 378
Gilliam, F. M.; 2246
Gilpin, H. D.; 828
Gilpin, J. R.; 1294, 1295
Gilpin, V.; 2097
Gipson, L. H.; 15, 467, 492, 522

Gleason, W. H.; 1171
Glenn, J. N.; 2686
Glicksberg, C. I.; 1296
Glodt, J. T.; 1457
Glunt, J. D.; 600, 854, 829
Gober, William; 1980
Goggin, J. M.; 16, 196, 297, 428, 468, 974, 2148-53
Goggins, L. M.; 1731
Gold, P. D.; 1803, 2834
Gold, R. L.; 442, 443, 469, 470, 471, 493, 1456
Gonciar, B.; 2154
Gonzalez, S. J.; 2649
Gonzalez, T. A.; 2517
Goodbody, A.; 2880
Goodyear, A. C.; 2155
Gore, E. H.; 2625
Gorman, M. A. F.; 332
Gottschall, A. H.; 1297
Goulding, F. R.; 1298
Goulding, R. L.; 1564, 2286, 2563
Goza, W. M.; 2083
Graff, M. B.; 429, 2586
Graham, T. S.; 1011
Graham, W. A.; 1981
Gramling, J. C., Jr.; 1792
Grandoff, V. C.; 1625
Green, A. A.; 2057
Green, E. E.; 333
Green, E. L.; 2743
Green, G. N.; 1866, 1867, 1868
Greenbie, J.; 2843
Greenhow, R.; 197
Greenlee, R. F.; 2156, 2157, 2158
Greenman, E. F.; 2159
Greenslade, M. T.; 680, 681
Grenelle, E. H.; 2288
Griffen, W. B.; 17, 379
Griffin, C. C.; 61, 773
Griffin, J. B.; 739, 1458, 2160, 2161, 2854
Griffin, R. W.; 830
Griffin, W. B.; 115
Griffing, J. R.; 1300
Grismer, K. H.; 2518, 2717, 2718, 2722, 2767
Griswold, O. T.; 908, 2509, 2892
Groene, B. H.; 831, 1096, 2332, 2744, 2745

Grubbs, D. H.; 2009
Guenin, E.; 334
Guerry, J. U.; 1524

Haarmann, A. W.; 523, 707
Haas, M. R.; 2162
Habig, M. A.; 1459
Hadd, D. R.; 1030, 1031, 2746
Haines, H. S.; 1732
Halbe, J. M.; 909
Halbert, H. S.; 601
Hale, N.; 116
Hall, W. H.; 1059, 1626
Halley, H.; 1627
Hallock, C.; 1301
Halsell, W. D.; 2310
Hamilton, H.; 910
Hamilton, P. J.; 524, 525
Hammond, A. E.; 335, 832, 911
Hammond. E. A.; 1733, 1734,
   2098
Hammond, J. M.; 1407
Hammond, S. L.; 1585, 1586,
   1587
Hand, S. E.; 1565
Hanke, L.; 117
Hanna, A. J.; 18, 19, 62, 198,
   241, 472, 1060, 1097, 1604,
   2329, 2424, 2876, 2907
Hanna, J. S.; 2299
Hanna, K. A.; 2907
Hanna, K. T.; 199
Hansen, A. M.; 1684
Hardaway, S. J.; 833
Hardy, A. V.; 1735
Hardy, I. D.; 1303
Hargis, M.; 2235
Harlan, R. C.; 494
Harlan, W. H.; 1736
Harley, A. F.; 154
Harman, J. E.; 380
Harney, W. W.; 2908
Harper, R. M.; 834, 1912, 1982,
   1983, 2844, 2845
Harrell, L. D. S.; 1737
Harrigan, A.; 2747
Harrington, J. C.; 2861
Harris, L.; 774
Harrison, B.; 200, 2163, 2164,
   2544
Harrison, F. K.; 655
Harshberger, E. L.; 2165
Harvey, F. L.; 1408

Hasbrouk, A.; 20, 708
Haskew, R. P.; 835
Hastings, D. O.; 836
Hatch, A.; 2447
Hathaway, J. A.; 2555
Harvard, W. C.; 1061, 1785,
   1869
Hawkins, J. M.; 336, 1237
Hawks, J. M.; 1304, 1305
Hayden, C. R.; 1172, 2748
Headley, J. T.; 242
Hebel, I. B.; 2084, 2531, 2835,
   2836
Hefferman, J. B.; 1151
Heilprin, A.; 1306
Held, R. E.; 118, 413
Hellier, W. R.; 2536, 2846
Helps, S. A.; 381
Hendry, B. L.; 21
Hendry, F. A.; 2749
Henry, E.; 1588
Henry, E. W.; 2750, 2751
Henshall, J. A.; 1307, 1308,
   1309
Hepburn, A.; 1409
Hering, J.; 837, 838
Hernandez Diaz, J.; 299
Hester, L. A.; 1870
Hetherington, M. F.; 2829
Hicks, J. D.; 1936
Higginson, T. W.; 337, 1098,
   1099, 1100
Higgs, C. D.; 382
Hildreth, C. H.; 2031, 2525
Hill, D. E.; 839
Hill, E. G.; 1173
Hill, L. B.; 2318
Hill, N. A.; 1410
Hill, R. N.; 1411
Hill, R. R.; 61
Hilliard, M. P.; 1460
Hine, C. V.; 1310
Hines, M. T.; 2247
Hines, N. C.; 1412
Hinkley, A. G.; 2626
Hinkley, N. E.; 414
Hinnebusch, F.; 1461
Hitchcock, E. A.; 912
Hodgson, M.; 1012
Hoffman, E. P.; 913
Hoffman, P. E.; 258, 259, 384
Holland, J. W.; 740
Hollingsworth, H.; 914

236

Kaufman, L. R.; 2392
Kearney, K. E.; 2403
Keasbey, A. Q.; 1315
Keegan, P. G. J.; 1468
Keen, M. W.; 1066
Keene, J. L.; 2368
Keene, O. L.; 2545
Keith, R.; 840
Kendall, J. S.; 659
Kendrick, B.; 1876, 2086
Kennedy, S.; 2168
Kennedy, W. T.; 2816
Kennerly, A.; 1663
Kennett, L.; 473, 495
Kenny, M.; 1469
Ker, H.; 1316
Kerr, W. B.; 474
Kersey, H. A., Jr.; 2169
Kershaw, A. J.; 1528
Key, M.; 688
Kiker, E.; 2170
Kilgore, J.; 1664, 2752
Kilpatrick, W.; 1915, 1957,
    1958, 1959
Kimber, D. K.; 2821
Kimber, E.; 445
Kimber, S. A.; 122
King, E.; 277
King, E. A.; 1552
King, G.; 301
Kinnaird, L.; 605, 689
Kinney, S. H.; 2872
Kinsman, O. D.; 1104
Kiple, K. F.; 2250
Kleber, L. C.; 338, 446
Kline, W. D.; 2688
Klose, N.; 2425
Knapp, J. G.; 1317
Knauss, J. O.; 841, 842, 1665,
    1798, 1799, 1877, 2338,
    2713, 2714
Knight, R. D.; 2506
Knipling, E. F.; 1739
Knotts, T.; 923, 2788
Kofoed, J. C.; 2600
Kohl, J. G.; 243
Korn, B. W.; 1628
Kriese, P.; 2331
Krogman, W. M.; 2171
Kruse, P.; 709
Kruse, R. C.; 72
Kuehl, W. F.; 27, 2376

LaDuca, C. E.; 1989
Laessle, A. M.; 1916
Lagergren, H. E.; 1415
LaGodna, M. M.; 1629
LaGorce, J. O.; 203
Laird, A. M.; 1858
Lambright, E. D.; 2358
Lamoreaux, L.; 2505
Lamson, H.; 123-5, 278
Laney, H. J.; 1630
Langdon, P. E.; 1740
Lanier, S.; 1318
Lanning, J. T.; 415, 675
Lanzas, P. T.; 158
Large, J., Jr.; 1319
Larkin, J. L.; 1154
LaRonciere, C. de; 339
Larsen, W. F.; 28
Lathrop, H. Q.; 1990
Latorre, J. N.; 568
Latour, A. L.; 660
Laub, C. H.; 1598
Laudonniere, R.; 340, 1239
Laumer, F. J.; 2863, 2864
Lawren, J.; 1960
Lawson, E. W.; 244, 279, 280,
    497
Lawson, K. S.; 392, 416, 475
Laxson, D. D.; 2172
Lay, C. F.; 1708
Layng, C.; 1961, 2035
Lazarus, W. C.; 2087
Lazear, E. A.; 126
Lazenby, M. E.; 1529
Leake, J. M.; 204
Leary, L.; 606, 776
LeChalleux, N.; 341, 1240
LeDiable, Captain; 1105
Ledin, R. B.; 2290
Lee, H.; 1320
Lee, W. H.; 1538
LeFevre, E.; 2343
Lehrman, I.; 1631
Leigh, Mrs. T. R.; 2650
Lente, F. D.; 1322
Leon, A.; 393
Leon, J. M.; 1991
Leonard, I. A.; 394, 395
Leonard, P. A., Jr.; 1506
Leo Xavier, Sister; 1471
Lewis, F. G.; 843
Lewis, M. D.; 2305
Lewis, S.; 2785

Lewis, T. H.; 303
Ley, F. P., Jr.; 2753
Ley, J. C.; 2388
Leynes, B. C., Jr.; 1937
Lightfoot, E. A.; 2173
Link, A. S.; 1878
Link, M. C.; 396
Linn, E. R.; 1992
Linneman, W. R.; 2610
Linschoten, J. H. V.; 1241
Lipscomb, O. H.; 1472
Lisenby, J. A.; 2251
Lloyd, D. G.; 29
Lockey, J. B.; 476, 498, 607-8,
    631, 844, 1567
Long, B. L. R.; 2298
Long, D.; 245, 1632, 1741,
    2010, 2011, 2036, 2567,
    2568, 2769, 2770
Long, E. C.; 205, 2415
Long, J. M.; 547
Long, R. G.; 2574
Longstreet, R. J.; 2615
Longworth, M. T.; 2689
Lonn, E.; 1155
Lorant, S.; 342
Lord, D.; 1879
Lord, M. M., Jr.; 2482
Lovejoy, G. W.; 1633
Lowe, E. R.; 260
Lowe, J. W.; 2012
Lowe, R. G.; 744, 778
Lowery, W.; 246, 343, 397
Luther, E. A.; 447
Lyon, A. B.; 1473
Lyon, E.; 384
Lyons, E.; 2848

McAlister, L. N.; 661, 690,
    691
McAvoy, T. T.; 73
McCall, G. A.; 926
McCarthy, J. E.; 975
MacCauley, C.; 2174
MaClahlan, J. M.; 1742
McClellan, J. E.; 1568
McCord, G.; 845, 2755
McCullough, M.; 2037
McDonald, J. A.; 1323
McDonnel, V. H.; 1880
MacDowell, C. L.; 2787
McDuffee, L. B.; 130, 2584
McGaughy, F. P.; 927

McGehee, E. M.; 1840
McGehee, J. C.; 1032
McGoldrick, Sister T. J.; 1569
MacGonigle, J. N.; 2899
McGuire, V.; 31
McIntosh, R. H.; 1800
McJunkin, D.; 2128
McKay, D. B.; 206
McKelvey, B.; 1177
McKenney, T. L.; 2175
McKinnon, J. L.; 2837
McLellan, D.; 2651
McMorries, E. Y.; 1106
McMullen, E. W.; 159, 2911
McMurray, C. D.; 1801
McMurtrie, D. C.; 32, 33, 548,
    1666
McNeer, M. Y.; 207
McNicoll, R. E.; 2176
McNulty, J. P.; 1474
McPhee, J.; 1993
McQuade, J.; 1324
McQueen, J.; 632
McQueen, R. A.; 746
McReynolds, E. C.; 2177
McRory, M. O.; 34
McVoy, E. C.; 2527
McWilliams, T. S.; 304
Mahon, J. K.; 478, 710, 720,
    928, 929, 930
Major, H. A.; 74
Malone, M. W.; 2569
Maloney, W. C.; 2570
Manier, J. T.; 2060
Mann, F. A.; 281, 2546
Manning, M. M.; 75
Mannix, D. P.; 2252
Manucy, A. C.; 76, 77, 127,
    261, 262, 573, 846, 2139,
    2652, 2690, 2858, 2862,
    2867, 2873
Marchman, W.; 128, 129
Marchman, W. P.; 2910
Margusee, J. E.; 2350
Marks, H. S.; 398, 399, 847
Marmon, K. A; 2178
Marsden, J. C.; 2620
Marsh, O. G. H.; 2583
Martin, J. W.; 2344
Martin, R. A.; 2726, 2801
Martin, S. W.; 848-52, 2345-49
Marx, R. F.; 2101
Mason, W. S. M.; 30

239

Massanet, F. D.; 393
Massari, A.; 2771
Massey, R. W., Jr.; 1994
Massolo, A. D.; 2404
Mattfield, M. S.; 1242
Maxwell, C. S.; 2601
May, E. C.; 2406, 1407
May, P. S.; 477, 2547
Mayo, L. S.; 2061
Mayo, N.; 1995
Mays, E.; 745
Meador, J. A.; 1014, 1015
Meek, A. B.; 931
Meginnis, B. A.; 1709
Mehling, H.; 2611
Meier, A.; 2253
Melish, J.; 1325
Mellon, K., Jr.; 1107
Mendelis, L. J.; 400
Mendenhall, H.D.; 1938
Mendoza Grajales, F. L. de;
263
Menendez De Aviles, P.; 264
Meredith, E. T.; 1033
Merk, J. L.; 2794
Merrick, G. E.; 2849
Merriman, R. B.; 401
Merritt, W.; 1743-8
Messick, H.; 1802
Meyers, L.; 940
Michael, M., Jr.; 1749
Micken, E. E.; 2826
Middleton, J. W.; 1803, 1804
Mier, R. E.; 2365
Milgram, J. W.; 747
Miller, E. L.; 2528
Miller, E. M.; 1605
Miller, G. J.; 1782, 1784
Miller, J. E.; 2179
Miller, L. W.; 2180
Miller, W.; 1141
Mills, J.; 1881
Miltimore, C.; 1687
Minor, W. R.; 1710
Miranda, F. de; 574
Mitchell, C. B.; 2062
Mitchell, M. C.; 1750
Mizner, A.; 1711
Mohr, C. H.; 1475
Moninger, A. V.; 2513
Monroe, J.; 711, 780
Monroe, M. B.; 2279
Moody, J. F.; 2827

Mool, J. B.; 1016
Moore, C. B.; 2850
Moore, J. H.; 853, 2691
Moore, M. M.; 1570
Moore, T. W.; 1996
Morales, D. J. V.; 662
Mordes, S.; 2653
Morris, A.; 1416
Morris, A. C.; 1634
Morrison, A. J.; 2327
Morrison, R. D.; 1912
Morse, M. E.; 2394
Moseley, W. D.; 1017
Motte, J. R.; 932, 933, 934
Mowat, C. L.; 79, 479-80, 499-
506
Mudd, N.; 1108
Mueller, E. A.; 2063, 2064,
2065, 2066
Muir, A. F.; 2396
Muir, H. L.; 2603
Muir, J.; 1417
Mullen, H. H.; 1939
Mulrennan, J. A.; 1751
Muniz, J. R.; 247, 1635, 2772
Munroe, K.; 1326
Murdoch, R. K.; 549, 609, 610,
611, 612, 633, 634, 635, 636,
698, 699, 712, 2254
Murga Sanz, M.; 282
Murphy, F.; 2417
Murphy, P.; 1882
Murphy, W. S.; 550
Musick, J. R.; 2692
Myers, J. R.; 2756

Nance, E. C.; 208, 1553
Nash, C. E.; 2612
Neill, W. T.; 80, 976, 2181-6,
2773
Nelson, P. V.; 1543
Nelson, W. M.; 1917
Newman, A. P. L.; 2781
Newton, E. W.; 183, 1712, 2654
Newton, V. M.; 1667
Ney, J.; 2632
Neyland, L. W.; 1606, 1607
Nichols, G. W.; 1327
Nichols, J. M.; 1109
Nichols, J. R.; 1918
Nichols, L. N.; 1668
Niemeyer, G. A.; 2623
Nightingale, L. T.; 209

240

Nistendirk, V. R.; 1688
Nolan, T. H.; 1067
North, H. R.; 2447
Norton, C. L.; 1328
Norton, H.; 1068
Norton, O. W.; 1110
Norwood, O.; 1018

Obenaus, K. M.; 1689
Ober, F. A.; 1330
O'Connor, M. J.; 36
O'Daniel, V. F.; 1476
Ogden, J.; 551
Ogg, F. A.; 663
Okenfuss, M. J.; 402
Olds, D. L.; 2882, 2883
Olney, G. W.; 1331
Olschkia, L.; 283
Olsen, S. J.; 1142
Olson, G. D.; 575
Omaechevarria, I.; 1477
Onis, L. de; 781, 782
Oppel, J. C.; 1213
Ore', L. J., de, Bishop; 1243, 1478
Ormond, J.; 2627
Osborn, G. C.; 552, 553, 1178, 1544, 1545
Otis, R. R.; 344
Ott, E.; 2822, 2875
Ott, E. R.; 1669, 2622
Over, F. A.; 284
Owen, W. P.; Jr.; 1795
Owens, H. P.; 2067, 2068, 2487, 2488
Owsley, F. L., Jr.; 713

Packard, W.; 1418
Padgett, J. A.; 554, 555, 556, 664
Page, D. P.; 1479
Paine, C. R.; 721
Paisley, C. L.; 1919, 1997, 2818
Palmer, A. J.; 1111
Palmer, N. A.; 1754
Palmer, H. E.; 1753, 2255
Palmer, T. Y.; 1754
Panagopoulos, E. P.; 481, 1636
Parker, D.; 1019, 1143, 1805, 1883, 1884, 2311, 2411, 2412, 2429
Parker, D. W.; 53

Parker, E.; 1806
Parker, H. H.; 937
Parker, J. F.; 1807
Parker, O. S.; 2454
Parker, R.; 2256
Parkman, F.; 345-50
Parks, A. S.; 1179
Parks, J. H.; 2383
Parks, P.; 2038
Parramore, A. E.; 1713
Parrish, C. J.; 2774
Parrish, J. O.; 938
Parsons, E. C.; 1637
Parsons, M. B.; 1808, 1809
Parton, J.; 748
Pasco, S.; 2420, 2815
Patane, J. S.; 1690
Patrick, E. B.; 211
Patrick, R. W.; 131, 210, 211, 613, 714, 783, 2319, 2400, 2480
Patton, L. C.; 1507
Paul, J. R.; 1755
Pazos Kanki, V.; 784
Peek, R. L.; 1180, 1181, 1182, 1183, 1184
Peeples, V. E.; 2659
Peithmann, I. M.; 2187
Pena y Camara, J. M. de la; 81
Pennington, E. L.; 576, 1508, 1509, 1510, 1511, 1512, 1513
Pent, R. F.; 2780
Perkins, S.; 749
Perres, M. J.; 1691
Perrine, H.; 1333
Perry, J. H.; 1426
Perry, W. L.; 1334
Peters, T.; 577, 578, 579, 1156, 2571
Petersen, J.; 2519
Peterson, M. L.; 2069, 2102
Pettengill, G. W., Jr.; 2039
Pfeifer, R. M.; 2390
Phelps, J. W.; 939
Phillips, G.; 2786
Phillips, P. L.; 2449
Phillips, R.; 1020
Phillips, U. B.; 854
Phinney, A. H.; 305, 715, 750, 1480
Pierce, C. W.; 2915
Pierce, P. N.; 940

241

Pikula, J.; 2806
Pink, H. R.; 2486
Pittman, L.; 557
Pizzo, A. P.; 2775
Plaisance, A.; 665
Plowden, G.; 2448
Poe, S. R.; 2868
Pohltecamp, D.; 1481
Porter, D. D.; 1112
Porter, E.; 1810
Porter, E. M.; 1021
Porter, E. R.; 351
Porter, J. Y.; 1756
Porter, K. W.; 941-3, 977-8,
  990-9, 2188-98, 2257-8
Porter, L. M.; 2638
Porter, R.; 2256
Portier, M.; 855
Post, C. J.; 1214
Potter, W.; 944
Pratt, K. F.; 1811
Pratt, R. H.; 2199
Pratt, T.; 2200, 2378, 2492,
  2634, 2851
Preble, G. H.; 945
Prentice, W. R.; 1144
Price, G. D.; 666
Price, H. D.; 1812, 2239, 2259,
  2260, 2261
Price, M. W.; 1157
Prichard, W.; 667
Priestley, H. I.; 248, 249
Priestly, J. B.; 1714
Prince, J. C.; 1554
Prince, S. C., Jr.; 2430, 2431
Prior, L. O.; 1885, 2262, 2423
Proctor, S.; 1035, 1069, 1070,
  1185, 1215, 1590, 1608, 1609,
  1610, 1611, 1638, 1886, 1962,
  2302, 2303
Pyburn, N. K.; 856, 1572, 1573,
  1574, 1612, 1613, 2283, 2284,
  2285, 2455, 2470, 2471

Quigg, J. E.; 946

Rachlis, E.; 2350
Rainey, F. G.; 2201
Raisz, E.; 160
Ramirez, M. D.; 1639
Ranson, R.; 212, 2306
Rattenberry, J. F.; 785
Rawlings, M. K.; 1640

Rawls, C.; 2548
Rawls, O. G.; 2070
Ray, S. H.; 1482
Rea, R. R.; 538, 558-63
Read, W. A.; 2202
Reams, G. B.; 1757
Reaver, J. R.; 1113, 1641
Redding, D. A.; 1540
Redfearn, D. H.; 2071
Redford, P.; 2613
Reding, K.; 265, 431
Redlinger, J.; 1483
Reed, A. H.; 2445
Reese, M. L.; 213
Reese, N. B.; 267
Reeves, F. B.; 2693
Reiger, J. F.; 1036, 1071,
  1073
Remington, F.; 1642
Renaut, F. P.; 668
Renz, J. H.; 83
Rerick, R. H.; 214
Reyes, E. L.; 1643
Reynolds, C. B.; 2694-7
Rhodes, F. A.; 1614, 1963,
  2395
Rhodes, H. G.; 1419
Rhyne, J. S.; 2812
Ribaut, J.; 1244
Rich, L.; 2783
Richard, M. J.; 1814
Richards, J. N.; 2782
Richards, R. L.; 947
Richardson, J. M.; 1186-95,
  1887
Richmond, Mrs. H. L.; 1715,
  2698
Rickenbach, R. V.; 1216, 1217
Rigby, T. C.; 1335
Rio Cossa, J. del; 614
Ripley, C. P.; 1888, 1889
Roady, E. E.; 2263
Roberts, A. H.; 948, 1073,
  1196, 1890, 2313
Roberts, D. C.; 1197-8, 2304
Roberts, J. M.; 2041
Roberts, K. L.; 1420, 1421,
  1422
Roberts, W.; 250, 580, 1245
Robertson, J. A.; 85, 86, 132,
  133, 306, 1484
Robertson, W. B. R.; Jr.; 2916
Robie, V. H.; 2585

242

Robin, C. C.; 1336
Robinson, A. A.; 1337
Robinson, E. L.; 2811
Robinson, L. F.; 1758
Robinson, T. R.; 2426, 2427
Robinson, W. M., Jr.; 1514
Roehrig, J. P.; 161
Rogers, B. F.; 1339, 1920, 2072
Rogers, J. S.; 1615
Rogers, W. H.; 1815
Rogers, W. W.; 857, 1037, 1075, 1139, 2043
Romans, B.; 1246
Roosevelt, R. B.; 1340
Ropes, L. G., Jr.; 1816
Roselli, B.; 1644
Rosen, F. B.; 1199, 1592
Rosser, J. L.; 1547
Roth, C. D., Jr.; 2572
Rowland, D.; 663
Rudloe, J.; 2917
Rudwick, E.; 2253
Ruffin, E.; 1038
Ruidiaz y Caravia, E.; 266
Rummel, V. C.; 1998
Rush, N. O.; 581
Russ, W. A., Jr.; 1200
Russell, C. C.; 449
Russell, M. H.; 2322
Russell, R. R.; 1022
Rutherford, R. E.; 615
Ryan, L. B.; 2073

Safransky, R. J.; 1891
Salamanca, L.; 2918
Salazar, P. de H.; 1485
Sanford, H. S.; 1892
Sanford, R. M.; 1074
Sanger, M. B.; 2510
Sanz, L. T.; 1468
Sapp, C. A.; 37
Sargeant, A. M.; 1341
Sauer, C. O.; 404
Saunders, H. R.; 38
Saunders, W. H.; 2103
Sawyer, J. J.; 1530
Scammon, E. P.; 1486
Schaal, P.; 2720
Scharff, R.; 2323
Schell, R.; 307, 2520
Schell, R. F.; 2203, 2777
Schellings, W. J.; 1158, 1218-

24
Schloenback, H. H.; 949
Schneider, M. P.; 2529
Schopf, J. D.; 1247
Schouler, J.; 751, 752, 753
Schroder, H. H.; 1342
Scisco, L. D.; 285, 286
Scott, H. A.; 2919
Scott, J. R.; 1531
Scott, K.; 2104
Scott, R. M.; 1114
Scott, R. C.; 1645
Scroggs, J. B.; 1201
Sebring, H. L.; 1818
Seckinger, R. L.; 162, 417
Seiber, T. D.; 2588
Seley, R. B., Jr.; 950
Sellards, E. H.; 39
Sellars, E. H.; 1575
Semingsen, E. M.; 2890
Serrano y Sanz, M.; 307, 405
Servies, J. A.; 40
Sessa, F. B.; 1921, 1940, 2605
Sewall, R. K.; 2699
Sewell, J. R.; 2074
Seymour, A. R.; 2819
Shambaugh, M. F.; 616
Shapee, N. D.; 2865
Shappee, N. D.; 1893, 2042, 2351
Sharf, F. A.; 2700
Sharp, H. R.; 2464, 2465
Shaw, B.; 87, 1693
Shaw, B. W.; 1692
Shea, J. G.; 41, 1487
Sheldon, J. M.; 951
Shelton, W. R.; 1423
Shenkel, J. R.; 2884
Shepard, B.; 2105
Sherlock, J. V.; 693
Shipp, B.; 309
Shoemaker, W. B.; 1344
Shofner, J. H.; 858, 1075, 1202, 1203, 1819, 1894, 1895, 1896, 1897, 2043, 2334
Shores, L. S.; 1694
Shores, V. L.; 859, 1617, 2759, 2881
Shubow, D.; 1964
Siebert, W. H.; 450-1, 507, 582-6, 1488, 1999, 2264-5
Silver, J. W.; 2356
Silver, M. H.; 1820

243

Silverstein, M.; 1821
Simmons, W. H.; 2204
Simms, W. C.; 979
Simms, W. G.; 352
Simon, T.; 1825
Simonhoff, H.; 1646
Simpson, C. T.; 1424
Simpson, F.; 1345
Simpson, J. C.; 215
Sims, L. H., Jr.; 1204
Sioussat, St. G. I.; 483
Skinner, A.; 2205
Skinner, J.; 637
Skinner, W. B.; 1076
Slaughter, F. G.; 251
Small, J. K.; 2206
Smiley, N. K.; 2408, 2573, 2574
Smiley, P.; 1647
Smith, C. L., Jr.; 1898
Smith, G. H.; 1648
Smith, G. W.; 1205
Smith, H. B.; 1822
Smith, H. D.; 2088
Smith, H. G.; 134, 406, 1491, 2207, 2705, 2706
Smith, J. A.; 1812, 1823, 1824
Smith, J. F.; 1023, 2000
Smith, J. R.; 952
Smith, M. C.; 1759
Smith, M. E.; 216, 1425
Smith, M. E. C.; 1532
Smith, P. H.; 587, 588
Smith, R.; 2266
Smith, T. L.; 1618
Smith, W. A.; 2795
Smith, W. B.; 1115
Smith, W. H. Y.; 1760
Smith, W. W.; 953
Snodgrass, D.; 217, 2549
Snyder, C. C.; 1761
Somerville, J. W.; 2075
Sosin, J. M.; 589
Souter, S.; 754
Southall, E. P.; 2267
Sowder, W. T.; 1751, 1762, 1763
Spain, R. B.; 1548
Sparks, J.; 353
Spellman, C. W.; 1492, 1493, 2208
Spoehr, A.; 2209
Sprague, J. T.; 954, 955

Spratt, J. W.; 354
Spurrier, S.; 2457
Staid, Sister M. E.; 2361
Stafford, F. J.; 2268
Stafford, R. C.; 956
Stakley, C. A.; 2269
Stallworth, H. F.; 2530
Stanley, J. R.; 2805, 2813
Stanton, E. P.; 2532
Staub, W. L.; 2828
Staudenraus, P. J.; 1116
Stearns, M. L.; 1899
Steck, F. B.; 310
Steinbach, R. H.; 2706
Steinhardt, I.; 1825
Stenberg, R. R.; 755
Stephen, L. L.; 2920
Stephens, M. C.; 860
Sterkx, H. E.; 669, 1117
Stern, D. S.; 1826
Stetson, J. B., Jr.; 135
Stimson, M. O.; 1346
Stockbridge, F. P.; 1426
Stockton, J. R.; 1922
Stoddard, H. L., Sr.; 2459
Stolee, M. S.; 1716
Stork, W.; 1248
Stout, J.; 508
Stout, M.; 508
Stover, A. J.; 1764
Stowe, H. B.; 1347
Straight, W. M.; 1765, 1766, 1767, 1768, 1769, 1770, 1771
Strichartz, R.; 1827, 1828
Strickland, A.; 1159, 1923, 2336, 2419, 2628, 2852
Stuart, M. F.; 1649
Stuart, V.; 1348
Sturgis, W. E., Jr.; 1829
Sturtevant, W. C.; 980-1, 2210-4
Sumner, W. G.; 756
Sunderman, J. F.; 861
Surber, E. L.; 2661
Swanton, J. R.; 311, 312, 313, 314, 2215
Sweet, F. H.; 1650
Sweet, Z. W.; 1077, 2620
Sweets, J. F.; 1900
Swenson, L. S., Jr.; 1924
Szaszdi, A.; 670

Tanner, E. C.; 2379

Tanner, H. H.; 90, 91, 92, 509, 510, 617, 618, 619, 620, 638
Tarbox, I. N.; 2453
Tarry, E.; 2381
Taylor, A. E.; 1901
Taylor, E. O.; 957
Taylor, F. H.; 1349
Taylor, G.; 590
Taylor, G. E. W.; 42
Tebault, A. G.; 218
Tebbel, J.; 722, 958, 982
Tebeau, C. W.; 136, 176, 219, 220, 2495, 2575, 2797, 2921
Temple, D. L.; 43
Ten Eick, V. E.; 2534
Tenney, J. F.; 2466
Tepaske, J. J.; 407, 418-20
Thielen, B.; 2576
Thoburn, R.; 1732
Thomas, D. H.; 93, 94, 862, 1078
Thomas, E. F.; 1695
Thomas, F. J.; 2589
Thompson, A. W.; 863, 1024, 1079, 1350, 2044, 2483
Thompson, B.; 669
Thompson, L. S.; 44
Thompson, W. E.; 1830
Thorner, R. M.; 1838, 2853
Thrift, C. T., Jr.; 1533, 1619, 2295
Tilden, P. M.; 1965
Tillis, J. D.; 959
Tindall, G. B.; 1941
Tingley, H. E. B.; 484
Tischendorf, A. P.; 1925
Tolle, R. L.; 1772
Tomberlin, J. A.; 1576
Torrey, B.; 1351
Townsend, E. W.; 2413
Townshend, F. T.; 1352
Travers, J. W.; 2635
Troetschel, H. T., Jr.; 1826, 2360
True, D. O.; 163, 164
Trumball, H.; 252
Trumbull, M. R.; 2371
Truslow, F. K.; 2922
Tucker, P. C.; 511
Turner, F. J.; 700, 701, 702
Tyler, D. F.; 1353
Tyler, M.; 960

Tyson, W. K.; 2001

Udell, B. S.; 1831
Ugarte, R. V.; 408
Ulmann, A.; 2723
Umble, J. S.; 1651
Upchurch, J. C.; 621, 694
Utley, G. B.; 1697

VanBeck, J. C.; 2217
Van Beck, L. M.; 2217
Van Brunt, D.; 1494
Van Camper, J. T.; 2707
Vance, M. M.; 1206
Vanderblue, H. B.; 1942
Van Holmes, J.; 2002
Van Ness, Major W. P.; 757, 961
Van Schaick, J., Jr.; 1427
Vasques, A.; 315
Venable, E. M.; 2374
Verner, C.; 1577
Vernon, R. O.; 2076
Verrill, A. H.; 1428
Vickers-Smith, L. D.; 2521
Vigil, C. M.; 268
Vigneras, L. A.; 269, 432
Vignoles, C. B.; 221, 222
Vinten, C. R.; 137, 2890, 2923
Vollbrecht, J. L.; 2708
Volney, C. F. C.; 1354
Vosburgh, F. G.; 2922
Vosburgh, J. R.; 2924
Voss, G. L.; 2077

Wager, R. E.; 2218
Wagner, H. J.; 2280
Wagstaff, W. S.; 2550
Waldby, H. O.; 1833
Waldo, H.; 2312
Walker, J. L.; 2089
Walker, H. P.; 962
Wallace, A.; 1698
Wallace, F. W.; 2219
Wallace, J.; 1207
Wallace, T.; 2925
Walter, S. T.; 2323
Ward, M. M.; 983
Wardle, H. N.; 2220
Ware, J. D.; 409, 622, 2474
Waring, J. I.; 1773
Warner, H. G.; 1355

Warren, F.; 1902
Warren, H. G.; 138
Warren, R. W.; 858
Waters, D.; 1429
Watt, M. G.; 2359
Watteyne, V.; 1356
Waybright, R. J.; 1834, 1835
Webb, A. S.; 963
Webb, D.; 2709
Webb, H. A.; 2221
Webb, W. S.; 1357
Webber, C. H.; 1358
Webster, D.; 787
Weidenbach, N. L.; 864
Weigall, T. H.; 1430
Weilding, P. J.; 2514
Weinberg, S. J.; 1039
Weiss, S. S.; 1858
Wellborn, C. G., Jr.; 1225
Welles, G.; 1145
Wells, G. W.; 1359
Wells, W. A.; 984
Wells, W. J.; 2354
Welsh, H.; 2222
Wenhold, L. L.; 355, 452,
2886
Wentworth, T. T.; 223, 2656
West, E. H.; 695
West, G. M.; 2662
West, W.; 1717
Westbury, W.; 2884
Westmeyer, D. P.; 2778
Whitaker, A. P.; 623, 624,
1926
Whitaker, M. A.; 1578
White, F. F., Jr.; 964
White, J. W.; 1360
White, L.; 2710
White, L. V.; 2577, 2578
Whitehead, W. A.; 2579
Whitehurst, M. K.; 2808
Whitfield, J. B.; 865, 1836-7,
1903
Whiting, H.; 1361
Whitman, A.; 866
Whitney, J. P.; 1362
Whitson, L. D.; 2580
Wickert, E.; 1431
Wickham, J.; 2711
Wilgus, A. C.; 139
Wilkinson, R. A.; 1363
Wilkinson, W. H.; 316
Will, L. E.; 2078, 2463, 2491,

2496, 2926, 2927, 2928, 2929
Willey, G. R.; 47, 2223, 2224,
2225
William, A. C.; 2830
Williams, A. P.; 2930
Williams, A. W.; 1146
Williams, E. H., Jr.; 1838
Williams, E. L., Jr.; 1025,
2270
Williams, E. R.; 1208, 1495
Williams, G. M.; 1718
Williams, I. M.; 965
Williams, J. L.; 867
Williams, J. Lee; 1364, 1365
Williamson, E. C.; 1120, 1839,
1904, 1905, 1906, 2271, 2316,
2335
Willing, D. L.; 2045
Willoughby, H. L.; 1366
Wilson, E. F.; 165
Wilson, F.; 2461
Wilson, F. P.; 1367, 2606
Wilson, J. R.; 1840
Wilson, M. M.; 986, 2226-31,
2825
Wilson, O. C.; 868
Wilson, R. D.; 869
Wilson, T. B.; 2272
Winter, N. O.; 1432
Winters, C. Z.; 48
Wintringham, M. K.; 2931
Wiren, G.; 1433
Withington, C. M.; 2552
Wolff, R. P.; 1927, 2607
Wood, R. E.; 1774
Woodford, M. M.; 1121
Woodford, S. A.; 967
Woodman, C.; 1209
Woodman, J.; 2553, 2554
Woodward, A. L.; 966
Wooster, R. A.; 1040, 1041,
1042
Worcester, D. E.; 564
Wright, A. H.; 2932
Wright, F. A.; 1841
Wright, G.; 1122
Wright, I. A.; 97, 453
Wright, J. L.; 454, 625, 656,
696, 724
Wroth, L. C.; 98
Wyllys, R. K.; 716, 759
Wysor, F. J.; 140

Yglesias, J.; 2789
Yoder, L. C.; 1943
Yonge, J. C.; 1080
Yonge, J. J.; 2281
Young, Captain H.; 760
Young, R. J.; 1928
Young, R. W.; 788, 968
Yulee, C. W.; 2484
Yulee, D. L.; 1043

Zabriskie, G. A.; 287
Zornow, W. F.; 1081
Zubillaga, F.; 1496
Zuniga y Zerda, J. de; 455

SUBJECT INDEX

(Numbers refer to entry numbers)

Adams-Onis Treaty, 761-88
Alachua County, 2790-95
Amelia Island, 2486
Anderson, Walker, 2281
Apalachee, during British occupation, 557; fortifications of, 431;
    Penas' expedition, 362-64
Apalachicola, 2487-88
Apalachicola Indians, 805
Arguelles, Martin de, 372
Arthur, Chester A., 1887
Atlantic Coast Line, 2014
Avery, Owen M., 2283
Avon Park, 2489
Ayala y Escobar, Juan de, 377

Baltzell, Thomas, 2284
banking, 1929-43
Baptist church, 1541-48
Bartow, 2490
baseball, 1922
Belle Glade, 2491
Bernard, Jesse T., 1020
Bethune, Mary M., 2289
Blodgett, John Loomis, 2290
Blout, William Alexander, 2291
Bloxham, William Dunnington, 1175, 1873, 2292-3
Boca Raton, 2492
Boring, Isaac, 2295
Bowlegs, Billie, 906, 941
Bowles, William Augustus, 656, 675, 678-9, 688-91, 696
Bradford County, education in, 1592
Branch, John, 2297
Branscomb, Bishop John, 2300
Brevard County, 2796
Brookville, 2493
Broward, Napoleon B., 2301-3
Broward County, medicine in, 1758
Brown, Joseph E., and the election of 1876, 1197, 2304
Brown, Thomas, 831, 2305
Brown Library, Brown University, Florida materials in, 98
Bryan, William Jennings, 1881

248

Bryant, William Cullen, 1261
Bulow plantation, 869
Burnham, Mills Olcott, 2306

Cabrera, Juan Marques, governor of Spanish Florida, 410
Caesar, John, 994
Call, Richard Keith, 851, 2307-12, in the 1836 campaign, 795;
    and the Seminole War, 898
Call, Wilkinson, 2313
Campbell, Doak S., 2314
canals, 859, 2047, 2051, 2059, 2072-4, 2076, 2078
Cape Canaveral, 2494
Cape Sable, 2496
Castillo de San Marcos, 2861-2
Catholic Church, 1434-96
cattle, 1966, 1972, 1990, 1998
Catts, Sidney Joseph, 1872, 1879
Celi Expedition, 356, 409
Chaires, Anna E., 1585
Chamber of Commerce, 1910
Chapman, Frank, 2315
Chase, Salmon P., 1057-8
Chester, Governor Peter, 530, 555
Chinsegut Hill Library, University of Florida, 87
Chipley, William D., 2316
cigar industry, labor problems, 2004, 2010-11; see also tobacco
citrus, 1968-71, 1973, 1979, 1987, 1993, 1996, 2003
Civil War, see War Between the States
Civilian Conservation Corps, 1900
Clarke, Elijah, 633
Clarke, George, 2317-8
Clements Library, University of Michigan, Florida materials in,
    58, 79, 90-92
Clinch, General Duncan Lamont, 946, 2319
Collier County, 2797
Constitutions, 1783, 1785, 1793, 1799, 1810, 1817, 1819, 1835,
    1837, 1839
Coral Gables, 2497
cotton, 858, 1013, 1974-5, 1997, 2000
courts, appeals, 845; in Territorial Florida, 824; Supreme Court,
    1777-8, 1808; and Samuel Douglas, 2332; and Thomas Douglas,
    2333; and William Andrew Hocker, 2374
Crane, Cora, 2321
Curry, William, 2322

Dade County, 2798-2800; boom in, 1930; education, 1588; medicine,
    1725, 1765
Dade Massacre, 896, 925, 948
Dania, 2498
Davis, Thomas Frederick, 2325
Daytona Beach, 2499
Debary, Frederick, 2326
Deherrera, Luciano, 475

Deland, 2500-1
Delius, Frederick, 2329-31
Democrats, 1847, 1878, 1904
de Soto, Hernando, 288-316
Dexter, Horatio S., 878
Disciples of Christ, 1553
Disston Land Purchase, 1168
Donax, 1965
Douglas, Judge Samuel, 2332
Douglas, Judge Thomas, 2333
Doyle, Edmund, 672
Drayton, William, 500
Drew, George F., 2334-5
Dunedin, 2502
Dunnellon, 2503
Duval, William P., 825, 2337-8
Duval County, 2801-3; medicine, 1726, 1743-4

education, 1555-78; elementary and secondary, 1579-92; of freed-
   men, 1188, 1209; higher, 1593-1619; of Seminoles, 2169-70;
   in Territorial Florida, 841, 843, 856; and Owen M. Avery,
   2283; and Thomas Baltzell, 2284; and John Beard, 2285; and
   Charles Beecher, 2286; and Doak S. Campbell, 2314; and
   Eleazer K. Foster, 2355; and K. L. Goulding, 2367; and Ham-
   ilton Holt, 2376; and George M. Lynch, 2392; and Samuel B.
   McLain, 2395; and Albert J. Russel, 2450; and William M.
   Sheets, 2454-5; and David Shellby Walker, 2470-2
Episcopal Church, 1497-1514
Eppes, Francis, 2339
Escambia County, 2804
Estero, 2504-5
Everglades, 2887-2932

Fairbanks, General George R., 2341
Farmers' Alliance, 1851, 1877, 1886
Fernandina, 2506
fiction, relating to Florida, 14, 99
Finegan, General Joseph, 1132, 2342
Flagler, Henry, 2019-21, 2343-51; and his church, 1538-9
Flags of Florida, 184; in the Civil War, 1143
Fletcher, Duncan Upshaw, 2354
Fletcher, Henry Prather, 1578
Florida Agricultural College, 1594
Florida Central Railroad, 2027-9
Florida East Coast Railroad, 2030, 2038
Florida Historical Society, 111-3, 128
Florida Keys, 2507-10
Florida Library Association, 1687, 1697
Florida Southern College, 1619
Florida State Library, 1677
Florida State University, 1596, 1601, 1617; library school, 1694
forest fires, 1967
Forry, Samuel, 903

Fort Brooke, 806
Fort Caroline, 2856-9
Fort Dade, 2863-4
Fort Gadsden, 2868
Fort Jefferson, 2871-2
Fort King, 2874-5
Fort Lauderdale, 2511-14
Fort Leon, 809
Fort Maitland, 2876
Fort Marion, 2877
Fort Myers, 2515-19
Fort St. Marks, 2882-3
Fort San Carlos, 2879
Fort San Luis, 2880-1
Fort San Marcos, 2886
forts, 421-432, 2854-86
Foster, Eleazer K., 2355
Freducci Map, 163
Freedmen's Bureau, 1162-3, 1166, 1178-79, 1186-94, 1199, 1209
Fruitland Park, 2521

Gadsden County, 2805; indian massacre in, 966
Gaines, General Edmund Pendleton, 2356
Gainesville, 2522-30; Baptist church in, 1545; Methodist church in,
    1522; Presbyterian church in, 1535
Genet and Florida, 697-702
Gibbs, Jonathan C., 1192
Gifford, John Clayton, 2360
Gilchrist, Albert Waller, 2361; inauguration of, 1884
Gorrie, John, 2362-65
Goulding, K. L., 2367
Granger Movement, 1865
Greeks, in New Smyrna, 481, 1622, 1636; in Tarpon Springs,
    1624; and the sponge industry, 1946, 1951, 1955

Haisley, William Penn, 2369
Halifax, 2351-2
Hamilton, Henry, 560
Hammon, Hiram F., 2371
health, see medicine
Hernando County, 2806-8
highway patrol, 2088
Hill, Erastus G., 1173
Hillsborough County, 2809-11
Historical Records Survey in Florida, 68, 95
Hodgman, Samuel, 2375
Hollingworth, Henry, 914
Hollywood, 2534
Holmes, James, 604
Holmes Valley, 2535
Holt, Hamilton, 2376; his writings, 27
horse racing, 817
Hoskins Library, Panama City, catalog, 22

Huguenots, 317-355, 374
Hunter, Nathaniel Wyche, 916

Ibarra, Pedro de, 417
Indian Key, 793; massacre, 922, 962; and wrecking, 2092, 2094
Indian River, 2536
Indians, 2107-2232; and the defense of Spanish West Florida, 655,
    657; and the English, 460, 463-4, 468, 478, 487, 491, 493,
    553; and removal, 717-24; and the War of 1812, 710, 713
Indigo, 386
Innerarity, John, 680, 682-6, 695, 741
Italians, 1644; in Tampa, 1639
Ithaca, 2537

Jackson, General Andrew, 725-60
Jackson County, 2812-3
Jacksonville, 2538-50; Civil War, 1070; medicine, 1746-7, 1752;
    Methodist Church, 1525; Presbyterian Church, 1534; and music,
    1718; railroads, 2026; Rotary Club, 1704; and the Seminole
    War (1835-36), 920; and the theatre, 1713
Jacksonville Historical Society, 123-5
Jefferson County, 2814-5
Jenckes, Edwin T., 2379
Jews, 1628, 1638, 1631
Johnson, Brandish W., 2097
Johnson, James W., 2380-1
Johnstone, George, 534, 554
Jones, George Noble, 854
journalism, see newspapers
Juares, Juan, 1447
Jupiter Inlet and Island, 2551-2

Kelly, Judge Richard, impeachment of, 1801
Key Biscayne, 2553-4
Key Largo, 2555
Key West, 2557-81; bibliography, 26; medicine, 1722-3, 1733-4;
    salvage, 2100, 2104; Spanish American War, 1210; and the
    theatre, 1701
Kingsley, Zephariah, 477
Kirby-Smith, Edmund, 2382-3
Kirk, Claude R., 2384
Ku Klux Klan, 1848

Labor, 2003-12; during reconstruction, 1169, 1189; and the cigar
    industry, 1213
Lake County, 2816; Baptist Church, 1543
Lakeland, Rotary Club, 1708
Laudonniere, Rene, 318, 321
law, 1775-1841, see also courts
L'Engle, Claude, 2386
Leon County, 2817-20; Civil War, 1066; courts, 1805; education,
    1591; land use, 1937; plantations, 837-8; printing, 1658, 1664
Levy, Moses Elias, 2387

Levy County, 2821
libraries, 1, 1670-98
lighthouses, 2048, 2050, 2055-7, 2077
Lockey, Joseph Byrnes, 2389-90
Lorimer, John, 558
lumber industry, 1980, 1984, 1986, 1992, 1994, 2001-2
Luna y Arellano, Tristan de, 225, 248-9
Lynch, George M., 2392

McGehee, John C., 2393
McGillivray, Alexander, 2394
McIntosh, General John M., 1185
McLain, Samuel B., 2395
McLaughlin, John T., 864
Macomb, David B., 2396
Mallory, Stephen R., 2397-2401
Manatee, 2584-5
Mandarin, 2586-7
Mangos, 1977
maps, 141-165
Marianna, Battle of, 1128
Marion County, 1659
Martin, John W., 1880
Marvin, William C., 2402-3
Masarytown, 2588
Mathews, General George, 646
medicine, 1719-74
Meigs, Montgomery C., 2408
Melbourne Beach, 2589
Melrose, 2590
Menéndez, Pedro de Avilés, 253-69
Mennonites, 1651
Merrick, George Edgar, 2409
Methodist Church, 1515-33, 2300
Miami, 2591-2607; Federal Music Project, 1716; public library, 1672, 1683; Womens' clubs, 1705
Miami Beach, 1552, 2608-13
Middleburg, 2614
Milton, John, 1103, 2410-12
Minorcans, 1621, 1625
Miranda, Hernando de, 413
Moultrie, John, 2413
Mount Dora, 2615
Murat, Achille, 2414-5
Murphee, Albert A., 1612, 2416

National Intelligencer, Florida material in, 8
Natural Bridge, Battle of, 1141
Negroes, 2233-72; education, 1188, 1209; in Gainesville, 2528; and Osceola, 979; and Florida Politics, 1868; and public library service, 1691; and Seminoles, 2151, 2192, 2194, 2196; and Seminole Wars, 987-999; in the Spanish American War, 1212; in Reconstruction, 1161-1209

New Smyrna, 2618-20; Greeks in, 1622, 1636; in the Civil War, 1077
Newhouse, John, 2418
newspapers, 1652-69, 1867; list of, 12, 57; in the Civil War, 1074; in Reconstruction, 1204; in the Spanish American War, 1225; in Tallahassee, 1011; in Territorial Florida, 842, 857; in World War I, 1889
Niles Register, Florida materials in, 5, 8
novel, see fiction

Ocala, 2621-2; Methodist Church, 1521; newspapers in, 1669
Ogelthorpe, General James Edward, 445, 448-9
Okeechobee, 2897, 2926-9
Oldsmar, 2623
Olustee, Battle of, 1123, 1131, 1135, 1140
Onis, see Adams-Onis Treaty
Orange County, 2823-4; medicine in, 1772
oranges, see citrus industry
Oritz, John, narrative of his captivity, 235
Orlando, 2624-5
Ormond and Ormond Beach, 2626-8
Ormond, James, 2419
Osceola, 969-86
Osceola County, 2825

Pacheco, Louis, 995
Palm Beach, 2629-35; Society of Four Arts Library, 1695
Palm Beach County, 2826-7
Palmetto, 2636
Panama City, 2367
Panton, Leslie and Co., 674, 681, 683, 685, 687, 692-3
Patrick, Rembert, 2421-2
Peacock, U. S. S., 706
Pena, Diego, 362-3
Pensacola, 649, 665, 2639-56; architecture, 1712; bibliography, 40; under the British, 528-30, 551; churches in, 1526, 1546, 1549; in the Civil War, 1076, 1080, 1125; fortifications of, 427, 653; maps of, 143, 146; labor problems, 1864, 2008; library association, 1675; medicine in, 1759, 1771; and Miranda, 564, 581; newspapers in, 1656; public library service to Negroes, 1691; railroads, 2031; rivalry for, 439, 441; Seige of 1781, 519-20, 550; seizure by Jackson, 735, 741; Spanish in, 379, 394, 451; in Territorial days, 823; theatre in, 1699; in the War of 1812, 707
Pensacola Bay, 438, 440
Perrine, Henry, 2424-7; killed by Indians, 922, 962
Perry, Edward A., 2428-31
Phelps, John W., 939
phosphates, 1947, 1962
Pinellas County, 2, 2828
Plant, Henry Bradley, 2434-8
plantations, 600, 606, 789, 791, 829, 837-8, 854, 1023, 1976
Point Pinella, 2627

Polk County, 2829
Ponce de Leon, Juan, 270-87; and medicine, 1761
population: in 1825, 814; in 1845, 816; in ante-bellum Florida,
    834; of Miami, 2595; of St. Augustine, 2678
Port St. Joseph, 803
Porter, Joseph Y., 2439-40
Powell, Levin M., 880
Presbyterian church, 1534-40
printing, 24, 32-3, 36, 1658
prisons, 2007
Proctor family, 2255-6
prohibition, 1949-50, 2594
Punta Gorda, 2658-9

racing, 1923
railroads, 2013-45; in the Civil War, 1046, 1075; and William D.
    Chipley, 2316; and David Yulee, 2482
Raney, George Pettus, 2442
Rawlings, Marjorie Kinnan, 2443-4
Reconstruction, 1161-1209
Reed, Harrison, 2446
Ribault, Jean, 325, 332, 343, 353
Ringling Brothers Circus, 2337-8
Robertson, James Alexander, 139
Rojas, Don Hernando de Manrique de, 355
Rolle, Denys, 506, 676
Rollestown, 457, 676
Rollins College, 1604, 1616; library, 1684
Romans, Bernard, 154
Roosevelt, Theodore, 1843
Ruffin, Edmund, 1038
Russell, Albert J., 2450

Saint Andrews, 2660-62
Saint Augustine, 374, 378, 407, 473, 475, 619, 853, 2663-2711;
    under the British, 503-4, 507, 585; Castillo de san Marcos,
    2861-2; Catholic Church, 1459, 1475, 1488; in the Civil War,
    1054, 1116; destruction by Drake, 436, 447; education, 843,
    1579, 1581; founding of, 234; map of, 146; medicine, 1745,
    1761, 1768, 1770; Minorcans in, 1625; Seige of 1702, 435, 455;
    sources on early history, 100, 122
Saint Johns River, 2052, 2070
Saint Joseph, 2713-5; in 1839, 835, see also constitution
Saint Lucie County, 2830
Saint Marks, 2716
Saint Marys River, 2061
Saint Petersburg, 2, 2717-9; public library, 1690
Salazar, Don Pablo de, 414, 416
salt making, 1155, 1963, 2524
Sanford, 2720-1
Sanford, General Henry S., 2451-2; and labor, 2003
Sanford Library, catalogue of, 82
Sarasota, 2722